Self Psychology and the Humanities

Reflections on a New Psychoanalytic Approach

Other Books by Heinz Kohut

*The Analysis of the Self: A Systematic Approach
to the Psychoanalytic Treatment of
Narcissistic Personality Disorders* (1971)

The Restoration of the Self (1977)

How Does Analysis Cure? (1984),
Edited by Arnold Goldberg
with the collaboration of Paul E. Stepansky

*The Search for the Self: Selected Writings of
Heinz Kohut* 1950–1978,
Edited by Paul H. Ornstein.
Two Volumes (1978);
Volume III forthcoming

Self Psychology and the Humanities

Reflections on a New Psychoanalytic Approach

HEINZ KOHUT

edited with an introduction by

CHARLES B. STROZIER

W · W · NORTON & COMPANY
New York   *London*

Published simultaneously in Canada by Penguin Books Canada Ltd,
2801 John Street, Markham, Ontario L3R 1B4
Printed in the United States of America.

The text of this book is composed in Baskerville, with
display type set in Baskerville. Composition and
manufacturing by The Maple-Vail Book Manufacturing Group.
Book design by Jacques Chazaud.

Library of Congress Cataloging in Publication Data

Kohut, Heinz.
Self psychology and the humanities.

Includes index.
1. Self—Addresses, essays, lectures.   2. Psychohistory
—Addresses, essays, lectures.   3. Psychoanalysis and
literature—Addresses, essays, lectures.   4. Psychoanalysis
and art—Addresses, essays, lectures.   I. Stozier,
Charles B.   II. Title.
BF697.K654   1985   150.19′5   85–10586

ISBN 0-393-70000-3

W. W. Norton & Company, Inc.,
500 Fifth Avenue, New York, N.Y. 10110

W. W. Norton & Company Ltd.,
37 Great Russell Street, London WC1B 3NU

2 3 4 5 6 7 8 9 0

For Matthew

Contents

SECTION III
Conversations With Heinz Kohut

Preface

Heinz Kohut (1913–1981) is one of the most important psycho-analytic thinkers of the 20th century. His three books (prior to this one) and three volumes of published papers essentially open up a new psychological approach, the psychology of the self, building creatively on Freud and the work of ego psychologists of the past generation. Kohut's work defines a new approach to the clinical data of observation, clarifies the empathic stance of psychoanalytic investigation, and modifies classical psychoanalytic technique. He is also a major thinker in the second half of the 20th century who, like Freud, grapples with fundamental issues beyond the clinical setting. For Kohut it is artificial to separate the therapeutic and scientific from the humanistic study of man. The consulting room may be a special kind of laboratory for the psychoanalyst, but a dream, for example, is no more nor less a cultural product than Picasso's *Guernica* or Shakespeare's *Hamlet.*

The conceptual design of this volume, as well as the arrangement of the papers, aims at presenting the richness of Kohut's thoughts on self psychology and the humanities. Some of these papers are altogether new, others familiar. Those intimately involved in self psychology may well want to skip Section II, which republishes four of Kohut's papers, but will surely find the rest of interest in whatever order it is read. The new papers of Section I and the interviews in Section III thus complement each other. Since dates are provided for each essay, readers familiar with Kohut's work may want to tie this material to his better known books and papers since the middle 1960s.

There is a point in the way the book is set up: to introduce Kohut's thought to readers who are not familiar with his varied writings. Unfortunately, there is no single monograph or set of papers in existence that provides such an introduction. This volume hopes to remedy that situation.

The first few papers range creatively over a number of central theoretical ideas—the self, themes of narcissistic pathology, and the nature of selfobjects—in the context of discussing humanistic and historical topics. Here theory is the backdrop. At center stage are the humble but heroic resistors to Nazism, Shakespeare's *Hamlet,* and the family in modern times. Section II reverses the emphasis. In these papers theory now occupies the foreground. Theoretical ideas that had registered at some level are now put into a larger and more unified psychological context. The humanities are now used as examples for the theory in the same way Freud used art and literature to enrich his papers and books. By grouping these papers in Section II, I hope to present Kohut's essential ideas on the psychoanalytic theory of the self. Thus, to take an example of the general difference in kind between Sections I and II, "On Courage" is concerned with the martyred heroes who quietly resisted Nazism. Here Kohut uses his theoretical concept of the "nuclear self" as a means of comprehending those particular heroes whose calm resistance so fascinated Kohut. In Section II, however, when Kohut discusses Winston Churchill in the paper "Forms and Transformations of Narcissism," it is simply as an *illustration* of the interplay between the grandiose self, the ego, and the superego in determining personality. It is not that one is better than the other. But they are different.

Two additional considerations guided the selection of the particular papers in Section II. First, in each of them one finds Kohut's most important previously published thoughts on history and the humanities. Thus, one finds in this section Kohut's ideas on Churchill, Freud and Fliess, charisma, and some of his ideas on Hitler, Kafka, art, and mothers and mothering, to mention a few. Equally important, however, these papers read together are a good basic introduction to self psychology. This is especially true of the two seminal papers, "Forms and Transformations of Narcissism" and "Thoughts on Narcissism and Narcissistic Rage." To understand these papers alone is the beginning of self psychological wisdom.

Section III then captures Kohut's reflective self. These interviews were the last he gave before his death and were directly related to the presentation of the material in the first two sections of the book. For example, in the interviews I asked him about the group self because that is a concept in Section II in "Creativeness, Charisma, and Group Psychology." The interviews are also personal; Kohut describes his education, his long-standing interest in history and the humanities, and his belief in the possibility of creative social and political change.

Origin of the Book

Any book has its own history, and this one is no exception. In general, the story of the story is irrelevant and to tell it is at best indulgent. But in the case of this book some description of origins is important for a reading of the text and an understanding of the dating of the various papers.

In the spring of 1980 Kohut first mentioned to me almost casually his "fragmentary writings on psychohistory." That fall, after one of his serious illnesses, I visited him in his apartment where he had several papers of different lengths carefully stacked on a table. They varied from a 300-page (triple-spaced) manuscript to a three-page insert, an aside that had been removed from its original source. After a brief talk I left with the manuscripts in hand, hoping that no car or train would run me down. After reading the papers, I suggested to him that he had the basis for a fascinating book but that it should be conceived for those readers who were basically not familiar with his work. It should thus consist of carefully edited versions of his original papers, a few of his previously published articles that together provide a good introduction to his thoughts, and some interviews concerning his most recent reflections on history and the humanities. He agreed enthusiastically and we went to work.

Kohut's death on October 8, 1981, left our project incomplete. The interviews had been conducted, but he had reviewed only a rough transcript of the first four and neither he nor I had edited his original papers. It is in the nature of the unexpected evolu-

tion of this book that my presence as editor is strong. I chose the
titles for the three papers, which I also heavily edited, eliminat-
ing redundancy and generally trying to shape each sentence and
paragraph to keep the whole faithfully Kohut's but as close as
possible to the way I believed he himself would have altered it in
revision. The interviews especially had to be thoroughly revised,
since nothing is rougher than the direct transcript of a taped
conversation.

In doing so I believe I acted as Kohut would have wished.
Kohut himself was a meticulous reviser and editor of his own
writings, as anyone knows who has seen a manuscript of one of
his published papers or books. The only paper in this collection
that was beyond the first-draft stage (and that not by much) before
his untimely death was "On Courage." In editing, I received quite
different recommendations from readers about what to cut and
what to include. In the end I had to make up my own mind.
Furthermore, I think he trusted my judgment in these matters.
He had obviously held onto the papers many years before asking
me to evaluate them. He also signed the book contract from his
hospital bed, two days before his death, thus bequeathing me
the project to finish as best I could.

The dating of the three previously unpublished papers deserves
some mention. "On Courage" is the most difficult to tie down.
Mrs. Elizabeth Kohut, Heinz Kohut's widow, remembers him
writing notes to himself for the paper in the late 1960s. I asked
him once when he wrote it and he replied vaguely that it was in
the early '70s; getting a more precise date was one of the many
details left hanging at his death. Kohut was equally vague about
when he wrote the paper I have titled "On Leadership." In one
conversation he dated it in the summer of 1966, when he could
link it to other events. However, in two other conversations he
referred to the paper as the intended concluding chapter to *The
Analysis of the Self*. That book was written between 1969 and 1971.
Furthermore, the paper includes a discussion of Karl Dietrich
Bracher's *Die Deutsche Diktatur*, which was published only in 1969.
The discrepancy in dating that such reports raised did not occur
to me before Kohut died. I have chosen the dating of 1969–
1971 because Kohut mentioned it twice and because of the
Bracher reference; it could just as well be from 1966, perhaps
drafted separately and later brought up-to-date and considered

for adoption as the final chapter for the monograph he was then writing. Finally, Kohut recalled clearly that he wrote "Self Psychology and the Sciences of Man" in the summer of 1978, just before an importance conference.

The Text

New ideas require new language. The years during which Kohut was writing the papers in this book, published and previously unpublished, were a time of rapid shifts in his terminology and conceptualization. Even a term as basic as "self" means one thing between 1966 and about 1974 and something quite different from then on. As editor I have naturally not interfered with such inconsistencies. I did attempt to make spelling and grammar consistent. Thus in "On Leadership" group-self becomes "group self" and in "Self Psychology and the Sciences of Man," "self-object" becomes "selfobject." Otherwise, I have tried to walk the very fine line between editing sufficiently to make the papers and interviews both publishable and readable and compromising the originality of Kohut's formulation.

In the texts presented in Section I, I have either folded most of Kohut's footnotes from the manuscript into the text or excised them. Where they seemed important to preserve as notes, they appear as he wrote them. His references to other sources are similarly carried over into the end notes. Occasionally, I have a note of my own, which is printed in brackets.

Acknowledgments

It would be difficult to thank Elizabeth Kohut warmly enough
for her help in preparing this volume for publication. She read
every word many times over, compared each new version I prepared against Kohut's original, and had numerous creative ideas
for shaping the whole. At times we disagreed, but each passage
so lovingly labored over profited in its final formulation. She
prodded me vigorously throughout to keep at it. There is no
question that, but for the assistance of Elizabeth Kohut, this book
would not be in existence in its present form.

I also want to thank Tom Kohut, Heinz's son, who teaches
history at Williams College. Tom read a final draft of the manuscript with an eagle eye and had much to contribute. He also
shared the manuscript with his colleague, Robert G.L. Waite,
who offered criticisms and suggestions.

Arnold Goldberg has helped me so often with so many crises
in connection with this book it would be difficult to thank him
enough. Needless to say, he has also read the papers at various
stages of their preparation and offered useful suggestions.

Along the way several friends and colleagues read drafts of
the papers, including Bruce Mazlish, Dan Offer, Mike Lennon,
Geoff Ward, and Ernest Wolf. Bruce Mazlish assisted further in strongly supporting the proposal that Heinz and I took
to Norton. Larry Shiner also helped a great deal with the introduction.

The psychohistory seminar that I lead at Rush Medical School in Chicago has seen all of this book over a two-year period and contributed much in the way of helpful comments. I am particularly grateful to Robert Zadylak, Katie Busch, Linda Belknap, Carolyn Skipper, James Crawford, Jamie Trujillo-Gomez, Casey Byrnes, Maynard and Doris Cohen, Betty Czekala, and George Fitchett.

At Norton two editors were encouraging, helpful, and smart. Ed Barber shepherded the book along until Susan Barrows took it over and pushed it to completion.

For years now Lisa Robinson has typed and retyped the papers in this book, not to mention voluminous correspondence relating to it. She did it all well and cheerfully.

Thanks, finally, to Cathy.

Charles B. Strozier
Springfield, Illinois
March 28, 1985

Introduction

The humanities in the broadest sense clearly engaged Kohut
personally and scientifically. In this introduction I first want to
discuss some of Kohut's early writings that are not included in
this volume. The first paper he wrote in psychoanalysis (he had
written some papers earlier in neurology) was an essay on Thomas
Mann's *Death in Venice*. Kohut withheld publication of the essay
until 1957 after Mann's own death, but he had actually written
the essay in 1948. The paper is subtitled "A Story About the
Disintegration of Artistic Sublimation" and focuses on the psychological meaning of Aschenbach's excessive love for the beautiful young boy, Tadzio. The pressures of death and loss of his
own creative power force in Aschenbach "the breakdown of sublimated homosexual tenderness and the nearly unchecked onrush
of unsublimated homosexual desire in the aging writer." (Ornstein, 1978, I*:125) Kohut generalizes in the essay on the nature
of artistic creativity and the "old and well substantiated psychoanalytic thesis" that artistic creativity is related to the feminine
principle; certainly, he concludes, Aschenbach's creativity is a
function of the presence or absence of either sublimated or
unsublimated homosexual strivings (I:126–27).

Kohut's first published psychoanalytic paper (1950) deals with

---

*Kohut's papers from 1950–1978 were collected in two volumes of *The Search
for the Self*, edited by Paul H. Ornstein. Hereafter references to these papers are
cited as "I" or "II" denoting the volume.

music and why one enjoys listening to it. The paper—written with Kohut's childhood friend, Sigmund Levarie, who by then was on the faculty of the University of Chicago—reflects Kohut's abiding interest in an understanding of musical expression. Kohut and Levarie note the long-standing concern among theorists and philosophers (since Plato and Aristotle) to clarify the psychology of music. All, however, have failed to adequately address the basic and simple question of why we enjoy listening to music. "As a complex psychological phenomenon," they argue (I:1–7), "the enjoyment of music should warrant the participation of the total personality. What remains obscure is something more specific: an explanation of the mechanism of the production of pleasure in the listener which will take into account the essential universality of this experience, as well as the circumstances which can prevent the experience from being pleasurable."

This approach to the subject then leads Kohut and Levarie to an analysis of an infant's complex experience with sounds, noting (I:141) how sudden noises produce fear and pleasure as experience "when psychological tension is relieved or when such relief is anticipated shortly." The actual experience of listening to music varies significantly. One can sit with closed eyes and open mouth and regressively drink in music as a suckling baby. Another might experience the evocation of the rhythmic sounds of the primal scene. And so on (I:143). Music liberates energies, organizes complex sounds, and demands a degree of mastery (though that varies enormously). Much of the essay examines these points in fine detail. There is something profoundly preverbal and liberating about the enjoyment of listening to music. Music enlarges one's identity to embrace "a whole primitive, nonverbal universe of sounds after the original threat is overcome." And in conclusion (I:158): "The ability to regress to this early ego state while at the same time preserving the complicated ego functions required to recognize and master the influx of organized sounds, is the prerequisite for the enjoyment of music."

Kohut followed this paper with scholarly reviews of books on music and then, in 1957, picked up again on the issue of listening to music as it related specifically to psychoanalytic therapy. The paper—"Observations on the Psychological Functions of Music"—applies the Kohut-Levarie model to a patient who had vague discomforts that he could only describe as an unbearable tension in his stomach, throat, head, or limbs (I:246). Kohut likened it to what Freud called the "actual-neurotic hypochondriacal core of schizophrenia," that is, some basic disturbance in the patient's psychoeconomic balance. The patient eventually was able to find a relief of tension in the experience of music. He resumed playing musical instruments that he had abandoned in childhood, began to compose music, and became an active participant in a musical organization (which, secondarily, also enriched his social life). It represented a kind of cure in music that went along with changes in therapy but occurred outside of analysis (I:249).

The culmination of Kohut's early concerns with literature and music came with the 1960 essay on the method of applying psychoanalysis, "Beyond the Bounds of the Basic Rule." This far-reaching essay remains a key statement on methodology in the entire realm of applied psychoanalysis, whether in literature, history, political science, or the arts. The examples in the essay are in fact generally from literature and the paper is actually constructed as just a review essay of four books, written for the *Journal of the American Psychoanalytic Association.* But the ideas and generalizations about applied psychoanalysis have significance far beyond such an apparently prosaic format. It is perhaps relevant to note here that the essay emerged from one of Kohut's many committee assignments in the 1950s during his active tenure in the administrative structure of the American Psychoanalytic Association. He made things his own in special ways in the act of appropriating them.

Applied psychoanalysis is a field awash with playful amateurism and lacking much scientific rigor. Its findings offer "an easy target for derisive condemnation by those whose emnity toward psychoanalysis has unconscious personal roots, and much of the most violent criticism the workers in applied analysis encounter can thus be understood as rationalized resistance" (I:276). Kohut notes the differing responses, based largely on idealizations, of Beethoven, as well as the complex ways a figure's life impinges on the observer's psychological being. Alexander Wheelock Thayer, in his biography of Beethoven, thus blocked on his subject when he had to describe Beethoven's relationship with his nephew. Thayer developed excruciating headaches which plagued him all day—even if he worked on Beethoven for only an hour. The block furthermore was quite specifically related to the issue of Beethoven and his nephew. During the time Thayer was unable to work on his Beethoven book he produced two scholarly books on other subjects. Similarly, Phyllis Greenacre can only account for the outburst of fury at Paul Schilder's 1938 study of *Alice in Wonderland* as part of a resistance and, in Kohut's words, "as a manifestation of an insecure capacity to sublimate those deep aggressions for which the nonsense created by Carroll's genius provides such a delightful catharsis" (I:278).

But it would be naive to blame the problems of applied analysis entirely on the resistances of readers, however true that may be in certain circumstances. Often the problem is that the worker is not really proficient in both fields. He thus often makes elementary errors, like those of humanists who abuse the psychological subtlety of psychoanalytic theory or the gross factual and contextual errors analysts often make when studying the humanities (e.g., Freud's error in his 1910 essay on Leonardo da Vinci, when he made a series of deductions based on a mistranslation of a single word; he should have used the original Italian). There is also a fundamental problem in that the worker in the field of applied analysis must operate without the essential ingredient of clinical psychoanalysis—free association (I:280–81). In some cases, of course, creative output resembles free association, but even in such cases there will always be absent, "the still more informative interplay of interpretation and resistance and the living ebb and flow of the transference." (I:281) Moreover, artists are motivated neither by therapeutic self-revelation nor by a close bond with the therapist that might prompt curative revelation. Indeed, as Freud said of Goethe, a whole corpus of work can serve the purposes of self concealment. Finally, Kohut considers the legitimacy of the aims of applied psychoanalytic work. Is it only to reduce behavior and motivation to their ultimate unconscious roots? His answer is basically that, however true at one time, that is neither the aim nor effect of better and more recent work in ego psychology (I:283).

The definition of concepts, issues, and methods in the field sets the stage for Kohut's careful examination of the four books under review. This middle part of the essay seems the least useful, but his conclusions to the essay are another matter. There Kohut draws back again and surveys the broad terrain of applied psychoanalysis. He distinguishes three types of studies: biography supported by psychoanalysis (or biography in-depth); psychoanalytic pathography, which revives a term from the earliest discussion of the circle around Freud; and the psychoanalysis of creativity, in which, "The research may be aimed at the elucidation of the contribution made by specific conflicts and other psychological constellations to the development, maintenance, and disturbance of normal or especially desirable ego functions." (I:301) This latter category is particularly interesting, for with it Kohut turns the spotlight on the applied analytic researcher himself as a way of understanding creativity in general.

> We know little about the psychology of creative psychoanalysts. It is likely that they are represented by different personality types; yet there is certainly one group among them in which a greater than average need for artistic expression during adolescence and early adulthood is finally channeled into devotion to the science of psychoanalysis. It is probably this group that tends toward the quasi-artistic preoccupation with a biographical branch of psychoanalysis in which imagination plays a greater role, and in which the subject that is investigated can be chosen by the worker according to his predilections and needs. The Beethoven book by the Sterbas and the two essays by Greenacre, especially the one on Carroll, are close to being artistic productions themselves. In these books, analysis, without losing its scientific rigor, again seems close to its poetic origins. (I:302)

This fascinating passage, bristling with self-reference, offers a fundamentally fresh perspective on applied analytic work, which he sees as itself an act of psychoanalytic creation. In this regard Kohut is fascinated with Freud's own creativity.

Among the previously published essays that appear in the middle section of this book is the essay, "Creativeness, Charisma, Group Psychology: Reflections on the Self-Analysis of Freud," which takes as its central challenge systematic self evaluation. "Creativeness" notes in its opening pages the enormously significant idealization of Freud that emerges from the close reading of *The Interpretation of Dreams* that is so basic to psychoanalytic training. "Such empathic closeness with total sectors of another person's mind," furthermore, "extending from conscious to unconscious levels," is a rare event in our lives and tends to leave in analysts a firmly established identification with Freud or, in reaction-formation, a rebelliousness against this identification. This emotional closeness to Freud makes the scientific study of his creativity difficult; indeed, as Kohut notes in a footnote

(II:797), the same issue affects the study of psychoanalytic texts in the curricula of training institutes.

There are many consequences to the intense idealization of Freud among analysts and the fact that they therefore share an important ego ideal. "A firm group self supports the productivity of the group" which gives any analyst a "sense of belonging to a living, developing body of scientific knowledge to whose growth he can contribute . . ." (II:799). Such group support, however, can also force a deadening conformity on members of a group. Many analysts will thus tend to be overcautious while others, responding to a "preconscious rebelliousness against the encompassing presence of an unchanging ideal" will welcome new ideas simply because they seem to offer liberation from a dimly perceived internal bondage (II:800). But on the whole the non-defensive idealization of Freud serves creative purposes for analysts by consolidating important and high ideals and muting the expression in the group of envy, jealousy, and rage. But the analyst's feelings for Freud must be understood, training analyses need perhaps to be more sensitive to such issues, and scientific self-scrutiny of Freud needs encouragement (II:803–804). There is, after all, in theory at least no group more scientifically and introspectively aware than psychoanalysts. Those skills need to be turned to advantage in the study of Freud and of groups themselves by examining the psychoanalytic community.

Kohut's concern with the method of applying psychoanalytic theory to the humanities reflects his ongoing interest in creative expression. After 1960 he was not again to write a sustained essay on a work of music, literature, or art. In a sense his agenda dealing with topics of theory and what he came to call self psychology crowded out any extended forays into applied analysis. Nevertheless, if one looks rather more closely it is quite clear the humanities remain crucial in Kohut's thought. "Forms and Transformations of Narcissism" (1966), which reappears in this collection, contains a revealing reference to Goethe but much more importantly provides a theoretical explanation for human creativity as one form of transformed narcissism. The essay opens with a sharp criticism of the "improper intrusion of the altruistic value system of western civilization" (I:427) and goes on to develop the specific ways in which empathy, creativity, humor, and wisdom express vital developmental self acquisitions. These concerns are then continued in Kohut's paper, "Thoughts on Narcissism and Narcissistic Rage" (1972), also in this collection, which frames the issue of narcissistic rage with a discussion of Heinrich von Kleist's 1811 essay, "On the Puppet Theatre" and makes pointed reference to two great literary examples of the insatiable search for revenge—Kleist's *Michael Kohlhaas* (1808) and Herman Melville's *Moby Dick* (1855). After such examples, the cases of Mr. A. and Mr. P. in the paper seem almost pallid by comparison (II:649–650).

This volume, in the third section of "Conversations," also captures the humanistic flavor of Kohut's more informal side. He weaves Kafka and Shakespeare into expositions of the self of modern man and discusses Picasso on the question of authenticity. Metaphors from the arts just as naturally as those from biology (e.g., that of oxygen as similar to the selfobject milieu) breathe life into Kohut's formulations of self psychology. And the traffic runs both ways between psychoanalysis and the humanities. Freud's essay on Leonardo da Vinci, for example, "was not primarily a contribution to the comprehension of Leonardo's personality and the vicissitudes of his creativity; it was a medium for the presentation of a particular form of homosexuality." Indeed neither can afford to ignore the other's specific methods, research, and results. Ideally the university itself should create an intellectual atmosphere in which both flourish (i.e., II:685–724, especially p. 722). In Kohut's mind at least, such easy exchange always existed. Thus to take one example from the "Conversations" Kohut (Chapter 11, March 12, 1981) moves from a somewhat technical discussion of empathy with seemingly psychotic patients to the difficulty of understanding another culture that becomes increasingly comprehensible as we learn its language and ways. That leads Kohut to a disturbing but important insight: "So long as another culture is totally foreign to us, it is like psychosis. It's so easy to say the Nazis were beasts and that Germany then regressed to untamed callousness and animal-like passions. The trouble is that Nazi Germany is understandable. There is an empathic bridge, however difficult to maintain."

In 1976 at a meeting with historians and other humanists, Kohut was asked about the relationship between the history of art and culture and developments within psychoanalysis, especially the emergence of self psychology. Kohut noted in reply that "The great artists of yesterday"—which is a somewhat vague chronological phrasing—"dealt with the experiences of people in the world of interpersonal love and hate and with the experiences of people in the sphere of the swings of narcissism to which a firmly cohesive, relatively strong self is exposed: the loves and hates, the triumphs and defeats of basically strong people were their subject matter" (II:780). But artists now—meaning basically in the 20th century—are focused on depicting the fragmented self and the formidable tasks of reconstituting it and the world. Thus in Kafka's *The Castle* there is a search for a place that cannot be found. In *The Trial* no one will define the basis for the guilt, but death comes anyway, without meaning. In *Metamorphosis* the self is suddenly and horribly estranged. Kohut also discusses Eugene O'Neill's *The Great God Brown* in this context (II:781). The play has at the end the "clearest expression of man's leading problem" in Brown's words: "Man is born broken. He lives by mending. The grace of God is glue."

The answer to this curious shift in artistic expression and its analogue in the move from Freudian psychoanalysis to self psychology lies in the historical changes in the family, especially in the quality of parenting. "In former times," Kohut says (II:781–2), "the involvement between the parents and their children was overly intense." The children were touched, cajoled, and generally stimulated by parents and / or a host of caretakers ranging from nursemaids to nannys to cousins and other kin in an emotionally rich world of love and ritual. Conflicts that emerged were in response to such "protracted emotional interplay." The Oedipus complex, while not strictly speaking an artifact of this interplay, was "artificially stimulated" by the overcloseness of parents and children. But in the 20th century the issue lies not in excessive stimulation but in an atmosphere of "emotional flatness and sterility." Children are alone and depressed, yearning for meaning, often turning to drugs, sex, noise or whatever to fill the void. In other words, cultural and scientific developments of profound significance are themselves artifacts of historical changes in the quality of parenting within the family. In other terms Kohut liked, the shift is from guilty to tragic man.

And that idea brings us to the centerpiece of Kohut's humanistic concerns—his absorption in history. "I am not a historian," he said once (II:686), "—unfortunately. If I had another life to

live, I think I would try to become one." Kohut's varied comments on history, although never presented systematically in a
single monograph of his own were extensive and noteworthy.
His 1960 essay on the method of applied psychoanalytic work
serves equally well to describe psychohistorical as psycholiterary
interpretation. Throughout his life he wrote several thumbnail
psychobiographical sketches of historical figures, including Kaiser Wilhelm, Hitler, and Winston Churchill. Psychobiography,
however, especially of political leaders, is part of a more general
theory of leadership that extends Freud's 1921 pioneering work
in this area and leads Kohut, among other things, to the beginnings of a plausible psychoanalytic conceptualization of groups.
"I am convinced," he said (II:686), "that a new and revolutionary science of history is the logical next step, the natural development that ought to follow the revolutionary step Freud took
with regard to the psychology of the individual."

    First, psychohistorical method. "Yes, of course," he said to the
question whether he saw parallels between the activities of the
historian and the psychoanalyst. He continued: "The psychoanalytic historian looks at his material in a way that is similar to the
way an analyst listens to his patient, except that there is no active
free association from the observed field. You don't tell historical
data: 'Never mind whether it's embarrassing or seems unimportant, say what you feel.' But the listening or the looking process
is the same; that's why it's beyond the bounds of the basic rule."
Kohut labors throughout the essays and conversations in this
volume, as well as in earlier writings, to define the parameters
of how historical and self psychological methodologies can be
blended. In the essay, "On Leadership," for example, Kohut is
at pains to consider the classic traditional historical explanations
for Hitler and Nazism by Karl Dietrich Bracher. Analogously,
Kohut gives due consideration to Kurt Eissler's odd idea (see pp.
61-62) that Freud's *Moses and Monotheism* uncovered a Jewish collective oedipal guilt and "like a good interpretation, freed the
Jews to create a homeland."

    Kohut's own views on psychohistorical method are in fact much
more nuanced, sophisticated, and interesting. Thus as early as
the 1960 essay on method, Kohut includes Edward Hitsch-
mann's collection of essays on political figures, *Great Men*, along
with the books on Beethoven and the essays by Greenacre, en-

abling him to say something methodologically about the work or product of a great man's life. That work may be scientific, literary, or political, but the same issues emerge for the psychological observer about the meaning of that work, the nature of creativity, and the relationship between public and private, that is, the personal and psychological sources of creativity, however expressed.

Kohut is keenly sensitive to the "tool and method" pride or snobbishness that keeps researchers fiercely loyal, indeed often in a parochial way, to their discipline. Such pride "refers to the increasing esteem in which a specific method developed by each branch of science in the pursuit of its goals tend to be held, to the awe, even, with which the devoted specialist ultimately looks up to the idealized methodology of his field" (II:690; see also II:677, and II:773). Disciplinary specialization tends to narrow our sights and restrict our vision. It takes us away from considering the purposes of knowledge. It is by now a dated view that scientific advances in any field are unto themselves, without purpose, direction, or meaning. Historical and scientific understanding especially provide "an intermediary step toward man's over-all goal to achieve increasing mastery over his destiny" (II:774; in this volume p. 164).

Throughout his writings Kohut finds in the deeper self psychological understanding of individual political leaders one expression of this common historical and psychoanalytic goal of "increasing mastery" over man's destiny. Thus, a favorite example of Kohut's in this regard is the figure of Winston Churchill. As a child Churchill seemed unusually pressured by the needs of his grandiose self to escape situations of apparent danger by reverting to flying fantasies. Once he even attempted to jump a ravine while fleeing from pursuing playmates in a game. It was days before he regained consciousness and months before he walked again. Churchill jumped, it appears, because at some level he thought he could fly (I:444, and here p. 110). Later, of course, Churchill often managed his escapes better, e.g., during the Boer War. His utter sense of invincibility undoubtedly gave him a serene sense of confidence that translated into actual success. He was in a sense ideally suited emotionally to lead the British in their darkest—and under his tutelage their finest—hour. He shared with the nation his own unshakeable belief in his psychological strengths. By extension, Kohut adds tellingly, once the victory over Hitler was complete, "the need [of the British] for a merger with an omnipotent figure subsided, and they were able to turn from him to other (non-charismatic) leaders" (II:828, this volume p. 110). Churchill was unceremoniously dismissed.

There is no doubt, however, that the historical figure whom Kohut most often discusses is Adolf Hitler. In "On Leadership" in this volume, Kohut picks up on his earlier characterization of Hitler as someone with a "healed over psychosis" (1971, p. 256) who had suffered enormous narcissistic injuries. Hitler made an attempt to work through or transform his narcissistic tensions in art but failed miserably. After that, during the Vienna period (1907–1913), Hitler lapsed into a period of lonely brooding and hypochondriacal preoccupation, from which he emerged with the conviction that "the Jews had invaded the body of Germany and had to be eradicated" (see p. 54). An important point about such insights is that Kohut's self psychological theory opens up categories of evidence previously ignored or at least underestimated by those interested in psychobiography. Many observers, relying on Freudian drive theory or some variant (for example, object relations theory), find themselves all too often attempting facile reconstructions of the early life experiences of historical figures. Furthermore, drive theory leads the unwary into the private and inaccessible realm of a figure's loves and hates, unconscious fantasies, and symbolic interactions with his or her contemporaries. Self theory, as well as Kohut's subtle formulations of psychohistorical method, encourages the investigator to avoid such pitfalls. It is the readily observable—the ideals and values, the grandiosity, the work, the fears, the rage, and the complex issues of self-esteem maintenance—that is of primary concern in self psychology. Such an approach hardly abandons what psychoanalysis calls the genetic perspective and what historians regard as the central question of origins. But Kohut gives new psychoanalytic meaning to matters closer at hand in time and more comprehensible in form. Kohut thus manages to recover for historians what is most usable in psychoanalysis.

Kohut's psychological views of historical figures, however, represent more than a contribution to the somewhat narrow field of psychobiography. He has also defined the outlines of a refreshingly new theory of leadership, one that systematically formulates the psychological relationship between leaders and followers. Kohut thus notes in "On Leadership" (p. 54) that the fluidity of the borders of Hitler's self made him unusually sensitive to similar motivations in others and that knowledge gave him the ability to manipulate his followers. His social surroundings became part of himself and in that merger he managed to manipulate and control. The severe narcissistic crises Germany suffered after World War I—especially defeat in battle, humiliating acceptance of responsibility for the war itself, and the dislocations of political and economic chaos—opened up most Germans to the special psychological message Hitler offered, to merger with his paranoid certainty as a safeguard against their own seemingly imminent fragmentation.

Speaking generally, Kohut argues that leaders like Hitler, even though suffering from an otherwise crippling narcissistic personality disorder, compensate with a "heightened grasp of the unconscious and preconscious tensions states, of the fantasies, wishes, and fears of the group" (p. 56). Kohut stresses that this bonding of leader and follower can occur only where there is complete affinity culturally and psychologically between the fantasies of the group and its chosen messianic and / or charismatic leader. Neither party, so to speak, can diverge from the original pact. Hitler's fanatical certainty allowed no deviation in the grandiose fantasies Germans harbored about him, fantasies of which he had a complete empathic grasp due to the fluid boundaries of his self. When Hitler sensed the Germans were pulling back psychologically from their merger with him (after 1942 in particular), he became sneeringly contemptuous of them. In the final debacle he even ordered Albert Speer to destroy German economic life; one senses a parallel here with the Götterdämmerung of Guyana when Jim Jones disintegrated in paranoid panic at the visit of Congressman Leo Ryan.

Kohut's formulation of leadership, based as it is on the psychological relationship between leader and follower, thus leads him into a theory of group behavior. For the question in historical situations like the one that produced Hitler is less his peculiar psychological makeup (though that matters decisively in grasping the shape of events) than the reasons for the surprisingly enthusiastic reactions of a cultured people to a vulgar demagogue. Few can now watch Leni Riefenstahl's film of the 1934 party rally, "Das Triumph des Willen" (The Triumph of the Will) and not feel the rapture and sheer loss of self of some 200,000 people in their leader, Adolf Hitler.

Kohut plays with the notion of a group self in a way that is directly analogous to his theory of individual psychology. Therefore the self-selfobject relationship of mother and child, for example, provides data for the group self's psychological needs, its use of leaders, and its handling of what Kohut calls cultural selfobjects (artists, historians, intellectuals in general). The point is not to deify or anthropomorphize the group with some magical new language. Kohut talks of the group self, though he is fully aware of the extreme heterogeneity and complexity in groups. No two people are alike, and certainly a nation includes a vast, almost baffling, array of diverging class, ethnic, political, social, and economic interests. It is hazardous to find a common psychological thread in such a tapestry.

But that is exactly Kohut's purpose. He argues, for example, in the first interview in this volume (p. 215 ff) that at some point in a group's common, usually national, experience a program is laid down. This occurs in the now distant past in a way that parallels the patterning of the nuclear self that emerges from the mists of earliest development. Did it gel completely? Was it weak or strong? Was it potentially fragmented? And Kohut continues: "Those are the questions we ask. Those are the things that Proust tried to do by his own efforts. It is all very different from the attempted cure of a classical neurosis. The analogue in history is to think in terms of group self. There is a basic self that at one time or another gels. It then points into the future and has its own unrolling destiny" (p. 218).

A group self, that aspect of common psychological experience of individual people in a group, maintains cohesion in its confirming merger with leader selfobjects. The unconscious fantasies of a group's grandiose self, "expressed in the transference upon the image of an appropriate leader" (p. 57), can serve cohesion in the group. Hitler's strut reflected German fantasies of grandiosity in the interwar period. Such grandiose feelings, however, are immediately apparent as compensatory for the raw shame and sense of worthlessness that lies beneath. As with the individual, the group self's merger with the idealized leader provides only fragile cohesion. There is everywhere the potential for fragmentation. Rage lies close to the surface.

Kohut's ideas as far as Nazi Germany is concerned draw us into the palpable world of Hitler's relationship with ordinary Germans. Kohut points to a complex set of connections between contemporary social and political pathology and its origins in the German family, for one of Kohut's most interesting notions in these papers is that the German family in the late 19th and early 20th centuries seemed to generate a pervasive and chronic depression. That depression in turn reflected potential self pathology and a proneness to narcissistic injury. The German group self, in other words, seemed primed to react with fury and rage to the events of 1918–1933, to sell their souls, so to speak, and turn to Hitler as their savior. Obviously such an idea is tentative. It is hardly offered as a dogmatic assertion. Kohut qualifies, hedges, even seems to apologize for the wide-ranging connections he is making. But it is the kind of psychological formulation that begins to explain why it happened in Germany and not elsewhere.

One can (and should) also read Kohut's concern with courage in the lead piece of this collection as an aspect of his thoughts on the group self. Ideals of genuine humanness lay buried in the Nazi period ready to be discovered, to grow, and to enhance the corrupt values of the authoritarian regime. As in Jaeggerstaetter's dream (see pp. 13), everyone was jumping on a train bound for hell. But at least his quiet dissent points the way to a more hopeful future and creates the possibility of healing some wounds in the fractured group self.

Courage, one might say, intrigues Kohut. Hans and Sophie Scholl and Frans Jaeggerstaetter define courage in the 20th-century world. That paper lay in Kohut's back drawer for a decade before he himself had the courage to publish it. At the very end, in the last interview, he generalizes: "You know, one needs courage. Always. Anything that is good needs courage." He goes on to talk of the mindless response to modern music, but his examples could be political or scientific just as easily as they are artistic. That same interview begins with a discussion of the Spartans at Thermopylae who lose their lives biologically but save their souls psychologically. It is possible.

Self Psychology and the Humanities
Reflections on a New Psychoanalytic Approach

HEINZ KOHUT

The Past Considered

1

On Courage

(early 1970s)

Courage and Heroism

As the depth psychologist surveys the currents of history he will inevitably have to confront the question of human behavior during periods of crisis. In particular he will have to face the task of defining the psychological constellation which allows an exceptional few to oppose the pressures exerted on them and to remain faithful to their ideals and to themselves, while all the others, the multitudes, change their ideals and swim with the current. What allows (or compels) some people to face death and even suffer it, rather than give up the openly professed loyalty to their ideals, to bear "witness" in traditional religious terminology? In what consists the courage of those who, though outnumbered or alone, will yet maintain their self and their ideals?

Some forms of courage need no explanation. Many people will act courageously when they have no choice, for example, as members of militant groups which insist on conformity or when they are fighting for their biological survival. The problem which has to be solved concerns those whose loyalty to the continuity of self and ideals becomes *more* important than biological survival, when, to paraphrase Alexander Mitscherlich (1963), the consistency of the structure of the ego enables a person to remain true to his goals and ideals, despite intimidation from without and within.

Courage can be defined as the ability to brave death and to tolerate destruction rather than to betray the nucleus of one's psychological being, that is, one's ideals. There are genetic, dynamic, and structural aspects of such fortitude, as well as certain auxiliary devices which the psyche employs in order to maintain its resolve.

The psychological study of courage in history is not a simple matter. When we scrutinize the personalities and the behavior of unusually courageous people, of those who as solitary martyrs uphold apparently hopeless and useless convictions, there is the possibility that we are dealing with mentally deranged individuals. I have no doubt that there are instances in which severely disturbed individuals, whose assessment of reality has been overpowered by psychotic illness, will drift into the role of political, ideological or religious martyrdom. Such individuals will often be given conspicuous punishment by an established regime and will attain in the long run the halo of sanctity. They will then be solemnly celebrated by a grateful posterity. Such figures, whatever their degree of psychological illness, may serve the curious role of scapegoats or enemies of the people for those in power and of martyrs and heroes for the powerless opposition. Analogously, at certain historical junctures, as the Mitscherliches have pointed out (1967), society will choose irrational leaders to take the responsibility for carrying out purposes for which responsibility can then be again disowned after the leader has disappeared. We tend to judge the wish for survival as paramount in the normal individual, especially when his behavior serves no practical end and leads to death. But the typical representative of historical heroism and martyrdom is not to be judged as necessarily pathological when assessed from a depth-psychological point of view, even though there may be the temporary presence of some grossly abnormal features in his thoughts and behavior and despite the apparently unrealistic nature of his actions.

One striking characteristic of unusually courageous individuals is that at certain critical moments or stages of their lives they create imagery concerning an all-powerful figure on whom to lean for support. This idealized figure may be a personified god or a prototypical historical figure or a charismatic person who is living in the present. The spectrum of such falsification of reality, employed in the service of establishing a courage-supporting relationship to an idealized figure, extends from (a) temporary delusions and hallucinations, via (b) grossly aggrandizing distortions in the evaluation of people who in reality have only ordinary and moderate endowment, to (c) an illusional, concretizing, vivid idealization of truly inspiring personages who are either temporally or spatially remote from the hero who, however, in his fantasy, will feel that he is deriving concrete support from leaning on them.

To the first group of falsifications or courage-supporting mechanisms belong experiences such as hearing the voice of God or seeing visions in which God appears as the hero. Such messages that the courageous individual receives are delivered from the supernatural powers with the aid of supposedly meaningful but, in fact, accidental occurrences. Some of these experiences are tradition-bound and standardized, like "the call" from a personified god heard at a specific time and place by those embarking on a career as missionaries.

A good example of the second type of falsification of reality engaged in by heroic people is the intense, unrealistic idealization of the physical, mental or moral powers of people who in reality possess only ordinary, moderate endowment. I call this phenomenon the "transference of creativity." A genius, frightened by the boldness of his pioneering discoveries and yearning to relieve his loneliness, creates for himself the figment of a vastly overestimated figure on whom he leans temporarily but whom he discards (i.e., from whom he withdraws his idealization) after his essential work has been achieved. During the transference of creativity itself, the genius projects his own mental powers onto someone else. He assigns his discoveries temporarily to that other person and feels humble toward and dependent upon this idealized protector, mentor and judge, who is in essence his own creation.[1]

---

[1] See in this context my reference (*The Analysis of the Self,* 1971, pp. 316 ff [and the paper in this volume, "Creativeness, Charisma . . . ," p. 171 ff]) to the relationship of Freud to Fliess and the general discussion of the fact that certain paranoid personalities with their absolute conviction of being right lend themselves to being used temporarily as overvalued, idealized figures. Certain paradigmatic experiments of great pioneering scientists may be considered as related phenomena in this context. These experiments, although unrepeatable in the form in which they are first described, are appropriate illustrations of some law of nature newly discovered by the genius. They are, however, not ordinary

In some of these examples (especially in those involving the relationship to hallucinated god figures) it may, on superficial scrutiny, seem difficult to draw a clear-cut line of demarcation with the psychoses. I will return to the topic of this differentiation later on when discussing certain individuals—specific examples of heroism and martyrdom—in whom such pseudo-psychotic features can indeed be found.[2] But the third type of falsification of reality, in which courage is supported through a leaning on or a merger with inspiring prototypical figures, does not generally raise serious doubts about the sanity of those who cling to these bonds, even though with this group one may occasionally encounter experiences of hallucinatory vividness and temporary delusion-like distortions.

It is not difficult to recognize that all these falsifications of reality, which are so dramatic at certain critical times in the lives of courageous individuals, are variations on the single theme of regression in the developmental line of a specific narcissistic configuration, that of the idealized, omnipotent selfobject. It is my impression, however, that in many instances of great heroism it is not an intensely cathected value system alone which is the primary motivation for the courageous thought or deed. As I will try to show, this motivation arises from the entire *nuclear self* of the individual and not from his values alone. The re-concretization of the ego ideal, however—that is, its (regressive) transformation into an omnipotent selfobject—becomes temporarily necessary as an auxiliary means by which the fulfillment of the nuclear self can be attained despite the most severe anxieties of dissolution to which man will expose himself voluntarily. The pseudo-delusions and pseudo-hallucinations of the hero are, therefore, created in response to a temporary great need; they occur as the outgrowth of conditions which resemble those of early childhood when, because of the psychological incompleteness which prevails at that stage, the young child's self-esteem regulation depends almost exclusively on the presence of selfob-

---

experiments (designed to facilitate discovery, or to prove a theory) but rather the expression of the genius' creative, concretistic thinking, which—during peak moments of his mental activity—make him confuse action with thought, persuade him that he has seen and manipulated in physical reality what in truth he has seen only with his mental eye.

[2] In this context see also the report of Miller (1962) concerning the experiences of political prisoners in Hungarian jails.

jects who admire the child or who allow the child to merge into their idealized perfection. Under certain anxiety-provoking conditions, then, the archaic need for support becomes so great that the omnipotent object will, regressively, arise out of the ego ideal and be, again, as it was once in early life, experienced as an archaic, prestructural, *external* power. Thus it may happen that an individual at the very peak of psychological independence—when he lives in fact more actively and expresses the goals of his nuclear self more completely than the average human being can ever hope to do—believes that he has no initiative and feels himself "lived" by influences from outside himself. The brave anti-Nazi farmer, Franz Jaegerstaetter, for example, who uncompromisingly went to the guillotine rather than take up arms for the evil forces of Nazi Germany, stated it thus (Zahn, 1982, rep. 1964, p. 128): "If God had not given me the . . . strength even to die for my faith . . . I, too, would . . . be doing the same [i.e., compromise with the Nazis] as . . . other Catholics . . ."

It seems apparent that courage cannot be easily explained as the personification and concretization of the ego-ideal. Nor does the hero simply mobilize irrational imagery and beliefs to support his rational, nonpathological pursuits. So what then prompts him to move forward, despite intimidation from within and without? He is compelled to proceed on his lonely road, even if it means his individual destruction, because he must shape the pattern of his life—his thoughts, deeds and attitudes—in accordance with the design of his nuclear self.

But what is this nuclear self for which I claim such an important place in psychological health and disease?[3] It is that continuum in time, that cohesive configuration in depth, which we experience as the "I" of our perceptions, thoughts and actions. There are those who would postulate that a self—*the* self—is the center of our being from which all initiative springs and where all experiences end. I, however, do not agree for the following two reasons: (1) To posit a single self as the central agency of the psyche (Levin, 1969; Schafer, 1973) leads toward an elegant,

---

[3] See Kohut (1971, pp. 179–186), for a clinical contribution to this topic, i.e., the discussion of the different dynamic significance of the overt grandiosity displayed by a specific patient's (vertically split-off) peripheral self, on the one hand, and the unmet demands of a hidden (repressed) but central, i.e., nuclear, self, on the other hand.

simple theory of the mind, but also toward an unwarranted de-emphasis of the importance of the unconscious. And (2) this def-inition of the self is not derived from psychoanalytic material but from conscious experience. The decision to assign to a single self the most central position in the psyche is not—at least not at the present stage of psychoanalysis—forced on us by the necessity to accommodate specific data obtained through psychoanalytic observation, but it is made by choice in order to fashion a rounded and cohesive theory of thought, perception and action. The con-cept of a unitary, central self is an axiom introduced into analysis from the outside.

There is, however, a second approach to the conceptualization of the self. Although it does not lead immediately to a theory of the mind which is as elegant and cohesive as the first, it has my vote. I prefer to define the self as an abstraction derived from psychoanalytic clinical experience, not excluding psychoanalyti-cally sophisticated observation outside the clinical setting. I con-sider the self as a potentially observable content of the mind.[4] If we choose this approach we will recognize the simultaneous exis-tence of different and even contradictory selves in the same per-son, of selves with various degrees of stability and of various degrees of importance. There are conscious, preconscious, and unconscious selves; there are selves in the ego, the id, and the superego; and we may discover in some of our patients incom-patible selves, side by side, in the same psychic agency.

Among these selves, however, there exists one which is most centrally located in the psyche, one which is experienced by the individual as the basic one, and which is most resistant to change. I like to call this self the *nuclear self*. It is composed of derivatives of the grandiose self (i.e., of the central self-assertive goals, pur-poses and ambitions) and of derivatives of the idealized parent imago (i.e., of the central idealized values). The nuclear self is thus that unconscious, preconscious and conscious sector in id, ego and superego which contains not only the individual's most

---

[4] See in this context my discussion (Kohut, 1959, p. 460) of our right to define "the Preconscious and the Unconscious as psychological structures not only because we approach them with introspective intention, but also because we consider them within a framework of introspected or potentially introspected experi-ence."

enduring values and ideals but also his most deeply anchored goals, purposes and ambitions.

The nuclear self, however, is not immutable. The task of modifying and even of transforming it is repeatedly imposed on us throughout life under the influence of new internal and external factors. The modifiability of the nuclear self—at certain developmental junctures like adolescence and old age or under the influence of crucial environmental changes—is not a sign of disease and must not, in and of itself, be evaluated as a psychological or moral defect. On the other hand, we may justifiably deplore some behavior as the manifestation of a psychological shortcoming and of moral infirmity—like the actions and attitudes of those who quickly and opportunistically adjust their convictions under the influence of external pressures. Such behavior does not involve an alteration of the nuclear self but represents merely an adaptation on the psychological surface. In such individuals the nuclear self ceases to participate in the overt attitudes and actions and becomes progressively isolated and is finally repressed or disavowed. The psychological outcome, which is unfortunately more or less characteristic of the psychological makeup of the majority of adults, is not an individual striving toward a creative solution of his conflicts concerning the redefinition of his basic ambitions and values but a person who, despite his smoothly adaptive surface behavior, experiences a sense of inner shallowness and who gives to others an impression of artificiality.

The heroic individual's nuclear self is, therefore, not necessarily characterized by its immutability. As a matter of fact the hero's willingness to die sometimes comes about as a result of a creative change in his nuclear self, a change by virtue of which he gets out of step with the goals, ambitions and values of his environment. The capacity of the nuclear self to undergo changes, whether they take place slowly or occur abruptly (as in mystical experiences of illumination) is fully compatible with that firmness of attitude so characteristic of courage.

Almost all heroic individuals face grave crises while they are still on the road to reaching the ultimate decision that they will remain faithful to their selves, whatever the cost. They are generally not beset by fear of the consequences they will suffer as a result of their actions. They seem unafraid of isolation, social ostracism or punishment. The crisis of courage is rather one of extreme narcissistic imbalance. They feel deeply frustrated, because inner and outer obstacles stand in the way of that total devotion to the central self which alone promises them the inner peace of narcissistic equilibrium.

Winston Churchill's nuclear self, for example, seems to have crystalized around derivatives of the grandiose self. For one thing, one of the most common specific ideational elaborations of the grandiose self, namely a flying fantasy, was active in him. He had a compelling need to be entrapped in order to prove his ability to escape, that is, to fly off.[5] Furthermore, his personality appears in general much less characterized by devotion to lofty ideals than by the conviction that he possessed unconquerable power. This he communicated effectively. His addresses to the nation and to the world, which did so much to strengthen the will to resist during the darkest moments of our century, were not in the main appeals to high ideals but, in their most effective aspects, expressions of his belief in the surpassing strength of those who defended civilization against the forces of evil. Finally, side by side with the awe-inspiring manifestations of his strength, courage and independence there remained in him a touch of the infantile—perhaps a residuum of the grandiosity of the oral phase—in the form of a childlike enjoyment of being catered to and of exhibiting his physical and mental attributes for admiration. Thus with Churchill, as is undoubtedly true for many other great leaders, it was the grandiose self and not the derivatives of the idealized imago which was the most important ingredient in a composition of his nuclear self.

Be that as it may, we can discern in Churchill a clear progression from a state of narcissistic imbalance to one of narcissistic equilibrium. He experienced a sense of great inner calm and relief when he became Prime Minister (Churchill, 1959, p. 227). It seems a state of narcissistic equilibrium established itself when he had the opportunity to live out again, in ultimate fulfillment, the deepest purposes of his self. He could then reenact in the arena of the whole world the apotheosis of a grandiose fantasy he retained from childhood: that of gaining freedom from

[5] [Editor: Kohut also talks about Churchill in this context in his essay, "Forms and Transformations of Narcissism," this volume, p. 110].

encirclement by blissfully soaring into the air.

In the decisions and actions of many other heroic individuals, however, the values of the nuclear self, rather than the subject-bound grandiosity, supply the decisive motive power for heroism. In the Austrian peasant Franz Jaegerstaetter, for example, it was clearly a set of religious ideals which led him to decide not to serve in the German army. His own touching account explains the long psychological road he had to travel from his initial moral challenge at the time of the invasion of Austria by the Nazis in 1938 to his final decision to accept death. He rejected all the compromises that were offered to him, especially that of noncombatant service in the German army, and calmly and "serenely"—the term often used by martyr-heroes or by those who observe them—went to the guillotine in 1943 rather than betray his Christian values.

The intensity with which Jaegerstaetter responded to the original challenge is illustrated by a dream which he recorded later. (It is certainly significant that this unsophisticated farmer not only remembered the dream, but that he recorded it. He must have realized that the content of this dream—including his own interpretation of it—dealt with events of psychological importance). Here is Jaegerstaetter's account of his dream in free translation (Zahn, p. 212):

> Right at the beginning I want to describe a brief experience during a summer night in 1938. First I lay awake almost until midnight even though I was not ill; but then I must have fallen asleep for a while because I was shown a beautiful railroad train which circled around a mountain. Not only the grown-ups but even the children streamed toward this train and it was almost impossible to hold them back. I hate to tell how very few of the grown-ups there were who resisted being carried along by this occasion. But then I heard a voice which spoke to me and said: This train is going to hell . . .

Jaegerstaetter reflected on the meaning of this dream. Ultimately he came to the conclusion that it depicted the Nazi invasion. It showed how everybody was jumping on the bandwagon, but that the movement which everybody joined was evil and that they all would be led to their utter destruction.

It is my impression that we are not dealing here with a dream in the full psychoanalytic sense of the word, that is, with a psychic phenomenon in which the preconscious concerns are merely the carriers for the true motivators of the dream, the dreamer's infantile wishes and conflicts. It seems instead that the dream is a thought sequence occurring during an altered state of consciousness, expressed through visual and auditory experiences of near-hallucinatory vividness. We are thus dealing with a phenomenon in which, in a reversal of the usual direction, it is the secondary process which pulls up the primary process and enlists it in its service.[6] Such an occurrence is evidence of a person's concentrated attention to an all-important task, that he is focusing all of his available energies upon a conflict or decision of the gravest importance. Indeed, such experiences testify to the fact that an individual is directly confronting an inner task of such magnitude that the vast majority of people would automatically avoid it, would sanely sidestep the tragic decision and—expressed in the imagery of Jaegerstaetter's dream—would run along with the crowd. Phenomena such as Jaegerstaetter's dream of the summer of 1938 are therefore not manifestations of psychological failure but, despite the unmistakable presence of archaic features, of a peak performance. The mental activity involved here strains the psychic apparatus to the utmost, without, however, doing it permanent damage. We should not refer to such phenomena in terms that stress the imperfections of the performance. We should instead give them a name which acknowledges that a hard task is joined by the depth of a psyche. We might therefore speak of such psychic activities as "hypercathected crisis thinking."[7]

Jaegerstaetter was not the only Catholic in the St. Radegund of 1938 who realized that his religious values were in conflict with the total loyalty demanded by the Nazis; nor was he the only one who felt that his homeland had been taken over by a power which was inimical to certain of its basic traditions. Still, whatever the content of the values and traditions of those who, despite initial reservations, joined the near-unanimous majority, their psychological equipment did not allow them to set the core

[6] The psychic activity described here is related to the one which creates the "dreams from above" (Freud, 1929) and to the processes to which Ernst Kris (1936) referred to as "regression in the service of the ego." Silberer's "functional phenomenon" (1909) also overlaps the area under consideration.

[7] [Editor: In Freud's early psychological writings, cathexis refers to the charge of affective energy attached to a given ideational content. A rough translation of "hypercathexis" would therefore be "supercharge" or, even freer, "intense."]

of their selves against the overwhelming presence of the opposing values and traditions of the Nazi movement. The remarkable psychological quality that individuals like Jaegerstaetter
possess is their capacity not to withdraw from an inner conflict
of extraordinary proportions. Their conflict concerns the performance of certain interrelated tasks. They must identify their
nuclear self, resist their tendency to disown it, and ultimately
resolve to shape their attitudes and actions in accordance with
the basic design of the nuclear self, despite inner doubts and
external threats and seductions. Some details in the performance of these tasks may seem regressive. But such details are
either the unavoidable vibrations of the psychological machinery
as it strains under the intense demands made on it or are in fact
supportive maneuvers, which remain unscrutinized because the
psyche's energies are totally committed to the central, creative
effort. Thus Jaegerstaetter's dream contains details in which his
resistant self seems to be supported by an external superior power.
(". . . I was shown a beautiful train. . . . I heard a voice which
spoke to me and said . . ."). But in the long run Jaegerstaetter
not only became clear about the meaning of his conflict and could
think about it rationally, but also began the painful process of
testing the appropriateness of his conclusions and plans by eliciting the opinions of those whom he considered to be his men-
tors and spiritual guides, those traditional agents of realism and
morality.

Such heroic individuals are therefore not psychotic. Nor are
the hallucinations and delusional commands which the hero
experiences as the motivators of his courageous actions and attitudes the manifestations of a dissolution of the self. The true
motivator which propels the hero toward the heroic deed is his
nuclear self; the hallucinated commands are merely temporary
auxiliary mechanisms, secondarily created to serve the purposes
of the hero.

In support of this claim I will discuss three features of some
heroic individuals which place them clearly outside the realm of
psychosis. The three features are: the presence of a fine sense
of humor; the ability to respond to others with subtle empathy;
and, generally at the time when the ultimate heroic decision has
been reached and the agonizing consequences have to be faced,
the suffusion of the personality with a profound sense of inner

peace and serenity—a mental state akin to wisdom. This is something which never fails to impress the observer, including even persecutors, torturers and executioners.[8] Heroes, in other words, achieve a high order of development in the narcissistic sector of their personality, and this developmental achievement is maintained during the decisive heroic period of their lives.

My examples of heroism are anti-Nazis who were active during the Second World War. They include the Austrian farmer, Franz Jaegerstaetter, and Hans and Sophie Scholl, who were two of the heroes of the Student Conspiracy in Munich in 1943. Specifically, I will discuss the presence of a sense of humor in Jaegerstaetter, of a high degree of empathy in Hans Scholl, and of serenity as a ubiquitous phenomenon present in all of these heroes but most noticeably manifested (and self-interpreted through a decisive dream) in Sophie Scholl. Finally, I will attempt to show the difference between two classes of heroes: those which I am discussing at this point—I will call them for simplicity's sake the *martyr heroes*—and those (exemplified in Nazi Germany by individuals belonging to such groups as the so-called Kreisauer Kreis and to the Oster-Canaris-Stauffenberg Circle) to whom I will refer as the *rational resisters*.

The presence of a genuine sense of humor constitutes one reliable indication that there is no severe impairment in the narcissistic sector of the personality. It speaks in particular against the existence of, or even against the propensity for, a psychosis. Genuine humor can be achieved only when primitive forms of grandiosity have been relinquished—whether the grandiosity had previously been bound to the subject's grandiose self or had been focused on an idealized (aggrandized) selfobject. A paranoiac's

---

[8] I will not here elaborate the reasons for my view that these features indicate the presence of a psychological state which is in certain respects the opposite of schizophrenic psychosis. Suffice it to say that we are dealing here with manifestations of the highest degree of mastery in the realm of narcissism (see the discussion of humor, empathy, and wisdom in Kohut, "Forms and Transformations," 1966, this volume, and in Kohut, 1971). That is, we are dealing with the very opposite of schizophrenic psychosis, a disorder which is determined by the disintegration of the patient's self and by a lasting regression of his narcissism (see Kohut, 1971, in particular, pp. 6 ff). It certainly gives food for thought, however, that there should be at least a superficial resemblance between the behavior of individuals who are paradigmatic of the highest sublimations of narcissism and those in whom the narcissistic sector of the personality has broken down. Mercier (1781–1788) expressed it suggestively in his famous phrase: "Les extrèmes se touchent."

coldly arrogant superiority and the hostile certainty of his own conviction about the powerful persecutor's inimical intentions are the very antithesis of a healthy humorous attitude toward the realistic limitations of oneself and of those one admires. It bears repeating that to be humorous is not the same as to be self-belittling or to be lacking in enthusiasm. Humor is fully compatible with a secure sense of self-esteem or with a warm devotion to values and ideals. It is, of course, true that there are times, outside of mental illness, when the serious, nonhumorous pursuit of the purposes of the self and a serious, nonhumorous devotion to ideals may be demanded of us. But when an individual has earnestly resolved to live in accordance with the central purposes of the self and in harmony with the highest idealized value and still preserve a sense of modesty and proportion, then we will feel that he has achieved a high degree of healthy mastery in the narcissistic sector of his personality. We can be certain that the core of his personality is sane and that the inner forces which propelled him toward heroic activity were not based on delusions when his ability to respond with humor is preserved in the face of the utmost sacrifices that man can make as he remains faithful to his nuclear self.

This was indeed the psychological state which prevailed in Franz Jaegerstaetter when he faced execution. Jaegerstaetter's letters to his wife from the prisons in which he was kept from March 2, 1943, until he was executed five months later on August 9, are a moving testimony to his modesty, his sense of proportion and his humor. He was neither self-belittling nor sarcastic, and he never lost his heroic resolve to suffer death rather than to compromise with evil. Jaegerstaetter's total correspondence should be studied by those who want to experience the full human resonance of his communications. Here a few samples will have to suffice.

In a letter written on March 19, Jaegerstaetter empathically imagines the strain which his imprisonment and the villagers' reactions to his anti-Nazi and anti-war stand must have imposed on his wife. He sympathizes with her concerning the amount of work that she now has to do because he is away. But then he adds, tongue in cheek (Zahn, p. 66): "I think it would be good for us occasionally to trade places for a week; such a rest would be good for you." Or, on April 4 he comments, with a touch of wry humor, about the food in prison (Zahn, p. 68): "Of course, you can easily understand," he writes, "that we are not getting fat on this diet; but that is not essential either, for they have not locked us in here in order to fatten us up."

The Scholls provide further evidence that many martyr heroes give evidence of a high degree of sublimation in the narcissistic sector. These two young Munich students were both executed on February 2, 1943: Hans Scholl was 22 at the time of his death and his sister Sophie Scholl was 19.[9]

As a student of medicine Hans Scholl was released from regular military duties, but from time to time he was subject to active service on the front. At the beginning of one of these periods of service, on the way to the Russian front, the train which transported his company stopped at a small station in Poland. There he saw a line of women and young girls bent over doing heavy labor at the railroad tracks. The women had the yellow star of David affixed to their garments. Hans jumped from the train and walked toward the women. The first in the row as he approached them was an emaciated young girl. He noticed her slender hands and her intelligent, beautiful face, which seemed to express unspeakable sorrow. He tried to think of something that he could give her. He remembered that he had his "K-ration" with him—a mixture of chocolates, raisins, and nuts—and he stuck it into her pocket. The girl threw it back at him, with a harried but proud gesture. Hans smiled at her warmly and said, "I would so much have liked to give you a little pleasure." He bent down, picked a daisy, laid it upon the food package, and put the gift at her feet. Then he ran for the train which had begun to move. From the train window he saw the girl once more, standing up straight, looking after him. The white daisy was in her hair.

[9] [Editor: Hans and Sophie Scholl were two of the student leaders of a small resistance movement in Munich University called the White Rose. Formed in the spring of 1942, the White Rose launched its rebellion against the lies of the Nazi regime on February 18, 1943. Thousands of leaflets were distributed and appeals to fight against Hitler were posted on walls and at the entrance to Munich University. The members of the group were quickly arrested and executed. At the university there was no protest and professors and students did not even petition for the pardon of the members of the White Rose. Kohut had clearly been reading of the student resistance movement when he was writing this paper; in a footnote he refers to Christian Petry, *Studenten aufs Schafott* (1968) and to the moving account by a surviving sister, Inge Scholl, *Die Weisse Rose* (1953).]

The journey of the true martyr hero leads him increasingly toward clarity concerning the essence of his nuclear self. The beginning of this journey may be marked by a shock-like recognition, which is often experienced as a revelation, i.e., as coming from outside. The revelation may occur at a time when some change of the external or internal milieu (including a basic alteration of the nuclear self) brings about a psychological disequilibrium. Suddenly there exists now a gap between the kind of behavior which would be in harmony with the self and the kind of behavior that is dictated by the demands of the environment. Once the martyr hero has become aware of his nuclear self (and of the inner and outer conflict situations to which he is brought by its demands), he can find no rest. At first it may seem that he is primarily afraid of the social consequences which he would have to face if he lived in conformity with the basic patterns of the nuclear self. His uneasiness, however, is in the main not due to the fear of the external forces which might oppose him; rather, his tensions are a manifestation of the fact that he is in a severe narcissistic disequilibrium until he has achieved the complete unification of his personality under the leadership of the nuclear self. As soon as the ultimate step in this direction is made and the ultimate decision has been reached (whether it be Churchill's becoming prime minister or Jaegerstaetter's resolve not to accept any further compromises with the demands of the Nazi war machine), the hero experiences a sense of relief and of inner peacefulness and serenity. These feelings are manifestations of the narcissistic balance which has come through the establishment of a state of complete harmony between the nuclear self and the rest of the personality.

In many of the martyr heroes, it is the set of central values and ideals, the heir to the archaic idealized object, which decisively defines the nuclear self.[10] Thus, the ultimate state of nar-

[10] In the present context it may be mentioned again that the martyr-hero's first awareness of the nuclear self, in those instances where this central structure is mainly defined by the hero's idealized values, comes to him frequently in the form of a pseudo-projection: the central set of his values becomes regressively transferred into the (prestructural) archaic omnipotent selfobject from which it had once originated. This archaic selfobject is then experienced as being on the outside. It makes its appearance in the form of a "call" or of other manifestations of a seemingly external power which shows the hero the road he must take, etc. It follows that heroic individuals in whom the nuclear self is more defined by the derivatives from the *subject*-bound sector of infantile narcissism than by the

cissistic balance in such people blends the personality with the central values of the self. When such an identification has been achieved, the martyr hero has a sense of profound inner peace (narcissistic equilibrium) and even the experience of conscious pleasure that his ideals and his total personality have now become one. The general psychological setting in which these emotions occur is one of calmness and clarity. We see neither the fuzzy mysticism which characterizes certain regressive swings in narcissistic personality disturbances nor, of course, the anxious and bizarre mental state surrounding the delusional contacts with a bizarre god and with other distorted omnipotent figures which we encounter in the psychotic.[11]

The most beautiful illustration of the essence of the experience of inner peace and serenity which the martyr hero achieves in the end is poignantly contained in the last dream of Sophie Scholl. It occurred during the night which preceded her execution. Sophie Scholl's dream should be compared with the dream of Jaegerstaetter. Jaegerstaetter's dream potrays the state of the psyche at the beginning of the martyr hero's road: It shows the first response of the psyche to the demands of the nuclear self, the first stirrings of recognition regarding the difficult road which lies ahead. Sophie Scholl's dream portrays the state of the psyche at the end of the martyr hero's road: It shows how the total personality is being given over to the essential sectors of the nuclear self, to the hero's idealized values.

---

derivatives of the archaic omnipotent *object* (Churchill may serve as an example of such a constellation), will not be likely to have experience of receiving a "call" from an archaic idealized figure at the crucial moment when they begin their irreversible journey in the direction which is dictated by their nuclear self but will experience an upsurge of inner power and certainty which propels them toward their goal.

[11] See in this context Kohut (1971), in particular diagram 1 on p. 9 and the discussion of the regression in the realm of the omnipotent object on pp. 6–10. The regression goes from (1) ideals, values and admired figures, via (2) the upsurge of mystical religious feelings in the narcissistic personality disturbances to (3) the experience of the powerful persecutor in the psychoses. It might be added here, which indeed goes without saying, that—after the lasting disintegration of the idealized selfobject has taken place (a process which constitutes the essence of schizophrenic psychoses)—the omnipotent object is reconstituted in the psychoses in two forms: either as a bizarrely hostile persecutor (e.g., the influencing machine, etc.) or as a bizarre power (e.g., the personified sun, etc.) which, nonhostilely, infuses strength or vitality into the psychotic patient.

Here is the account of Sophie Scholl's last dream.[12] After she had been aroused from her sleep to face the day of her execution, she told the following dream to her cellmate. In the dream, she said, it was a sunny day, "and I carried a child, dressed in a long white garment, to be baptized. The path to the church led up a steep mountain; but I held the child firmly and securely. Suddenly there was a crevasse gaping in front of me. I had barely enough time to deposit the child on the far side of it, which I managed to do safely—then I fell into the depths." After Sophie had told her dream she immediately explained its meaning to her companion. The child, she said, is our leading idea ("unsere Idee")—it will live on and make its way to fulfillment despite obstacles ("wird sich durchsetzen").

Her behavior during the rest of the day (she was executed in the afternoon) testifies to the total absorption of her personality by her idealized values. Everything that is reported about her is in harmony with a sense of total narcissistic balance. She was calm and peaceful throughout the day. Her skin was glowing and fresh, her face radiant, with an expression of "wonderous triumph." Her lips were of a deep glowing red. She went to her execution without a trace of fear.

Normality and Rational Resisters

The contrast between the martyr-heroes and the resisters is great. In most cases we can more easily empathize with the rational

[12] [Kohut notes that his free translation of the dream follows Inge Scholl's report in *Die weisse Rose*, 1953]. In the true martyr heroes such dreams are not part of a system of denials (e.g., the denial of having failed in their realistic pursuit; the denial of the reality of the imminent destruction of the self), but an expression of the triumph of the nuclear self. The physiological signs of glowing health, in particular the vascular suffusion of the skin and of the visible mucous membranes (see the description of Sophie Scholl's appearance during the last day of her life), are strong supports for this assessment of the martyr's psychological state. Sophie Scholl's dream, as was true for Jaegerstaetter's, is, therefore, a "dream from above." The contributions from the unconscious, in other words, while surely of interest, do not determine the dream, and their uncovering would not give us the dream's essential meaning. It follows that we are, in such instances, not dependent on the free associations of the dreamer but can trust the dreamer's, generally unambiguously given, own explanation. In this context note my earlier discussion on pp. 13–14 of Jaegerstaetter's dream and of the phenomenon which I called "hypercathected crisis thinking."

resisters. It is nevertheless extraordinarily difficult to characterize them psychologically. First of all it must be admitted that normality is often a (almost unfathomably) complex state—more complex at any rate than those forms of pathology which rest on regression and primitivization. Secondly—a consideration which is correlated to the preceding point—the actions of the individuals in this group are predominantly determined not by demands which emanate from the depth of their nuclear selves (although this basic aspect of their personalities, especially the code of their superegos, is of considerable importance), but by the decisions of their autonomous or dominant egos. Such persons will, therefore, be realistic in their assessment of the social reality which they want to influence through their actions and in their evaluation of the means at their disposal. The actions which the rational resister will undertake in order to achieve his social and political ends will thus be shaped by the cognitive processes of his ego. Unlike the martyr-hero, he is not likely to achieve that unswerving resolve to pursue his aims at all costs, which is so true of those propelled by their nuclear selves.

The rational resisters are generally of greater interest to the student of historical, political and social events than to the depth psychologist. The impact of their successes and failures tends to exert a greater influence on the currents of actual events than the deeds of the politically often inexperienced and naive martyr-heroes who, at least for a considerable span of time after their martyrdom, appear to have hardly been noticed and whose self-sacrificing attitudes and acts are covered over by the noisy incidents of the day. It might, therefore, be assumed that the depth-psychological assessment of the rational resisters holds little promise and that we should instead examine the greater or lesser realism of their plans and the effectiveness of their actions— in other words, their influence on the course of the crucial events of the times. Nevertheless, I believe the psychology of the rational resisters—of individuals, in other words, who may in fact become significant actors on the historical stage—lies clearly within the purview of the depth psychologists.

Although rational resisters can surely be differentiated from the martyr-heroes, their personality organization is hardly uniform. As stated before, they all share one feature: their decisions and actions—whatever their deeper motivation—are predominantly determined by the cognitive functions of their ego. Members of the German resistance came from areas as diverse as politics, religion and the military. Some were uncertain, cautious, hesitant and emotionally anemic in their conspiratorial pursuits. Others—most of all von Stauffenberg, the actual leader of the famous conspiracy against Hitler and the courageous human instrument who himself, on July 20, 1944, deposited the briefcase with the explosives next to the Führer—were driven by a greater inner fire and were more willing to disregard risks. They were more certain that they had to act against the prevailing evil, whatever the consequences.

One could group rational resisters on a sliding scale in terms of the greater and lesser autonomy of their ego. On one end of the scale we would find those individuals in whom one could assume that the psychological surface has made itself independent of the psychological depth and in whom the ego is thus not only the arbiter of the means and ends of their actions but also the matrix of their motivations. On the other end of the scale we find those in whom the psychological surface, as judged by their behavior, appears to be in broad contact with the psychological depth. In this group, as was true in the first, the ego also assesses the means and ends of the contemplated actions and screens the motivational pressures which arise from the depth. In contrast to the first group, however, the ego is not the autonomous source of the motivations. The ego is here in its decisive activities guided by the deeply anchored pattern of the nuclear self and is drawing its power from it. One would assume that those resisters whose actions emanate from the autonomous ego would be ineffective because of the lack of vigor of their motivations in situations demanding total commitment. In contrast one would assume that the second group, i.e., those in whom the psychological depth and surface form an unbroken continuum, constitute the greatest potential threat to a totalitarian regime. In the specific case of the resistance activities in the Third Reich, it was indeed this group which came nearest to carrying out a successful coup. And it was only due to a few unforeseeable, accidental occurrences that von Stauffenberg's plan failed and that the conspirators had to suffer a horrible tortured death at the hands of the Nazis.

To make clear statements about a significant correlation between the psychological structure of certain individuals and their potential influence on the events of history leads us into a new and essentially uninvestigated territory. There is no need, however, to feel unduly apologetic concerning this step, because there is no claim whatever that a comprehensive understanding of man's behavior on the stage of history has been achieved, not even with regard to the explanation of the narrowly circumscribed topic concerning the effect of a few unusual individuals. But I do believe that this approach will enable us to ask further meaningful questions and plot the direction of promising further investigations. For example, it would be interesting to know a great deal more about the interplay of early trauma and trauma mastery in the narcissistic realm and how this tends, in combination with the appropriate biological endowment, to produce the unusually firm nuclear self.

In making such proposals, however, it must be admitted that we have entered an area which has traditionally been considered as lying outside the scope of the psychoanalytic investigator: the treacherous ground governed by our evaluative judgements of normality and abnormality, of psychological health and disease. These are difficulties, however, which I will simply sidestep in the present context. I have attempted to advance psychological evidence in support of the proposition that the behavior of some of the resisters discussed in the preceding part of this study constitutes psychological health—should we speak here of *abnormal* psychological health?—and I will not burden my investigation with considerations regarding the propriety of introducing normative factors into the realm of a scientific investigation. What had to be faced, however, was the disconcerting question whether the courageous deeds of the bravest of the resisters might not have rested on the bizarre basis of a covert psychosis, whether the courage of the heroes, the titanic strength of their nuclear self, was not a manifestation of a severe narcissistic regression leading to a breakdown of the self and to the replacement of the self by a delusional structure which then, accidentally as it were, had led them to the fearless performance of those deeds in the political and social arena for which we now pay them our respect.

As can be gleaned from my examination of the personality organization of the martyr-heroes and of the rational resisters, I am not concerned with the question whether there are indeed examples of heroic individuals whose nuclear self disintegrated and was replaced by a delusional substitute that directed their action on the stage of history. I have no reliable evidence at my disposal to give a definitive answer to this question but I think that such instances do indeed exist—and probably not in small numbers. Among the saints and the heroes of history are some who, when examined with the penetrating instruments of modern depth psychology, would indeed be found to have been in essence impelled by delusional force. Clinically, these individuals would most likely be diagnosed as covertly psychotic or considered "borderline cases," for their cold, unswerving strength rests on a nonhuman, psychotic nuclear self. Here, too, is a promising area for investigations of historical figures by depth-psychological means. But it is an area which, in the context of the present considerations, I can safely leave on the side.

I am not denying the possibility that there exist psychotic individuals who can influence both contemporaries and posterity and thus leave their mark on history. But it was my intention to demonstrate that there are some, at least among the martyr-heroes (i.e., a group made up of individuals whose mental health is most likely to be questioned and who will be most suspected of being not only mentally unstable but in essence psychotic), who are in possession of a firm nuclear self, whose unusual behavior, far from being unwholesome and pitiable, is in fact powerful and exemplary. These are people whom we can admire without hesitation and whom we might wish to emulate within the limits of our own strength. I believe that I have been able to adduce sufficient evidence concerning the personality of the touching Austrian farmer Jaegerstaetter and of Hans and Sophie Scholl, the two young people who were leaders of the student conspiracy in Munich, to feel certain that their firmness of purpose did not emanate from a psychotic structure but from a strongly cathected, powerful and cohesive self. Jaegerstaetter's wry humor during his imprisonment, Hans Scholl's subtle empathy with a suffering human being, Sophie Scholl's serenity, her glowing narcissistic equilibrium even as she was confronted with death—all these features argue forcefully on the side of the conclusion that we are dealing, in these instances at least, with individuals who were enabled to maintain their heroic attitudes by virtue of the strength of the healthy narcissistic foundation of the personality.

The Nuclear Self

I hope that the examination of courageous individuals, of heroic figures in history, has taken us some distance along the way toward the clarification of the position of the nuclear self in the human personality and of its function in the life of the individual. But there is still a great deal that may seem to have remained unclear. One might argue, for example, that the definition of the nuclear self rests on a kind of circular reasoning. We postulate that the nuclear self occupies the most central position in the personality and that other selves occupy positions which are more peripheral or more superficial in relation to the central one and, by implication at least, are less genuine. On the other hand, we conclude that the self which ultimately determines the admirable actions of the martyr-heroes is the nuclear self, because only the genuine, structurally most centrally located self could have such a powerful positive influence on the personality. There is a logical fallacy here in first hypothesizing courage to be a central characteristic of the nuclear self and then proving the hypothesis by demonstrating the unswerving courage and persistence of some exceptional, saint-like persons whose attitudes and deeds we see as the manifestation of their nuclear selves.

These are compelling arguments which cannot be disproved within the confines of a system of pure logic. But I do believe that the validity of the processes of fact-finding of empirical psychology can be gauged by these standards. First I would like to specify that, although my illustrative examples concerned certain individuals whose actions I personally happen to admire and whose values and goals are similar to my own, my explanatory attempt concerns at this point only the ability of the heroic individuals to perform their actions, not the moral or social validity of their standards and goals. Secondly, steadfastness in the face of maximal threats and intimidations is not the only distinguishing and characteristic quality of the nuclear self. While I have no doubt that it is in general only the central self which is likely to prove itself indomitable in the face of torture and death, there might be instances when a defensive stance, resting on an image of the self which is located in a peripheral or superficial area of the psyche, is kept up for a long time and may in very exceptional cases be maintained even in the face of ultimate sacrifice. The gripping novel *Jud Süss* (1925) by Lion Feuchtwanger can perhaps be considered as a fictitious illustration of such an occurrence. Thus—to put the previous statements in a milder form—while it may appear to be very likely that the solitary martyr-hero is living out the pattern of his most deeply anchored and most central self, we must search for criteria which apply not only in these extreme cases but also in less dramatic ones.

Indeed, as I have indicated earlier, there is at our disposal another set of data which lends strong support ot our hypothesis. This supportive evidence is obtained through the psychological investigation of a person's path toward the full dominance of his nuclear self, through the scrutiny of the depth-psychological significance of the steps which lead to the final equilibrium at the point when the central narcissistic structure achieves its total victory and a tranquil joy pervades the total personality. The careful empathic scrutiny of this last stage of quiet triumph in the face of death will protect us in particular against resorting to a routine, nonspecific judgment, i.e., dispensing with the evidence obtained from the actual psychological manifestations of the martyr-hero's experiences and explaining the progressive course of his development directly in the terms of a biologizing drive-psychology. The consummate peace achieved by the hero is, at least in certain instances, not the result of the instinctual gratification of a masochistic wish—the fulfillment of an expiatory death-wish (the victory of self-destructive aggressive strivings in the service of the superego, for example)—[13] but the ultimate ascendancy of a firm and life-affirming self.

It must be admitted furthermore that any judgment made outside of systematic therapeutic analysis concerning the question whether certain actions or attitudes of an individual are the manifestations of his nuclear self will, of necessity, remain open

[13] There were undoubtedly instances among the martyr-heroes of the anti-Hitler resistance in which self-destructive forces played a role in the psychological makeup of the resister: e.g., in the form of self-punitive activities, instigated by the superego as punishment for the rebellion—however justified—against a person—however evil he might be—who had come to stand in the father's stead. There are, for example, indications that, as a subsidiary component at least, such a self-punitive factor may have been active in Hans Scholl on the crucial day of his apprehension. See Petry (1968), pp. 107–123.

to some doubt.[14] We do, however, not need to feel ashamed of our insecurity. It is not due to the possibility that we might have fallen prey to faulty reasoning and circular definitions, but relates to the fact that we are dealing with data which we observe and assess within the framework of an empirical science. Our decision whether, in any given instance, we are seeing the manifestations of the nuclear self, or whether we are seeing the manifestations of a peripheral or superficial self, must therefore rest on the conscientious psychological scrutiny of the data at our disposal, work which is, as usual, a two-step procedure: (1) the careful collecting of the relevant empathically observed psychological data by a trained mind, and (2) the meaningful ordering of the data thus obtained by fitting them into a theoretical framework (i.e., psychoanalytic metapsychology) which is attuned to the nature of the subject matter.

During psychoanalytic therapy, for example, the psychoanalyst would no more allow himself to decide definitely which of the various selves that a patient might present during the early stage of the treatment is the nuclear one than he would, at that stage, allow himself to make fixed judgments about the central and genetically determining childhood conflicts. To be sure, in each of these two areas a seasoned analyst's experiences with similar cases will elicit certain tentative expectations in him (on the basis of the assessment of early transference manifestations, for example); but he will not permit his perception of further material, containing evidence contrary to his first impressions, to be distorted by his earlier conjectures.

I must stress again that that self which had at one time been the nuclear self does not necessarily retain the central position. Despite the fact, however, that a previous nuclear self has now become peripheral, its investigation is still important to us if we wish to understand the present nuclear self. Some of the qualities of a previous nuclear self may still live on within the present one. The analyst will, therefore, attempt to achieve the more or less complete tracing of a developmental line from early forms of the nuclear self—at any rate from preceding forms—toward the present one.

To give an illustration: The manifestations of certain aspects

---

[14] [Editor: For a further discussion of problems of applied analysis, see Kohut, 1960, "Beyond the Bounds of the Basic Rule".]

of a particular patient's[15] presenting self appeared to be clus-
tered around his devotion to liberal political ideals and around
his ambition to be the admired protector of the persecuted and
powerless. In his childhood he had been brought up in a fundamentalist religious and politically conservative atmosphere.
During analysis the question arose (stated here in very simplified
terms) whether this patient's "liberal self" was a reaction formation and therefore a surface self (the outgrowth of a rebellious
attitude toward parental pressure), or whether it was the percep-
tible aspect of his nuclear self, i.e., of the present nuclear self as
it had developed out of the childhood nuclear self.[16]

Only long-term, conscientious observation during analysis can
provide us with the data on which we can base the answer to
such a question. To pursue further our clinical illustration, we
will, for example, try to plumb the depths of our patient's "liberal self." In attempting to assess, however, whether a particular
psychological structure indeed constitutes the nuclear self (or at
least an aspect of it), we must base our decision neither on the
criterion that the nuclear self ought to be in harmony with the
rest of the personality nor on the idea that there should reign
inner peace as soon as the patient has recognized his nuclear
self. On the contrary, the analytic investigation of the nuclear
self will almost always reveal inconsistencies between this structure and the rest of the psyche. Although these discoveries might
create discomfort, they are likely to be beneficial in the long run,
because the mobilization of psychological work through the

[15] While I have a specific patient in mind here (Mr. P., who is mentioned in
Kohut, 1971, and Kohut, 1972b), I am not primarily giving a clinical description
at this point but am simply taking certain data from the clinical material referring to this case in order to illustrate a specific problem encountered in psychoanalytic practice.
[16] One could also formulate this alternative in the terms of (secondary) ego
autonomy: one could ask, in other words, whether or not certain ego functions
which had originally been motivated by rebellion (to be specific: active attitudes—e.g., to be helpful to the weak—acquired in defense against loathed or
feared passivity) had now become ego-syntonic and autonomous (secondary
autonomy). I am strongly inclined to think, however, that it is more appropriate
(i.e., more in tune with the clinical facts, and more advantageous from the heuristic point of view) to conceptualize the normally integrated nuclear self not as
occupying only a delimited portion within the ego but as forming a whole sector
of the psyche in depth, specifically in that part of the psyche which I like to refer
to as the area of progressive neutralization (Kohut and Seitz, 1963). The nuclear
self is, therefore, a configuration which dips deeply into the unconscious during
each of the several stages of its development.

increasing awareness of these inconsistencies and conflicts opens the way to creative resolutions.

Changes in the personality may now take place.[17] There is a possibility that the patient may relinquish certain goals which had not been in tune with the basic pattern of the nuclear self and thus alter his overt actions and attitudes. There may also gradually occur a genuine transformation of the nuclear self. But despite everything there is finally the possibility that a harmonious and internally consistent personality cannot be achieved, and that some deep rents in the psychic structure must remain unmended.

We will come back to the last-mentioned possibility shortly, when we turn to the depth-psychological assessment of tragedy. In the present context, however, it is important to repeat that the whole personality can hardly ever be expected to live in harmony with the nuclear self.[18] The peripheral and suface selves are those of easy adaptation and comfortable consistency. The psychological question is not whether the psychic structure under consideration is in a state of conflict or of peace with the rest of the personality, but whether it is shallow or deep. The analytic examination of the nuclear self—in contrast to the examination of peripheral selves—leads always into the psychological depths and, as the deeper layers are gradually penetrated, to the discovery of a dynamically and genetically meaningful pattern.

The clinical investigation of the man with the "liberal self," for example, revealed a plethora of conflicts and inconsistencies.[19] Nevertheless, there is no doubt that the "liberal self" formed (an aspect of) the meaningful center of his being. His liberal convictions and the enthusiasm with which he had always supported liberal causes and followed liberal leaders were intense. When these goals and ideals were investigated in depth during analysis, rebellious attitudes vis-à-vis persecutors and rage about being victimized made their appearance. These attitudes accounted for the rigidity of his beliefs and for the fanaticism with which he

[17] [Editor: In the original, Kohut refers to the "non-self areas of the personality," which probably means the "non-nuclear self areas of the personality." However, in the context of the paragraph such an obscure distinction is more clearly expressed as one between the nuclear self and the total personality.]

[18] The martyr-hero's ultimate serenity is, of course, an exception to this rule.

[19] See, for example, the description of this patient's ambivalence toward those whose protagonist he wanted to be, Kohut (1972) [this book, p. 144].

pursued his political actions. They also interfered occasionally with his ability to help the persecuted, because an old wish for revenge was at times lived out under the guise of helpfulness.

The core of his "liberal self," however, the core of his wish to help the persecuted and disadvantaged, was deeply anchored in his personality. Its three major components had resulted from: (1) an early empathic identification with the humiliated and helpless because he, too, had felt humiliated and helpless as a child; (2) the effective (transmuting) internalization and partial integration of messianic religious ideals (not only held up to the child by the mother—who, it seems, had remained in awe of her own messianic father—but also represented by the father who had indeed been a genuine idealized selfobject for the little boy); and (3) the partial integration of grandiose fantasies (to be his mother's protector and rescuer) to which his mother had responded with reasonably appropriate pleasure and pride in his early years.

A full integration of these grandiose fantasies and archaic idealizations into the adult personality under the dominance of a realistic ego had not been achieved by the patient, and a number of opposing psychological attitudes (acquired, for example, under the impact of his mother's sadistic attacks on him when he wanted to make himself independent from her) interfered with the ability of this central sector of his personality to translate its pattern into consistent attitudes and actions. All these defects were confronted in the course of the analysis. They entered into the transference and became part of the working-through processes. At no time during the analysis, however, did the presence of these obstacles obliterate the patient's progressive political stance to reform our society and his self-concept as the champion of the oppressed. Neither the patient nor the analyst felt tempted to devalue the manifestations of these basic constituents of his personality and to see them as "mere" defensive activities, instituted in order to counteract his hostility, for example, or to overcompensate for infantile feelings of helplessness.

Many clinical complexities can also occur with the activation of unconscious guilt in the analysis. In most cases it is the analysand who insists repeatedly that certain genuine aspects of his nuclear self are merely defensive or, at any rate, that they originally arose in a defensive context. While the analyst must always listen carefully and consider the possible truth of the patient's assertations, he will—after he has convinced himself that it is the patient's current self-devaluation which is defensive and not those aspects of his personality which are at present under scrutiny— institute the only appropriate move at his disposal: He will communicate to the patient his impression of the presence of unconscious guilt that may be a source of his self-devaluation (and of a "negative therapeutic reaction"). He will then sit back and observe the consequences of his interpretation as manifested by the patient's further associations.

It should go without saying that there also exist many instances of socially commendable behavior of the patient as citizen which are in fact defensive moves during an analysis and serve the patient's acting-out, e.g., to deflect some transference impulses from the analyst. Furthermore, in certain analyses even some well integrated, valuable and approvable activities—autonomous ego activities, in other words—will temporarily give way during the therapeutic regression as infantile patterns are being reactivated in the transference. If the relinquishment of secondary autonomy is circumscribed and if it is actively undertaken by a patient's strong ego in the service of the ultimate goals of the analysis, there is no need to interfere with the temporary regression. The ego functions will return after the analysis of the infantile genetic pattern has been completed and, as a matter of fact, will tend to be even stronger and less subject to regressive transformations than before.

*   *   *   *

Throughout this paper I have been trying to increase the understanding of the psychological significance of the self by illuminating it—its position, its functions, its fate—from various points of view. It was with this goal in mind that I discussed such diverse examples as, on the one hand, the ascendancy of a historically paradigmatic nuclear self, the self of the martyr-hero, and, on the other hand, the vicissitudes of a self revealed in the clinical situation, which has no impact on public life and no significance with regard to the events of history.

I realize that the results of my efforts will not satisfy those whose primary aim is to achieve simple and elegant formulations in the psychological realm. My present examinations may have clarified certain aspects of the subject matter under scrutiny; they have, however, not led to elegant and simple statements of general validity. On the contrary, it may be claimed with some justification that the variety of approaches to the problem of the significance of the self in the personality increases—at least initially—not only the phenomenological complexity of the field but also the difficulty of framing appropriate theoretical formulations. I feel, however, that a formulation which puts *"the"* self into the center of the personality as the initiator of all actions and as the recipient of all impressions exacts too high a price. Instead of openness to new impressions, instead of the healthy capacity to experience surprise at seeing the unexpected, instead of the challenge of creating new theories as new data become available, the scientist who bases himself prematurely on comprehensive simple theories will find that they tend to become a hindrance to perceiving the new. It is like what happens when a Believer, who has posited the God-concept as the ultimate explanation of reality, reaps the benefit of finding himself, with unscientific certainty, in a fully intelligible universe.[20]

If we instead put our trust in empirical observation, using introspection and empathy as our tools, we will be open to a bewildering increase in the complexity of the relevant phenomena. Instead of the single self of conscious experience, which has always been around, we will encounter a variety of incongruous and inconsistent phenomena. We will see different selves, each of them a lasting psychological configuration, each experienced as absolute and as the center of the personality, not only in different agencies of the mind but also side by side within the same agency. We see these various selves fighting for ascendancy, one blocking out the other, forming compromises with each other, and acting inconsistently with each other at the same time. In general, we will witness what appears to be an uneasy victory of one self over all the others. But we will also see that some individuals are more capable than others of tolerating the active, creative conflict of inconsistent selves, without having to resort to undue defensive maneuvers or to the achievement of a psychological synthesis at all costs.

The discovery during analysis of various selves in the same

[20] See in this context Freud's remark (Freud, 1914b, p. 77) on ". . . the difference between a speculative theory and a science erected on empirical interpretation."

individual is at times similar to the discovery of various configurations in the well-known experiments regarding various fig-
ure-ground configurations. At one moment the observer discerns
one configuration which has complete validity and forms a convincing "Gestalt." Yet, after an imperceptible shift in the focus
of the observer's attention, there appears another fully valid
configuration which crowds out the first.

There is an additional factor which has to be taken into account
if our appropriate neutrality toward the multiplicity of selves
within the same personality is not to mislead us. It may be taken
as a basic law that, within the realm of narcissism, the observing
psyche tends to experience each mental content as absolute. This
is true whether the mental content is observed with the aid of
direct introspection or through vicarious introspection, i.e., via
empathy. We experience each of the selves that is at any given
moment in the focus of our observation as unique and absolute.
As a matter of fact it is a characteristic faculty of the healthy
psyche that it will experience narcissistic content as unique, single and absolute, even if it is simultaneously in the possession of
data which should be expected to interfere with this experience.
A healthy person's insightful *knowledge* that he harbors various
selves is, therefore, not the same as the sense of fragmentation
which is the essence of the schizophrenic *experience* of multiple
selves. The first is the result of an achievement of cognition, the
second occurs in consequence of a lack in the capacity to imbue
the relevant psychic configurations with a sufficient amount of
narcissistic investment.

We thus tend to believe in the absoluteness of our experiences. Yesterday's fashions (like yesterday's selves) look ludicrous, strange and incomprehensible. A new style at first strikes
us as foreign and unacceptable. But after we have come to know
it the formerly strange, ludicrous or repulsive is transformed: It
shares now in that basic sense of absoluteness and perfection
which every healthy person has retained in the storehouses of
his experience, the grandiose self of childhood that survives in
the depth of the personality.

During the analysis the need for the ascendancy of one absolute self will bring about a (potentially creative) struggle among
the contestants. "May the best self win" will be our hope. But
which is the best? There are no foolproof criteria and no easy

answers to this question. Nevertheless, the findings of depth psychology will open broader vistas on this problem than those which are accessible by conscious contemplation. There may be no objective standards which determine "the" best self; however, depth-psychological investigation may well lead us to a self which is deeper than the others, has more genuine genetic antecedents than the others, engages broader aspects of the personality than do the others, and most importantly, is more completely the expression and continuation of the two great narcissistic configurations of early life: the grandiose self and the idealized parent imago. Indeed, if I should dare to offer a tentative definition of the nuclear self, I would say that it is the one which is derived from these two structures and draws its strength from them. I would have to add, however, that this self, as it strives to realize its ambitions and to live up to its ideals, must have become integrated into the total personality. Specifically, it must have come under the domination of the ego, since it is the task of this agency of the mind to integrate a person's psychologically rooted strivings with biological givens, on the one hand, and with the exigencies of the social environment and of the historical moment, on the other.

I will thus define the nuclear self as a specific psychic configuration available to introspection and empathy. Psychic configurations which we call self are, as we know, the representation of mind and body, of mental and physical functions. They are experienced as being continuous in time, unitary and cohesive, and as possessing stable spatial dimensions. The nuclear self, however, is that *specific* self which fulfills two further conditions: (1) It is the self which is the carrier of the derivatives of the grandiose-exhibitionistic self (i.e., the potential executor of the goals, purposes, and ambitions which are in genetic-dynamic contact with the original aspirations of the grandiose-exhibitionistic self); and (2) it is the self which has set its sights on values and ideals which are the descendents of the idealized parent imago.

It is my firm conviction, based on considerable relevant clinical experience, that the analyst capable of focusing his attention on the nuclear self and its vicissitudes will be able to grasp an important dimension of human psychological life. And I am furthermore convinced that the analyst's attention to the self is of great practical importance, that—stated in the negative—a neglect of this dimension of human life in the analytic situation is to the detriment of the ultimate well-being of the analysand.

When one suggests a viewpoint which deviates from the accustomed one, it is best not to become defensive but to trust that the test of clinical application will provide the necessary support. Still, in order to forestall unnecessary and unwarranted clashes of theoretical opinions, I will stress again that the analysis of the self must not be looked upon as a replacement of the traditionally emphasized analysis of the drives and of structural conflict but accepted as an additional approach, undertaken within the established framework of depth psychology. Traditionally we see our analysands—and those whom we scrutinize "beyond the bounds of the basic rule"[21]—as beset by (structural) conflicts. Conflict solution is enhanced if the conflicts are raised into consciousness. The most important regulator of the psychological activities in the realm of conflicts is the pleasure principle (including, of course, its extension, the reality principle), and, on the whole, the most important processes in this realm are the internalized conflicts between the (oedipal) drive-wishes of the id-ego, on the one hand, and the drive-curbing prohibitions of the superego, on the other hand. The psychological understanding of man as seen within the conceptual framework of the drive-conflict approach of psychoanalysis is related to that traditional outlook on human problems which is evoked by such terms as guilt and restitution, sin and redemption, crime and punishment, and the like. I will, despite the great variety of phenomena that are involved, characterize this whole outlook on human psychology by saying that it focuses on *guilty man*.

But there is another dimension of human existence which must be taken into account. It is the fateful matter of whether one's nuclear self is able to express its basic patterns within the span of a lifetime. We are dealing here with psychic functions that are not regulated by the pleasure / reality principle but which are subject to forces "beyond the pleasure principle." I will once more disregard the great variety of phenomena that are here involved

---

[21] [Editor: Kohut referred to the psychoanalytic interpretation of non-clinical material as "beyond the bounds of the basic rule." See his essay by that title, Kohut (1960).].

and characterize this second outlook on human psychology by saying that it focuses on *tragic man*.

Courage and Tragedy

Analysts, beginning with Freud, have felt strongly attracted by the mystery of tragedy, which they have explained largely in terms of a psychology of passions (drives), inner conflicts concerning these passions (structural conflicts), and punishment for transgressions motivated by passions (the victory of the self-punitive forces in the superego and the ascendancy of the death instinct). In this view of tragedy, which sees man as striving for happiness through love and work, man comes to grief because he cannot master his unruly passions and must ultimately bow to the inevitable victory of the life-destructive forces as embodied in his aggressions, in his guilt, and in the inevitable end of his biological existence.

A psychoanalytic psychology of the self is able to provide us with a fresh chance to comprehend tragedy. I will step directly in *medias res* and make my central assertion: The art of the tragic—whether sung, told, or written as in the great epics; whether through music, on canvas, in stone, or on the stage—is concerned with man's attempt to live out the pattern of his nuclear self. And the tragic hero who is the protagonist of the great tragedies, which must be counted as among the most precious cultural possessions of mankind, is a man who, despite the breakdown of his physical and mental powers (e.g., Oedipus) and even despite his biological death (e.g., Hamlet), is triumphant because his nuclear self achieved an ascendancy which never will, indeed which never can, be undone.

Surrounded by the incessant flux of the human condition, confronted by the necessity of admitting the impermanance of all things dear to him, compelled finally to acknowledge the finiteness of individual existence not only in the abstract but also as it concerns his own beloved self, man comes closest to narcissistic fulfillment when he is able to realize the pattern of his most central self. The effacement or the death of the tragic hero is thus not an incidental occurrence. Its essential meaning is not to be seen as punishment for a code-transgressing deed, which sets in motion the pattern of guilt and retribution. It is instead a necessary component of the hero's achievement, for it is only in death that the hero's narcissistic fulfillment attains permanence. The survivors weep about the hero's fate, but the raised body of the hero as it is carried to the funeral pyre is not lamented as the remains of defeat would be. It is admired as the symbol of the hero's narcissistic triumph which, through his death, has now become absolute.

Every individual has two courses open to him and every individual, in one way or another, follows both of them. In his ordinary day every man lives by the pleasure and reality principles: He is the man of work and love. But no man is excluded from participating in the tragic dimensions of life. No man, however apparently insignificant his self-fulfilling goals and the idealized aspirations of his nuclear self, is at all times fully absorbed by the toils of work and by the pursuit of time-limited pleasures. There will be periods, or at least moments, in the life of every man when he becomes aware, even if only dimly, of a yearning that does not relate to the attainment of the pleasurable discharge of drive-wishes but to the compelling urge to realize the deep-rooted design of his nuclear self. Man is propelled by both of these forces, and human life lacking either of them is incomplete.

Society, too, needs tragic man. The tragic man senses the destiny of a people and of his potential role as it relates to this destiny. Ordinarily, leaders will be of the "work and love" type. In extraordinary times, however, in times of deep crisis, it will be a tragic man who will rise to lead and inspire a group whose deepest group-self—the confluence of the nuclear selves, i.e., of the basic ambitions, goals and ideals of the individuals who make up the group—has been threatened and needs to assert itself.

All art, including tragedy, is wish fulfillment. But our enjoyment of tragedy does not come from the pleasurable participation in the victory of a drive (the death instinct). That would be analogous to our enjoyment of the pleasurable participation in the wish-fulfilling world conjured up by the art of the happy ending. Simple comedies please us through the vicarious enjoyment of fulfilled libidinal wishes. Other branches of the art of the happy ending present us with artistically disguised denials of the reality of our limitations and frustrations. There is a great variety of ways by which the art of the happy ending, through more or less sophisticated means, is able to entertain the man of work and love. Our enjoyment of these art forms is derived from our temporary acceptance of the artistic assertion that a drive-wish has been fulfilled or from the functional analogue of this process, the artistic denial of the pains and frustrations of life. Tragedy, however, has another function: It gives the spectator, reader, listener or beholder the opportunity to experience, in temporary identification with the tragic hero, the unfolding, expansion and triumph of his own nuclear self.

It is a significant (and largely unexplored) fact that civilized man feels timid vis-à-vis the profound strivings of his nuclear self and that his ego seems fragile when it is faced by its demands. Civilized man has learned to work, he tries to obey the restrictions necessitated by communal life and yet, despite work and restrictions, he manages, directly and indirectly, to obtain a modicum of fulfillment of his drive-wishes. But the fetters of communal living have curtailed his freedom to express his deepest self even more than they have interfered with the opportunity to discharge his drives. Indeed, I believe that there are forces at work in this realm which are even more restrictive than the inhibiting precepts of civilized society. From the beginning of our awareness these forces have made us fearful of developing our self-expressive initiative and our creativeness. Perhaps from infancy onward the unfolding of our central selves has evoked frightening envious anger, which is a manifestation of the wounded narcissism of those around us. The full assertion of our nuclear selves is thus for most of us beyond the scope of our courage. We withdraw from our innermost goals and ideals, and we falsify and dilute them. It is in this sphere then that the buffering of art allows us a tolerable experience of self-affirmation in the form of our participation in the self-expression of the tragic hero on the stage. Great tragedy, as exemplified most tangibly in the tragic drama, is a repeatable, and thus a dosed, experience. It allows us, therefore, to participate in the emotional development of the tragic hero from doubt to decision and from dejection to triumph as his nuclear self attains realization and is made permanent through death. Paradoxically, the spectator, participating in the ultimate self-realization of the tragic hero, experiences his own self as more vigorous and cohesive than he ever can in his real life.

The primary function of tragedy is thus not to supply us with wish-fulfilling daydreams in the area of our drives. This function is fulfilled by other forms of art which, for simplicity's sake, I have called the art of the happy ending. It should go without saying that I intend no value judgment by this comparison. Not all tragedy is great art. As a matter of fact, in viewing tragedy one will often feel keenly the truth of the old statement that there is but a step from the sublime to the ridiculous. Nor is wish-fulfilling art, that of the happy ending, by any mean necessarily second-rate in its formal execution and concerned with topics that are of no relevance to man. To use a specific example: work and love man is also moral man. Non-tragic art may, therefore, not only provide wish fulfillment to him through crudely direct drive satisfaction (such as is delivered by pulp magazines and peep-show movies) but also give him the narcissistic pleasure of identifying with the moral protagonist, of sharing in his victory over the forces of evil, and of feeling temporarily relieved of the tension between his own ego and superego. As he identifies with the personified superego of the work of art in which he immerses himself, his ego will feel calm and virtuous. In the narcissistic sphere work and love man gleans from the art of the happy ending wish fulfillments like the childlike aficionados of the grandiose deeds of Superman, which are the direct descendents of ubiquitous fantasies emanating from the grandiose self of childhood (their admixture of oedipal features and of simple morality places them in early latency) and he also, through the tales of gallantry, heroism and honesty, attains a vicarious narcissistic wish fulfillment in the realm of his ideals and values. The ego of work and love man, the man of drives and structural conflicts, is, after all, exposed not just to the pressure of his drives. He also suffers from being exposed to the demands of his superego and from having to bow to the fact that his control of the environment is incomplete. Thus wish fulfillment through the art of the happy ending can be achieved in a variety of ways and by appealing to diverse aspects of the personality.

Neither sophisticated means, however, nor even the portrayal of higher goals make tragic art. Self-fulfillment is not necessarily moral, and true creativity—which, I believe, always requires the full participation of the nuclear self—is not necessarily a matter of conscientious work. The tragic hero may be moral in the usual sense of the word; our values and ideals may coincide with his. But he may also be a great sinner, a man who steps beyond the bounds of the morality of his times and his society. The question is not whether the hero is a sinner or saint; the question is whether, in that segment of his life curve that is portrayed in the tragic drama or novel, the innermost pattern of the hero's self is struggling for expression and ultimately reaches its goal.

The heroes of the novels of Dostoevski, for example, are beset by unsolvable conflicts. They suffer, they fail. They may be sinners and cowards. Some are physically ill and many die. What then redeems them? In what way do they give us that pleasure of a self-enhancing participation in another's experience which I tried to describe? It is the very perfection of the portrayal of these personalities which gives us this pleasure. All of Dostoevski's figures, from Raskolnikov and Prince Myshkin to Smerdyakov attain firmness and permanence as they live through their tortured lives. Each of them is a self that will endure as long as tragic man is responsive to art, as long as there are men whose nuclear selves cannot ever find full expression, as long as there are men who gladly suffer the pressure of unfulfilled drives, the frustration of their wishes, and even the suffering of being torn by guilt, if only they could feel themselves as a firmly coherent unit which is able to experience the joys and sufferings of life in the full reality and firm cohesion of the self.

In the tragic art of antiquity, in the epics and tragedies of Greece, the protagonists' fate, their life and death, their triumph and downfall, is starkly presented to the participating audience—painted, as it were, in the primary colors of emotionality. It is a decisive element of the tragic art of the Greeks, reflecting the tragic quality of their conception of life, that each individual fate, as it unrolls before the spectator, the listener or the reader, appears to follow inexorably a predestined course. Even in death or in the total prostration of defeat we sense the fulfillment of the destiny of an innermost self. The outcries of the bereaved survivors are, therefore, at bottom the expression of profound admiration for the hero's achievement, and the moans of the defeated hero are unself-conscious and strong. The audience leaves the theater, the reader closes the tome containing the tragic epic, with a sense of (participating) prideful exaltation.

The greatest tragic art of western civilization of more recent centuries—from Shakespeare to O'Neill, from Dostoevski to Melville—while in essence fulfilling the same functions as the tragic art of Greece, does not and cannot use the direct approach to the participating selves of modern audiences. Our selves have become too fragile. Even in art we cannot tolerate, as could the Greeks, the participation in the almost openly portrayed fulfillment of the pattern of the nuclear self of the tragic hero. We need the screen of greater disguise. We need greater dosing, more refinement, a larger admixture of neutralizing reflection, and a plot which rationalizes the hero's inner propulsion toward his triumphant downfall and transfigured death. It is only in the very greatest of the tragic works of modern times—*Hamlet*, for example, or *Moby Dick*—that the motor which drives the action toward its inevitable conclusion lies, unrationalized, entirely within the hero. It is our timidity vis-à-vis the essence of the tragic, our wish not to recognize the inevitability of unrolling fate, which accounts for the fact that we are trying to keep such art an emotional arm's length from our selves and that we are wont to consider it as not fully intelligible by declaring it mysterious.

Disregarding anachronisms, I do not believe, for example, that Hamlet's fate, as it slowly progresses toward his deed and death, would have been as mysterious for the Greeks as it has remained (or perhaps as it has increasingly become?) for modern man. By insisting that Hamlet is mysterious, modern man disavows the fact that he knows it is the hero's innermost self which strives toward its ascendancy. The hero's death is not punishment for the deed but, in its essence, a part of the fulfillment. The curve of Hamlet's life, as portrayed in the play which has fascinated the best minds of modern depth psychology (from Freud and Jones to Eissler),[22] is therefore no more, but also no less, than modern man's version of the road which the tragic hero has traveled from time immemorial, *per aspera ad astra*, to his triumphant death. Hamlet's death is the triumphant fulfillment of his reconstituted nuclear self, and his weaknesses, hesitations and temporary failures are like the climber's toils and sighs as he

[22] [Editor: Freud first outlined his theory of *Hamlet* in 1900 (1900a, 4: pp. 264–66). Jones first published his essay on *Hamlet* in 1910; later (in 1954) he published an elaborated version as *Hamlet and Oedipus*. Kurt Eissler's 1971 study is entitled *Discourse on Hamlet: A Psychoanalytic Inquiry*.]

struggles to reach the peak. Horatio's touching final words ("goodnight, sweet prince") are not the adequate response to great achievement. They are a concession to the sentimental needs of that part of the audience which cannot tolerate the identification with the triumph of undiluted heroic self-fulfillment. It is Fortinbras' last command ("let four captains bear Hamlet, like a soldier, to the stage") which contains the recognition of the greatness of Hamlet's life and which acknowledges the reality of the hero's self-fulfilling triumph.

Hamlet, as I have noted elsewhere (Kohut, 1971, pp. 235–37), has the tremendous task of first rebuilding his nuclear self and then realizing the transformed pattern of the new self. Hamlet's old self, that of his late adolescence, was an idealistic one which did not acknowledge the presence of evil in his world. He had been a princely paradigm, beloved by the populace for the pureness of his idealism. The murder of his father, however, and the involvement (perhaps even complicity) of his mother in the crime demand from him the transformation of his whole world view. Faced with this staggering task, he attempts to deny the full reality of his recognition that the recent events give the lie to his idealistic outlook on the world. The recognition remains at first ego-alien; it is not he who has understood, it is the father's ghost who informs him of the horrible truth. The full force of recognition that the evil deed has been done is thus at first partly deflected; the inner recognition is disavowed, the information is reprojected and experienced as a message received from the outside. It is only gradually that he learns to accept and integrate the fact of the existence of the ultimate evil. The enormous task of rebuilding a new self that is structured in conformity with the changed world in which he now finds himself absorbs all his energies during most of the action of the play. It strains his psychic powers to the utmost, leading to a state of diffuse tensions of which his (pseudo-)insanity, his outbursts of rage, his sarcasm, and his seeming confusion are either direct manifestations or indirect symptoms. The inner task, however, is eventually accomplished and his new disillusioned self is built. Hamlet admits to himself that the world in which he lives, the world of the royal family, is evil.

Once this inner work has been done, however, there is a remarkable but fully intelligible change in the play: Its focus shifts from Hamlet as a person to the unrolling of a multiplicity of actions. Although the pitch of action-tension is at its peak, the psychological tensions which up to this point had absorbed the audience seem to evaporate; there is relief, even relaxed frolicking, as in the amusing scene with Osric in Act V, scene 2, which by its very lightness increases the tragic impact of the final events. It is as if the actors of the drama can now relax, as if the anonymous power of destiny has taken over for them, moving them through predestined motions onward toward the predestined goals. It is at this point that *Hamlet,* despite its psychological refinement, comes closest to the spirit, the simplicity, and directness of Greek tragedy. Following the unemotional steps of courtly etiquette, the duel is arranged and performed. With the gravity of an ancient religious ritual, the deed of revenge is done and like puppets in a puppet-show the several characters of the play succumb, one after another. It is then that Hamlet, dying, comes to life again, surveys past and future and, in a final act of timelessness, gives his vote to Fortinbras as the man who is to fill his place. Hamlet dies, but his triumphant self-fulfillment ennobles the survivors, who can now go about the business of restoring the health of the state.

It is illuminating to compare *Hamlet,* the greatest tragic drama of Christian civilization, with the tragedy of the life and death of Jesus of Nazareth, the Christ and Saviour of western religious belief. Despite some striking overt differences in the two life spans, there is much similarity. Both heroes are idealistic and beloved adolescents, both face the evils of the world, both turn away from their mothers although their mothers never cease to admire them, both appear to age rapidly as they are confronting the world of evil, both have their periods of doubt and despair, and both die in early manhood. In both cases their death coincides with the fulfillment of the deepest pattern of their nuclear selves, that is, in both instances seeming defeat is actually a narcissistic triumph. The hero's funeral which is ordered for Hamlet is, however, hardly more than a symbolic allusion to his triumph. The resurrection and ascension, symbolizing the full merger with the father ideal, is the glorified narcissistic triumph which permanently transforms the humiliated, suffering seeker into the God.

Stripped of dogmatic belief and sentimentalizing additions, the story of the gospels may, therefore, be regarded as a prototype of modern tragedy, as a link in that chain of the portrayals of western tragic man which leads from Sophocles to Shakespeare to O'Neill, and from the *Dying Persian* in the Thermae Museum to Grünewald's *Christ on the Cross* to Picasso's *Guernica*. The Marys faint and cry; the Pharisees, the men of work and love and everyday morality, sneer at the hero; Pilate, the wielder of worldly power, will not interfere with the unrolling of the predestined life, despite his wife's dreams. The hero's friends detach themselves one by one in order to survive as death approaches. And then, after one last weakness and doubt, as in all great tragedy, there comes the final fulfillment and the ultimate consummation of the nuclear self of the hero. The rest—the mythological details of the moment of death, the empty tomb, the reappearances is symbolism. These are secondary additions, yet they remain in meaningful symbolic contact with the essence of the story, for they tell in various ways of the hero's narcissistic triumph, of his immortal divinity.

I know that one must not simplify the complexities of a powerful religious creation by separating one strand from the intricate web of the overall pattern. But it is indeed my conviction that the tragedy of man forms the very center of the stories told by the evangelists. The older tradition of the epic of the warrior hero has remained alive to serve as a paradigm for the prototypical hero of western civilization. But the story of Jesus—the Judaic tale of a hero's loyalty even unto death, to the deepest pattern of his self—has influenced, in various ways, every western hero, whether on the field of battle, in artistic and scientific faithfulness or, as described earlier, in the historically modest deeds of the, mostly unsung, Jaegerstaetters and Scholls.

Courage and the Nuclear Self

The application of psychoanalytic findings in general needs no excuse if it is carried out with discretion. I am also certain that the psychology of the self is of special relevance in this context. Still, the question may, and perhaps should, be raised whether undertakings like the present one (specifically the preceding investigation of martyrs and heroes and of the psychological significance of tragedy) serve any practical purpose. Phrased differently, the question could be asked whether, by virtue of studies like the present one, man's influence over his inner and outer environment has been expanded, whether his self-control has become enhanced, and whether his autonomy and dominance have been increased vis-à-vis the inner and outer forces which surround that area of choice and decision to which he gives the name of "I."

I believe that a tentative answer to these questions can be given; at least I will attempt to make certain predictions. As far as the control of the external environment is concerned, it must be conceded with regret—at this point independent of the validity of my various specific findings—that my research into these matters must be considered as purely preliminary. These are preparatory reflections, in anticipation of the time when depth psychology and its scientifically revolutionary methods and discoveries will be taken seriously not only in the area of the psychopathology of the individual but also in the realm of action, i.e., in the arena of history, of politics, of social concerns. This time may not be far off; limited attempts to integrate undiluted depth psychology with other branches of the sciences of human behavior have already been made, though I must admit that the time has not yet come.

Surprisingly enough, however, the first beneficiary of investigations of the present kind will be the clinical psychoanalyst, the therapist with individual patients. Freud (1910a) in his investigation of Leonardo da Vinci, for example, whatever the validity of some of the details of some of the historical reflections contained in his essay, employed his study as a vehicle to transmit to his colleagues a new understanding of the role of narcissism in a certain type of homosexuality. Using his analysis of the personality of Leonardo as an illustration, he communicated his simple, yet crucial, discovery that certain homosexuals are propelled toward a specific kind of love-*object* by their libidinal fixation on a beloved childhood *self* which they could never relinquish. This great insight has so far opened new doors neither to the experts in art history nor to those in art criticism and the field of aesthetics; it has, however, given an important new understanding of a number of character types (not confined to instances of overt homosexuality) to the psychoanalytic clinician and psychiatrist, which has vastly increased the therapeutic leverage of certain specific interpretations and constructions in the clinical situation.

The same can be claimed with regard to the present work, although I must, of course, await the verdict of those who will actually undertake to test it. What I have in mind here is not primarily the application of the findings which I have reported so far. These may, or may not, prove useful for others in individual analysis or in individual psychotherapy. The question whether one is courageous or cowardly, for example, gives cause for concern to many analysands. And every analyst is familiar with the two phenomenological faces of the narcissistically vulnerable person's behavior: his tendency toward timidity, loss of heart and shrinking retreat, on the one hand, and toward boastfulness, arrogance and provocative aggressiveness, on the other. I have no doubt that the findings contained in certain parts of the preceding examination (of the martyr-heroes, for example) will, directly and indirectly, be of tactical aid to the psychoanalyst when he tries to assist his patients by expanding their understanding of themselves and of their behavior as it relates to the problems of courage, caution and fear. The study, for example, of the personalities of individuals who displayed unusual heroism under trying circumstances should protect the psychoanalytic psychotherapist from these two interrelated specific mistakes: (1) the error of trying to combat the patient's timid or provocative attitudes through exhortations or active moral pressure; and (2) the error of rejecting as resistance the analysand's (temporary and transitional) transference need for praise or for identification with the idealized parent imago. The analyst's understanding that beneath both the lack of courage and the boastfulness lies the patient's essential pathology—the insecure cohesion of his self—will assist him in interpreting to the patient the meaning of his behavior, the dynamics of his need for identifications with idealized figures and for mirroring approval. The understanding of the essentials of the pathology will also direct the analyst's attention toward the crucial aspects of the patient's childhood memories as they emerge in the transference. He will thus ultimately be able to make relevant genetic reconstructions concerning the origins of the basic psychopathology: the specific interactions between child and adult which interfered with the appropriate supply of narcissistic sustenance to the consolidating self through the availability of mirroring-approving and idealizable selfobjects.

Even more importantly, however, is the influence which the lessons derived from the study of historical man have on our outlook on the goal of analysis in general. It helps us determine, for example, whether the patient is suffering from the symptoms and character deformities which are due to narcissistic personality disorder or from those which are due to the pathological forms of structural conflict. Every man confronts a range of problems in the area of the continuing change, expansion and development of his self, which is *par excellence* the goal to which one might refer as the realization of the basic pattern of the nuclear self.

It must not be deduced from the fact that I used extreme cases—certain martyred resisters and the paradigmatic tragic heroes created by the greatest poets of world literature—that the realization of the basic pattern of a person's nuclear self is an esoteric ideal only, unattainable to the average individual, and that an acknowledgment of its relevance as a possible therapeutic goal in analysis would therefore constitute an unrealistic burden to the average patient. On the contrary, there is good reason to believe that, appropriately conceived, a modicum of self-realization lies well within the grasp of most individuals, and that to accept the limitations of this process facilitates the acquisition of a modicum of wisdom.

But I will make first a perhaps surprising claim. I've come to the conclusion that the realization of the pattern of a person's nuclear self is to some extent independent of the degree of an individual's psychopathology. Some individuals, despite the presence of the conflicts and symptoms of even severe forms of psychoneurosis, are leading fulfilling and significant lives. On the other hand, some individuals, despite the absence of neurosis, lead empty, shallow and restricted existences.[23] The fulfillment of the basic pattern of the nuclear self may be of personal significance only. As a matter of fact, I believe that even some of the socially most significant activities of the great actors on the

---

[23] See R. Grinker's description of homoclites (1962).

historical and cultural stage are motivated more by certain deeply anchored, even idosyncratic, psychic configurations than by a conscientious openness to the subtleties of the social situation and by a responsiveness to the needs of the historical moment. Be that as it may—and the etiological factors which account for great achievement are certainly multiple and varied—in the clinical situation, as it is experienced by the analyst in his daily practice, we must not expect that the patient will strive necessarily for objectively unusual achievements when he becomes able to define the aims of his nuclear ambitions and ideals.[24]

Conclusion

Certain qualities and functions of the nuclear self, once this structure has been fully formed, cannot be comprehended unless the self is conceptualized as an independent, autonomous unit. There are other, broad areas of the personality outside the nuclear self. But once it has been laid down, the nuclear self strives to fulfill itself. It moves, from the time of its consolidation, toward the realization of its ambitions and ideals, which are the ultimate descendents of the child's grandiosity and exhibitionism and of his strivings to emerge with an idealized selfobject. And if an individual succeeds in realizing the aims of his nuclear self, he can die without regret. He has achieved the fulfillment of the tragic hero—not the painful death of guilty man who strives for pleasure—but a death which is "beyond the pleasure principle."

Guilty man wants to achieve redemption and reform himself and society. But an individual's deepest ambitions and ideals, once congealed to form the nucleus of his self, will drive and lead him with a force which, though hidden in most of us by conflict, fear and guilt, in its essence is independent of fear and guilt, of expiation and reform. Tragic man's death is not caused by guilt. It is not suicide, nor is it self-destructive. It is more closely related to a "death-instinct" than is the striving toward

[24][Editor: At this point in the manuscript Kohut included a case history of nearly 6,000 words, that of Mr. R. It is being omitted because (a) it is of marginal relevance to the discussion of courage; (b) Kohut himself indicated to me on July 16, 1981, that he questioned whether the case should be included; and (c) the case appears in print elsewhere in Volume III of *The Search for the Self.*]

death experienced by guilty man. The death attained by tragic man must not be conceived, in analogy to Freud's conception of a psychobiological antagonism between Eros and Thanatos, as being in opposition to life. It is an integral part of the life curve of the self.

2

On Leadership

(1969–70)

The years that I devoted to organizational tasks in psychoanalysis[1] have made me more keenly aware of the role of narcissism in the public realm: as a spur for constructive planning and collaborative action, if integrated with and subordinated to social and cultural purposes; and as a source of sterile dissension and destructive conflict, if in the service of unneutralized ambition or of rationalized rage. For an analyst to report his observations concerning the role of narcissism in his own field, especially about its destructive influences, is, however, hardly appropriate within the framework of an objective scientific communication. He would lay himself open to the suspicion that he is grinding his own axe under the guise of pursuing a dispassionate technical investigation and, even if he could perform the feat of truly setting aside personal bias, his conclusions would hardly carry conviction. I would therefore restrict myself to res-

---

[1][Editor: For many years Kohut helped provide curricular and institutional leadership in the Chicago Institute for Psychoanalysis. He also served on a number of important committees of the American Psychoanalytic Association, and in 1964 served as President of that organization. In later years, he used to describe himself in that period of his life as "Mr. Psychoanalysis," that is, as a preeminently conservative leader of traditional, Freudian psychoanalysis. This essay, "On Leadership," written in the late 1960s, came at a time when he was shifting his attention away from organizational tasks and toward research and writing in what he came to call self psychology. This essay, as indicated in the Preface of this book, was first conceived as the final chapter of his book, *The Analysis of the Self* (1971). However, for reasons that are not entirely clear, Kohut decided not to include it in the final version of his manuscript.]

tating the view which I expressed in 1964 (I, p. 392), that a ". . . readiness for attitudes of mutual disrespect and contempt among colleagues . . . reflects perhaps the fact that we have not yet been able to push our explorations of the infantile roots of narcissism as far as those of infantile object-directed libidinal and aggressive attitudes." If this view is correct, the immediate blame would tend to be directed against the training analyses which we are conducting for not securing the ascendency of the ego over the narcissism of the future psychoanalyst. But even if the insight gained in their training analyses could be relied upon to determine the future conduct of analysts, the fault lies not predominantly with the technical shortcomings in the management of training analysts or by their more careful instruction. It is due instead to the lacunae which exist in our basic knowledge concerning narcissism, this important, yet still insufficiently explored, sector of our field.

Freud (1937, pp. 221–22) regarded untameable aggression as the primary cause of human destructiveness and suffering. When he discussed a concrete example of the irrational antagonism which one analyst (probably Sandor Ferenczi) had developed against another (Freud), he put the blame on the incompleteness of the work done in the training analysis. He felt the analysand's aggressions, embedded in the negative transference, either had not manifested themselves sufficiently or had not been recognized and understood. To be aware of the contribution of narcissism to disunity and destructive conflict does not, of course, deny the presence of an aggressive drive, that is, of an innate biological propensity to attack and to destroy. The depth psychologist, however, must not resign himself solely to the pessimistic recognition of irreducible psychobiological drives. It is surely part of his task to study the complete interaction between drive, psychic structures, and the environment. But he must also study narcissism, which sometimes is able to harness aggression to constructive purposes, while at other times serves as the vehicle for the most destructive activities of which man is capable.

Michael Kohlaas by Kleist and *Moby Dick* by Melville demonstrate the enormity and relentlessness of the rage which may ensue subsequent to the shameful experience of a narcissistic injury in the narcissistically vulnerable individual. In the clinical setting in particular, every seasoned therapist will search for the specific affront that was experienced by a narcissistic patient who shows signs of prolonged anger during the analysis. In the social field (including psychoanalysis), an often quite narrowly circumscribed narcissistic injury turns a former friend into a malicious enemy who spends all his intellectual and emotional energies carrying out a vendetta against a group or a profession, much as he may rationalize his behavior and justify his purposes by adducing other motivations.

One of the difficulties of a psychoanalytic explanation of historical events (and other social phenomena) is the complexity of the interplay of various groups in producing social or historical action. The apparently passive tolerance in larger groups of the takeover of leadership and initiative by smaller groups may actually be more active than meets the eye. Thus, small pathological, or otherwise highly special and unusual, aberrant groups may be "passively" permitted to assume leadership in order to reach a goal which the majority may wish to disown yet also to reach. For example, people motivated by "normal" competitiveness and jealously may tolerate the merciless killing of the competitor by a paranoiac group which, after it has done its work, is itself condemned and removed from the social scene. These considerations not only are relevant with regard to the explanation of specific social phenomena, like the behavior of the German masses, the powerful Socialist Party, the Army, or the Church toward the Nazis before, during and *after* the Nazi regime in Germany, but also point the way to a promising direction of remedial social action by psychology. The paranoid or otherwise aberrant minority is "incurable" by insight. The hope for "social therapy," however, is that it will raise the awareness of other groups concerning their motivation and their use of the minority for their own unconscious purposes.[2]

Take, for example, the role which narcissistic injury may have

---

[2] [Editor: In the original manuscript Kohut had this entire paragrpah as a long footnote. It seemed significant enough to include it in the text of the paper itself. However, at the end of Kohut's original footnote he had in brackets the following cryptic note to himself: "Elaborate here with reference to Bracher—a bow to Bracher, yet insistence on the pervasive influence of psychological factors." The "Bracher" book Kohut is referring to in this obscure note is Karl Dietrich Bracher, *Die deutsche Diktatur: Entstehung, Struktur, Folgen, Des Nationalsozialismus* (1970), which Kohut had been reading carefully in the period just prior to writing this paper.]

played in Hitler's unending destructiveness. After his failure to transform narcissistic tensions in art, Hitler appears to have lapsed into a period of lonely brooding and hypochondriacal preoccupation, from which he emerged with the conviction that the Jews had invaded the body of Germany and had to be eradicated.[3] It is paradoxical on first sight that wounds suffered from an attack on an individual's most private psychological possessions, his grandiose fantasies, should produce vast social consequences. It seems that in certain narcissistic types the fluidity of the borders of the self not only leads to great narcissistic vulnerability with the tendency to perceive impersonal and accidental occurrences as personal slights, but also produces a specific sensitive perception of similar motivations in others and with it the ability to manipulate them. Narcissistic leader figures of this type experience the social surroundings as a part of themselves. The mere fact that other groups, nationalities, or races are different from themselves and do not react as they expect them to react is a deep personal afront, a frightening, inimical disturbance of their solipsistic universe. The situation can only be remedied by wiping out those who dare to be different. Yet the same perception of the social scene makes such a leader sensitive to the perception of emotional identities. He can discover similar small or dormant motivations in others, which he uses skillfully by identifying with them and bringing about an identification with him. He melts them into his personality so to speak and brings them and their actions under his control as if they were his limbs, his thoughts, and his actions.

Freud demonstrated (1921, pp. 67–143) that identification with the leader's ego-ideal creates group cohesiveness, mutual identification, and diminution of aggression between the members of the group. Such groups are, I believe, held together through a bond of idealizing love and are capable of constructive action. The groups which are formed around the personality of a paranoid leader, however, are not tied together by the convergence of their idealizing love, by an ego-ideal held in common. They

---

[3] [Editor: At this point in the manuscript, Kohut refers to Heiden (1966) and to Bullock (1964). In the margin of the manuscript Kohut wrote the following note to himself: "But insert here Hitler's dread of regular work in this period, i.e., his absolute commitment not to be deflected from some vaguely sensed destiny."]

are principally united by their sharing of an archaic narcissistic conception of the world that must destroy those who are different and by the identity of their grandiose fantasies embodied in their leader. They are held together by a common grandiose self.

To say that constructive groups, such as Freud had in mind, converge in their purposes through a shared ego-ideal, while destructive forces, such as those of 20th century fascism, have coalesced by dint of the magnetism of a shared grandiose self is largely correct but inexact: Constructive groups may well hold certain ambitions in common and the heightened self-esteem which the individual derives from feeling himself at one with a group with whose sense of power and pleasurable display of self-confidence he identifies is by no means incompatible with self control, civilized behavior, and creative purpose. Mixtures of identification of the aim-inhibited derivatives of the prestructural omnipotent object and the grandiose self are undoubtedly present in all viable and productive groups. This would include small teams of individuals working toward limited political, mercantile, or scientific tasks to large nations and populations who want to improve the territory in which they live and to leave a better world for their children. What decides the cultural value of the group is not the predominance of one of the narcissistic structures over the other (based as it were on the biased value judgment that ideals are morally superior to ambitions) but the relative archaism or maturity of these configurations and the relative degree of ego dominance over them. It is nevertheless true that the most culture-destroying forms of mass behavior—e.g., of those masses under the sway of the dictatorships of our century—emanated from groups which were predominantly amalgamated by the identity with the archaic grandiose self. Even here there are undoubtedly exceptions. Individual members of these groups relate to the leader in mystical religious devotion, betraying the presence of archaic forms of the omnipotent object; others use overt idealization as a cover of their reactivated archaic power-grandiosity; and still others mobilize truly idealizing cathexes. Yet the bulk of mass movements form themselves around shared archaic grandiosity after the previously existing aim-inhibited and ego-controlled shared form of self-confidence (national prestige) and the previously existing aim-inhibited and ego-controlled communal ego-ideal (religious values) have been destroyed or debased.

The overwhelming quality of the forces which have formed the destructive nationalistic movements of this century and the power and efficacy of their vengeful actions must thus, I believe, be understood as the result of the narcissistic bond established between the personality of the leader and the psychological tensions of the masses. Certain charismatic leaders appear to have been exposed to narcissistic deprivations in early childhood that prevented the gradual modification of their grandiose self and its integration with the reality ego, thus depriving this structure of one of its most important constituents. Since it is through the reality ego that a person's relationships with others are mediated, the defectiveness of this structure—experienced as alternate states of grandiosity and inferiority—leads at first to severe degrees of social isolation. One might say that the presence of the unmodified grandiose substructure interferes with the ability to acknowledge the existence of other individuals as independent centers of initiative and thus to perceive them as separate from himself and as distinguishable one from the other.

What differentiates the leader, however, from others who suffer from interpersonally crippling personality disorders is the fact that, while his capacity to perceive and distinguish individuals and to relate to them as a friend and companion is impaired, the leader develops a heightened sensitivity to the anonymous group and its motivations and is able to relate to it intensely. The socially impoverishing tendency to perceive people as types and chichés rather than as individuals, which is found so frequently in the narcissistically fixated,[4] is compensated for by a heightened grasp of the unconscious and preconscious tension states, of the fantasies, wishes, and fears of the group. It should not be forgotten, however, that this power of the gifted leader can be effectively engaged only in the area in which the fantasies and wishes of the masses are like his own. He is completely unable to

[4] See in Kohut (1971, p. 150) the examples of patient G. who told me that all his playmates had known his name while he had not known theirs, and that of patient H. who as a child had the fantasy that all people were his servants. Both of these patients were as adults quite lacking in the capacity to understand others as individuals, and both harbored strong group prejudices and were in general inclined toward thinking of people in terms of types and clicheś.

understand groups that are different from his own, and he fails to understand even his own group when it begins to be motivated by strivings which do not spring from the grandiose fantasies that they hold in common with him. The leader's inability to perceive and to understand human reactions beyond a certain range is not recognized by him as a limitation, even though it is a serious shortcoming that often contributes to his ultimate downfall. He declares as contemptible motivations and attitudes which are not identical with his own. Thus he develops along with his great understanding of the masses a steadily increasing contempt for them. Hitler identified intensely with the German people as long as they shared his ambitions but became contemptuous of them when they did not completely fall in line with him.[5]

The unconscious fantasies of the group's grandiose self, expressed in the transference upon the image of an appropriate leader figure, thus can play at times a crucial role in its cohesion. The leader of such a group is not primarily the focal point of shared values, as Freud suggested, but self-righteously expresses the group's ambitions and extols its greatness and power. Along with the various political, social, and economic factors that account for the irresistible attractions which nationalistic movements are able to exert at certain historical junctures there is thus a psychological one. At certain historical moments there exists a widespread painful awareness of narcissistic imbalance in large segments of a country's population. Shame propensity and readiness for rage are ubiquitous. Individuals seek to melt into the body of a powerful nation (as symbolized by a grandiose leader) to cure their shame and provide them with a feeling of enormous strength, to which they react with relief and triumph. Old fantasies of omnipotence seem suddenly to have become reality; all are proclaiming the invincible strength of the nation, and he who dares to question the omnipotence of the group and the omniscience of its leader is an outcast, an enemy, a traitor.

But how do the psychological conditions arise which make whole populations susceptible to the lure of the omnipotent leader?

[5] [Editor: In the manuscript Kohut refers at this point to Hitler's table talk (*Tischgespräche*, see "References" under Hitler, 1941–1944). The suggestion in the manuscript is that Kohut intended to elaborate further on that reference.]

What accounts for the widespread feeling of narcissistic defect and the passionate desire for its relief through the restoration of a feeling of heightened self-esteem and power?

The answer to this question has been sought by some in psychological factors which influence the childhood experiences of a whole generation in such a way as to produce a specific vulnerability to subsequent historical events. Wangh, for example (1964) believes that the group of young adults who flocked to the banner of National Socialism in the early thirties were particularly vulnerable to the traumata inflicted by the severe economic depression which existed at that period because their fathers' absence in the war during the early years of their lives had sharpened their Oedipus complex upon their fathers' return, had increased their readiness to experience anxiety because of their mothers' anxiety during their fathers' absence, and had in general interfered with the stability of their superego and sense of identity.

Wangh's interesting speculation deserves greater attention than I am able to give it in the present context. I will only mention that, on the basis of my clinical experience with narcissistic personality disturbances, I would lay the main stress on different factors as possibly contributing to a predisposition to join the Nazi movement in the group examined by Wangh. I would emphasize that the child retains the image of an omnipotent father because, in the absence of the father, he lacks the opportunity for the gradual discovery of the father's shortcomings.[6] The childhood circumstances, furthermore, which Wangh describes contain also the following relevant element. The father's return, after a boy had ruled the roost for a number of years, ends with traumatic suddenness the child's prolonged state of grandiosity, with the usual deleterious result that, on the one hand, the unmodified grandiose self lives on in a split-off and / or repressed position while, on the other hand, realistic self-esteem receives no nutriment from the depth of the personality.

The complexity of historical developments appears to surpass the limits of the human mind. One sympathizes with the wish of some historians to restrict themselves to the dispassionate and objective recording of events, rather than searching for the

---

[6] See *The Analysis of the Self,* pp. 82–84.

explanatory factors that may even potentially lead to the anticipation of historical occurrences and to man's greater control over
his historical destiny. Yet who is more familiar than the depth
psychologist with the unending complexities of objective factors? And who else has discovered that a seemingly unmanage-
able wealth of detail can become intelligible, show recognizable
patterns, and lead to predictability and increased control? With
all the acknowledged limitations of his science, the depth psychologist is indeed able to achieve a degree of conceptual mastery over his field because, *in collecting his data,* he makes use of
the fact that the observing instrument is attuned to the field which
it observes; in other words, he employs introspection and empathy (Kohut, 1959). Can the field of history be observed in an
analogous way? Is history man-made or do we here see forces at
work which shape man's destiny beyond what would be psychologically graspable and explainable?

It would seem reasonable to work under the assumption that
there must at least be aspects of history which are potentially
intelligible when approached with the aid of the insights of depth
psychology, independent of the fact that forces which are beyond
psychology where drives, biological development, and the circle
of life and death are givens to which the psyche reacts but which
can neither be explained psychologically nor influenced by psychological means. It is enough that we recognize the limits of
psychology and learn to know the areas where we can only mod-
ify, transform, mitigate what is a nonpsychological given and even
those areas where we must resign ourselves to achieve no more
than contemplation and resignation that there exist powers which
are beyond human influence.

With regard to the specific topic which I intend to use as a
proving ground for the explanatory power of the concept of the
regression within the narcissistic sector of the personality—the
rise of destructive aggression in Hitler's Germany—the problems of finding explanations are staggering for both the depth
psychologist and the historian. Karl Dietrich Bracher, for example, has written an instructive book on the subject matter under
scrutiny, a treatise which not only brings home the complexity
of factors and the intricacy of their interrelationship but which
clarifies like nothing else that I have seen the uncanny effectiveness of the total machinery of destruction through an organiza-

tion of states within states which permitted remnants of the old to carry on a complex organized pseudo-life, while the unspeakable was going on. How the driving forces of Hitler's absolute convictions pushed things inexorably forward while the surviving civilized fragments of older regimes could manage not to see or to disavow the significance of what they saw, all this becomes much more understandable—also psychologically!—after one has studied Bracher's opus. Yet, what are the etiological conclusions of this monumental achievement? Bracher de-emphasizes the explanatory value even of the "results of the historical and sociological observations" and, in this context, does not even mention psychological factors which are, after all, ubiquitous. Instead he stresses the crucial importance of the "immediate process of the take-over of power (by the Nazis) under the novel conditions of our era. . . ."

While, as a depth psychologist, I am by no means willing to throw in the sponge, I will admit that the emphasis which Bracher lays on the processes which led to the Nazi take-over of power in 1933 leads indeed to extremely illuminating results. Among other things, it helps us understand the increased paralysis of the democratic and constitutional forces toward the pseudo-legal tactics of a determined minority.

But must one really rule out the contributions of depth psychology here? Could our control over man's historical fate not be increased through psychoanalytic understanding? Not, of course, at the very moment when the dynamics of historical development grind inexorably toward the next immediate stage (as at the time of Hitler's take-over from the helplessly reluctant conservative forces of Paul von Hindenburg and Franz von Papen and with the passive tolerance of the still huge and powerful social democratic party), but through long-term shifts which are produced by influencing the psychological propensities of populations.

What are the possible approaches to the understanding of group phenomena by which psychoanalysis might contribute something useful? I will mention a few, rather unsystematically, only to show the variety, before I offer my own.

First of all we can expand on broad impressions about the power of psychobiological forces and apply them, beyond the individual whose depth psychological study has led to these impressions, to mankind as a whole. This was, of course, Freud's purpose in his studies of culture, in particular, in *Civilization and Its Discontents.* It seems to me that the very breadth and depth of such insights into man's nature set also the limits of their usefulness. Just as no psychoanalyst would approach the average clinical problem by talking about the strength of the given drive equipment and the flimsiness of the forces of the ego, so also there are limits to the application of the insights of psychoanalysis to the phenomena in history. Both on the stage of individual therapy and in the arena of history we recognize that the power of psychobiologically given factors will set limits to what can be achieved through insight and through efforts which are based on insight. But the insight which we will strive to obtain will not be concerning the most general area of the overpowering strength of the primitive forces of nature in human life but concerning specific details of drive elaboration and drive control which must be patiently observed with the aid of the analytic instrument.

Wangh's attempts to explain the readiness of a specific age stratum in the German population to embrace national socialism is an example of such a study. It is an undertaking that deserves respect, independent of whether it can be proven that the fact of belonging to a temporarily fatherless generation during the First World War is indeed an ascertainable crucial variable in the nexus of the crucial historical events.

K. R. Eissler (1963) has furnished the paradigm of yet another depth psychological approach to the understanding of historical events. He suggested that the history of groups (nations) could be studied as if it were the psychological history of an individual, and he courageously undertook to apply to large groups certain psychological correlations which have proven their explanatory value in the understanding of the individual's mind and of the individual's behavioral propensities. He thus believes that nations can suffer traumata in their early history (parallel to the childhood trauma of the life of an individual). As a consequence of such childhood traumata, repressions can take place, and as a further consequence of the repressions, symptoms, tendencies to irrational acts, to special characterological sensitivities, etc., can develop, just as in the formation of the personality of the individual human being. Ultimately Eissler expresses his belief that, as the uncovering of the repressed through psychoanalytic interpretation enables the individual patient to shed former symptoms and inhibitions and to control former tendencies toward certain rigid reaction patterns, so also with groups and nations. He thus argues that Freud's *Moses and Monotheism,* by uncovering the communal unconscious oedipal guilt of the Jews, acted like a successful interpretation and permitted the Jews to establish a homeland in Israel.

I am well aware of the danger of one-sidedness and of the loss of a balanced scientific perspective and I know that this danger becomes especially great in areas where a multiplicity of factors participates in the production of the phenomena which we attempt to explain. Under such circumstances it is tempting to lift one set of factors from the whole intricate pattern of causes, to declare that it is primary and fundamental and to assign a secondary and subsidiary role to other influences. The depth psychologist, in particular, who day in and day out observes the manifestations of the enormous power of unconscious motivations, will naturally be inclined to look upon unconscious psychic factors as the decisive, essential, and only valid forces in the life of individuals and of groups. This temptation to espouse a narrow attitude of biased one-sidedness toward the explanatory power of depth-psychological insights the psychoanalyst must, of course, resist. And he must forever keep in mind as he employs the methodological skills and the insights which he has obtained in the long years of patient observation and study of the individual on what a precarious path he is now trying to advance. Extreme caution is indeed justified in such an undertaking, despite the pressing need for insightful psychological contributions to man's role in history, lest we discredit not only ourselves but our science. Yet, realistic caution must not become cowardice—and the risks must be taken.

In the analysis of narcissistic personality disturbances, I have repeatedly observed a specific, well-circumscribed psychological chain of events. The frustration of a patient's higher forms of narcissistic satisfaction leads to regression along both axes of the grandiose self and the omnipotent selfobject.[7] But there is also regressive development in aggression from higher levels of controlled aggression that are mobilized in support of a person's

[7] See the *Analysis of the Self* (1971), especially diagram two, p. 97.

ambitions and of his wish for acclaim and success to that specific
form of regression experienced in a specifically regressive perception of the environment that I have called narcissistic rage.
This regression, especially when it is prolonged, leads to a variety of untoward and potentially dangerous consequences in the
life of the individual. It also seems to be a factor of the gravest
impact when it takes place in the group. This is especially true
in one of history's most destructive agents—the nation. The most
malignant human propensities are mobilized in support of
nationalistic narcissistic rage. Nothing satisfies its fury, neither
the achievement of limited advantages nor the negotiation of
compromises, however favorable—not even victory itself is
enough.

The defect from which the enraged person suffers is an internal one. The offender is experienced as a foreign body in an
archaic world that must be populated only by obedient selfobjects. He regards the offender's mere otherness as an interference with his own omnipotent control of a narcissistically
experienced world. Curiously enough, closer scrutiny always
reveals that the enraged person harbors only a vague concept of
"the enemy," who, in the logic of primary process thinking, is
replaceable. The goal remains the total extinction of an enemy,
who is experienced as absolute at each moment in time. No appeal
to reason or pity can interfere with this goal, because there is no
capacity to be empathic with the enemy, to see a fellow human
in him.

Narcissistic blows are unavoidable and the propensity to respond
to them with rage is ubiquitous. The question, then, is what historical circumstances will provoke a large part of the nation (like
the Germans under the Nazis) to develop increased narcissistic
vulnerability and become susceptible, on the one hand, to
undertake a supra-individual, nationally organized vendetta of
merciless persecution, genocide, war, and destruction and, on
the other hand, to pursue a vision of total control over the world?
It is likely that many factors must converge to produce such a
result. The presence, for example, of a gifted pathological leader
or the absence of a gifted non-pathological leader might well
decisively influence the course of events. Yet historical crisis
influences group regression, independent of a leader's influence, in a variety of ways. There is a first stage of painful increase

of narcissistic tension with propensity toward shame, hypochondria, and depression. This is followed by a regressive movement
in the narcissistic realm, manifested partly in the sector of the
idealized omnipotent parent imago and partly in the sector of
the grandiose self. The first line of regression leads to such manifestations as inclinations toward vague mystical religiosity (the
following of sects at the fringe of true religion, for example) and
the search for an external embodiment of the omnipotent selfobject into whom one can merge. The second line of regression
leads to the reinforcement of archaic grandiosity, attitudes of
intolerant certainty, arrogance, and the extolling of an external
embodiment of the grandiose self in the nation. Ultimately the
stage is set for the coalescence of both tendencies: The individual finds triumphant relief from the narcissistic tension as his
grandiose self expands into the powerful group and as the leader
becomes the omnipotent selfobject with whom the individual
merges.

It goes almost without saying that the loss of national prestige
after the defeat in the First World War deprived many individual Germans of a great deal of pride in their self-group (the
group established on the basis of a grandiose self held in common). There was in addition the loss of self-esteem for untold
millions from unemployment, currency inflation, and decreased
social standing for the civil service and for other large parts of
the middle class. Like the individual patient whose need for
acclaim is not responded to, the potential for regression in the
area of the grandiose self must have increased strongly for many
Germans in the years after the First World War. Some parts of
the population—organized, class-conscious workers and certain
groups of intellectuals (some of them Jews)— attained new pride
in themselves. Yet for the rest, in primary-process logic, it seemed
the victors had taken narcissistic gratifications from them. Furthermore, the traumatically rapid devaluation of both Christian
and traditional tribal values (as embodied in and held by the
aristocratic officer caste) contributed strongly to the narcissistic
regressions, in particular toward archaic forms of the grandiose
self and toward archaic forms of rage.

There were many, of course, within Germany who were able
to maintain themselves despite the current of regression which,
with apparently irresistible power, sucked in people from all walks

of life: aristocrats like Claus Schenk von Stauffenberg; professional soldiers like Henning Tresckow; Socialists like Julius Leber; members of the clergy such as Dietrich Bonhoeffer among the Protestants and Alfred Delp among the Catholics; and finally such moving examples of inner independence and political resistance as the simple farmer Franz Jaeggerstaetter and those noble students, Hans and Sophie Scholl.

It is not easy to be dispassionate here. The inclination is strong to restrict oneself to staying within the limits of a morally buttressed rejection of the evil leaders and their followers and an affectionate and admiring response to the martyrs who died for their convictions. But the depth psychologist knows the task which is assigned to him, and this knowledge must help him transcend these limits. Even in the arena of historical action—and perhaps especially here—he must not only judge but also examine, understand, explain. He will envy, but he must not share the philosopher's attitude exemplified by Martin Buber (1967, p. 67), who in accepting the Frankfurt Peace Prize said this about the Nazi evildoers: "I am sharing only in appearance the dimensions of human existence with those who have participated in those misdeeds."

If the depth psychologist is to make a contribution to the understanding of man's role in history and his control over his destiny, then he must try to extend his empathic observation not only to the victims but also to the persecutors, not only to the martyrs but also to their torturers. He must discover the human, all-too-human, whether in the normal (as measured by traditional standards) or in the psychopathological, in the good or in the evil. Furthermore, he must not focus only on the historically distant past. There, it is true, our emotional involvement declines, but so also does our empathic attunement. The depth psychologist must overcome his reluctance and direct his empathic attention to that more recent past in which he is still deeply involved.

Who were those who served their former commitments and joined the new source of power and pride? The backbone of the Nazi party—and also the main source of the new German elite—was the lowest stratum of the middle classes: people who on the whole had few values to love but who were driven by the tension of untransformed exhibitionism and unformulated ambitions.

Some of the older generation realized, of course, the extent to which the traditional value system had been undermined and tried to appeal to their sons. But the damage had been done and the appeal was weak or came too late.

A touching letter to Joseph Goebbels (1897–1945) from his father (Manvell and Fraenkel, 1960, pp. 14–15) may be presented as an example of these psychological tensions. The then 22-year-old Goebbels, a Catholic by birth, had written to his father that he was increasingly moving away from religion. To this the father replied on November 9, 1919: ". . . I may assume that you have not yet lost [your faith] . . . but that you are tormented by doubts . . . no-one, especially no young person, is ever . . . spared such doubts; . . . there is not victory without a struggle. Hence, to make this a reason for keeping away from the Holy Sacrament is a grievous error; for who would claim at all times to have approached the Table of the Lord with the childlike pure heart of his very first Holy Communion."[8] Thus Father Goebbels tried in vain to persuade his son to retain the traditional religious values of the family. But neither he nor many others of the older generation were successful in this aim. The devaluation of the established religions, the fall of the monarchy, the defeat of Germany, the rise of the working classes, the loss of prestige and the internal devaluation of the aristocracy and the officer class—all combined to weaken traditional shared ideals. Narcissistic tensions rose and narcissistic regression ensued. Personal and sociocultural factors were, of course, inextricably intertwined. Goebbels' deformity and his unhappy love affairs at the time of the quoted correspondence with his father, for example, undoubtedly contributed to the severe psychological crisis which he then experienced and which nearly drove him to suicide less than a year later. Thus Goebbels closed his "Last Will" of October 1, 1920, with the words: "I part without regret from a life that has become for me no better than an inferno."

But it is not only the personal and idiosyncratic that can account for widespread shifts in attitudes. Psychologically significant

---

[8] I am here quoting only briefly from Father Goebbels' long and persuasive letter. That there existed a very intense relationship between Goebbels and his father can be clearly deduced even from this single document. But we are at this point focusing on data of individual biography only insofar as they are illustrative of the historical current.

changes in the sociocultural arena absorb the personal. Psycho-analysis itself as a form of individual psychotherapy is not likely to reach sufficient numbers of the population to influence broad sociopolitical attitudes and historical tendencies. Nevertheless, psychoanalytic insights that are applicable to the relevant socio-cultural factors may yet have a chance of increasing our control over the destructive forces of history, which have played greater havoc with humanity than all of nature's floods and plagues. An understanding of the need to supply values that are within the reach of large numbers of the population, for example, as well as to provide a framework within which the prestige needs of the average man can find a modicum of fulfillment, may become as important for the constructively thinking statesman, political leader, or public administrators of the future as, let us say, his grounding in economics or in the design of organizational schemes.

Many of those in Germany who could no longer maintain their narcissistic equilibrium were ready to see in Hitler and in the National Socialist Party a chance for the deployment of the nar-cissism of the archaic grandiose self to which they had regressed. This was possible because Hitler's programs, though clearly promising the fulfillment of the crudest narcissistic aims of power and domination, were yet disguised, however thinly, as a system of ideals. In other words, the Nazi propagandists and the fra-mers of the Nazi ideology (like the obscurantist Hans Rosen-berg) claimed that they were motivated by the highest ideals. The very frenzy, however, with which the leader figure was extolled, the emphasis on his absolute power and his omni-science, betrayed that he was not a symbol for values but that he represented a concretization of the grandiose self of the masses.

The negative image of the "international Jew" (and to a lesser extent the related images of international Jewish communism, international Jewish Christianity, and international Jewish democracy) reflected the poverty of lovable ideals in Nazism. The "vulgarized Darwinism" which was called upon to justify the extermination of fellow men was, apart from being wrong, not a beloved ideal but a delinquent ego's attempt to justify its mis-deeds. A repeated feeling of narcissistic triumph came when vic-tory seemed to confirm the grandiosity of the communal narcissistic self. However, the unavoidable knowledge of the unprecedented persecution of the helpless was denied. As Alexander and Margaret Mitscherlich (1967) have clarified, the fact that the misdeeds were committed in a state of *social repression* is clear evidence that the social ego failed to live up to cherished ideals and yielded instead to the combined pressures of narcissistic urges and the seduction of an external force posing as an ego-ideal.

It should be mentioned that the prolonged lassitude of the powers outside of Germany, especially their self-deceiving failure to acknowledge the seriousness of the Nazi threat, was accompanied by the same uncertainty about the traditional values which had paralyzed a potential opposition in Germany itself. It was only under the threat of an invasion and occupation that England realized fully its love for its endangered traditional values and turned to an inspired and articulate leader who symbolized and expressed them (Glover, 1940). The United States, too, again, under the leadership of an articulate man who stood for traditional values, began to realize the similarity of its ideals to those of Britain and supported the fight against the enemy of humanitarianism. The re-mobilization of values made these nations willing to fight for their survival and inspired individuals to give their lives for a cause which had not become imbued with their own narcissism in the form of their idealizing love.

The rational ego is indispensable for the individual and the group during times of quiet and solid progress. However, under circumstances when civilization is threatened by those who are driven by the vengefulness of offended unmodified fantasies of grandeur, rationality alone is all too often ineffectual. "The voice of the intellect is soft but persistent," Freud said (1927a, p. 53), but unaided and alone it cannot stem the tide of irrationality during periods of crisis. The rational purposes of the autonomous ego lack the courage-inspiring quality needed for heroic action. Rationality must be amalgamated within a vital system of idealized values, and it must draw strength and courage and achieve the capacity to take risks, even the willingness to die, from the supra-individual narcissism of the ego-ideal. When pitted against the forces of narcissistic rage, our more immediate—and not unreasonable—hope must be that the union of those held together by the identity of their cherished ideals is stronger than the union of those held together by the identity of their archaic ambitions. Only then can the conditions be recreated in which the persistence of the voice of the intellect again has a chance to assert itself.

It is a strange and puzzling fact that after nearly two thousand years in which generation after generation has been exposed, from childhood on, to the teaching of the loftiest ethical system of altruism, Western man is capable of unspeakable cruelty and of total disregard for the fate of his fellow man. Can the failures of Christianity be fully explained by the tenacity of the aggressive drives? Can we assuage our doubts by the belief that the excesses of the 20th century western man are only the last revolt of selfishness, cruelty, and lack of concern before final pacification is accepted and the ultimate victory of object love is won?

Analysts have learned some important lessons in the therapy of the individual about the limits of interpretation. Change requires time. The psyche, it seems, must consolidate each gain before another is undertaken, with the aid of a process which we call "working through." If this psychoeconomic element is disregarded and the psyche is instead exposed to demands for rapid changes, a surface adaptation will take place. The newly established function, although impressively strong at the moment, can only be maintained with continued effort and with the support of the therapist. It will therefore be brittle and easily swept aside when the therapist withdraws his support or under the pressure of changed circumstances. In the therapy of narcissistic personalities, a carefully paced analytic procedure leads to the improvement of the total functioning of the personality through the transformation of the narcissism into ideals, humor, wisdom, creativity, and empathy. Could the relative failure of Christianity to produce a reliable civilizing effect on Western man be understood in analogy to the results of overambitious individual therapy? Is the sudden appearance of barbarity after periods of a seemingly secure cultural equilibrium comparable to the sudden reappearance of old symptoms and impulses which we encounter in those patients (or in their children) who have made psychological surface adaptations, either under the insidious pressure of the therapist's premature interpretations or in consequence of his undisguised educational exhortations? The psychological demands which Christian ethics have made upon Western man may very well be considered as excessive, or at least as traumatically premature. In essence, Christian ethics are not satisfied with the ego's domination over the grandiose self and with the integration of its demands with the interest and goals of the ego; Christianity insists on the complete neutralization of the grandiose self and of the egotistical purposes of the personality. ". . . If you love only those who love you," Jesus preaches in the Sermon on the Mount (Luke 6, New English Bible, 1961), "what credit is that to you? . . . if you do good only to those who do good to you, what credit is that to you?" What clearer contrast could be imagined between the manifestation of the grandiose self, which are to be rejected, and the fullest object love, which must be attained, than that drawn so beautifully by Paul in his First Letter to the Corinthians (1:13): "I may speak in tongues of men or of angels," Paul writes, "but if I am without love, I am a sounding gong or a clanging cymbal. . . . Love is patient; love is kind and envies no one. Love is never boastful, nor conceited, nor rude; never selfish, nor quick to take offense. Love keeps no score of wrongs; does not gloat over other men's sins, but delights in the truth. There is nothing love cannot face; . . ."

The survival of Western man, and perhaps of mankind altogether, will in all likelihood be neither safeguarded by "the voice of the intellect" alone, that great utopian hope of the Enlightenment and Rationalism of the 18th and 19th centuries; nor will it be secured through the influence of the teachings of the orthodox religions. Will a new religion arise which is capable of fortifying man's love for its old and new ideals? The transformation of narcissism into the spirit of religiosity, i.e., the tradition-bound communal amalgamation of nonrational elements to man's systems of values, has often been capable of inspiring people to the heroic deeds on which at crucial junctures survival always depends. Could it be that a new, rational religion might arise, an as yet uncreated system of mystical rationality which could take the place of the religions of the past? Undoubtedly such a religion would initially have no appeal for the masses, but new religions are at first probably always only for the few (or even only for one?) who, thus inspired, are subsequently able to inspire others. There are, even in our time, instances of heroic men of constructive political action who have achieved a transformation of their narcissism into a contentless, inspiring personal religion. Is this the type which humanity will have to produce in greater numbers in order to survive? Dag Hammarskjöld, (1965, p. VII) an example of this type, describes his contentless mysticism in the following words: "Faith is a state of mind and of the soul . . . the language of religion is [only] a set of formulas which register a basic religious experience . . ."

I am not advocating the conversion of psychoanalysts. Our circumscribed contribution to civilization rests squarely on our capacity to keep our heads clear and not to be swept away—not even by a *constructive* mysticism. Yet, having assessed the dangerous historical situation, it behooves us to survey the existing highly differentiated personality types and to attempt to ascertain which ones among them give promise to serve as leaders or prototypes in mankind's struggle to overcome the destructive propensities of untransformed narcissism.

Mankind cannot take two developmental steps at once, and to expect from it the capacity to transform narcissism into object love, or to achieve rational control over its unmodified narcissism, betrays an underestimation of the tenacity of narcissistic fixation and of the intensity of the destructive forces that can be loosed by narcissistic rage. However, when the means for destroying all life on earth is available, the control of man's destructive propensities in general, and of those most dangerous ones emanating from his unmodified narcissism in particular, will have to be effected without delay.

Is there any hope? Reason would suggest that the chances are slim. The transformation of narcissism into ideals and rational purposes can hardly be achieved by large numbers. There is only a limited possibility for an expansion of the human capacity for humor, acceptance of transience, wisdom, creativity, and empathic understanding. Yet it is possible that we are misjudging the difficulty on the basis of our experiences with individual therapy. Humanity as a whole may have resources available for which no parallel appears in psychoanalytic practice. Not all of humanity needs to change, but an outstanding leader who has achieved a new internal solution may sweep along the rest. Amalgamation with mystical modes of thinking may support drive control and rationality. And, last but not least, a new form of psychic equilibrium may arise in the psychological field under the impact of supreme danger, which corresponds to the occurrence of a mutation in the biological field.

To speak of the possibility of a new, original, creative and effective solution to the problem of the disposal of the forces of unmodified narcissism may seem like pinning one's hopes on the appearance of a miracle. Yet, is it not conceivable that a new and higher form of narcissism might arise? Is it not conceivable that the frequency of neurosis in modern man is a pathological forerunner on the way toward a creative solution of the seeming impasse of the narcissistic demand? No one knows the answers to these questions. But I do believe that the psychological solution to the ultimate problem of narcissistic destructiveness will not be found in a simple assertation of normality. The normal and adapted may be pleasant, lucky people who suffer little and are no great bother to others. But what is called psychic normality is often a sterile balance. Each case of psychopathology, on the other hand, is not only an individual maladaption, but also an instance of the attempt to find a new solution to man's psychological problems.

At the very end of Kleist's essay on the *Puppet Theatre,* the dancer makes a statement which comes close to the preceding speculation by bringing into proximity the problems of the schizophrenic (who is loving his self and fears he has been a lifeless puppet) with an evolutionary solution. "When consciousness as it were has reached its utmost extension," he says, "then harmony is recovered." And he continues, "Human beauty is greatest when it is unconscious or has infinite consciousness—in the puppet or in God." "That means," the author asks, "that we have to eat again of the tree of knowledge to become innocent once more?" "Yes," replies the dancer, "that is the last chapter of the history of the world."

3

Self Psychology
and the Sciences of Man
(1978)

On Self Psychology

The basic premise of the psychoanalytic psychology of the self is the defining position it assigns to empathy and introspection. This emphasis makes psychoanalysis, despite Freud's ambiguity with regard to the issue of empathy and introspection, what it has always been in its essence, the first scientific psychology of complex mental states. Self psychology is instrumental in ushering in a new phase in the history of psychoanalysis: the move from a preoccupation with the elaboration and refinement of the established theories to one of renewed emphasis on the gathering of primary data, a return to the empathic observation of inner experience.

The renewed preoccupation with the collection of primary data of observation does not, however, imply a neglect of theory. On the contrary, by reemphasizing careful observation, the self psychologist reestablishes the mutually enriching interaction between theory and observation that characterizes all empirical sciences. Creative observation, as I should like to call it, is always interwoven with theory—it is directed by some vaguely perceived new orientation and is followed by the increasingly more precise formulation of new theoretical tenets and by the gradual evolution of a new theoretical framework. Some outlines of the changes in theory that self psychology is bringing about can already be discerned: a shift from the previous emphasis on quasi-biological "drives," and secondarily, from the study of the psychological conflicts that arise concerning their expression and their taming, to the positing of primary configurations that are already complex from the beginning ("molecular" not "atomic"; "organic" not "inorganic"; "psychological" not "biological"). These complex primary configurations are the "self" and its "constituents." Self psychology does not work with a framework of biological drives and a mental apparatus. It posits a primary self which, in a matrix of empathic selfobjects that is held to be as much a prerequisite of psychological existence as oxygen is for biological life, experiences *self*object greatness (assertiveness; ambitions), on the one hand, and self*object* perfection (idealization of one's goals; enthusiasm for one's ideals), on the other. Drives are secondary phenomena. They are disintegration products following the breakup of the primary complex psychological configurations in consequence of (empathy) failures in the selfobject matrix. Subsequent to serious and prolonged or repetitive failures from the side of the selfobjects, assertiveness becomes exhibitionism; enthusiasm becomes voyeurism; and joy changes into depression and lethargy. Zonal eroticism is pursued in an isolated fashion (oral, anal, phallic-genital) instead of being experienced as the various pleasure goals of a joyfully assertive total self. It aims either at consolation and soothing or has as its purpose the attempt to regain the lost sense of the aliveness that characterizes the active, healthy self.

The shift from a drive psychology to one centered on the primacy of the ambitions and ideals of the cohesive self leads to a different understanding of time in psychoanalysis. The classical viewpoint of the time axis was implied in the reconstruction of the individual past, but the emphasis was more on process and structure—on the analytic process penetrating to the repressed and on the layers that resisted penetration—than on the time axis along which the events in the life history of a person evolved. Expressed aphoristically, classical analysis discovered the despair of the child in the depth of the adult, that is, it established the actuality of the past, while self psychology has discovered the despair of the adult in the depth of the child—the actuality of the future. The child whose self is stunted by the selfobjects' failures is, in his depression, mourning an unlived, unfulfilled future. Each moment of experience is decisive in determining whether some suffering and depression may be in essence a step toward ultimate fulfillment or sterile and thus part of a tragic failure. Experience can only be evaluated against the assessment of the total course of a creative and productive or noncreative, sterile life cycle.

The value-laden terms—fulfillment, creative, productive, sterile, noncreative—employed in the foregoing, are in need of clarification in two directions. First, they do not refer primarily to the values of society, although they may, of course, be influenced by the current values; rather, they refer to an inner program, i.e., to the pattern of the nuclear self. Secondly, the evaluation does not rest on the retrospective historical assessment of an individual's life but on the mobility of inner potentialities and the readiness for achievement. The individual misfortune of a creative life accidentally cut short is psychologically not significant in our context—indeed its occurrence may bear out its potentialities by leading others to take up where the move was interrupted.

These considerations encouraged me to believe the psychoanalytic psychology of the self will help narrow the gap between psychoanalysis and the other sciences of man. For most of the 20th century, psychoanalysis has been a hope and promise to students of the experiences, thoughts, and actions of man outside the realm of psychopathology. But it has also been a disappointment. The distance between on the one hand, the explanatory scope of a psychology that examines man and his activities as a mental apparatus which deals successfully or unsuccessfully with the expression, the curbing, and the sublimation of drives and, on the other hand, the field of the shared significance of the creative aspirations of man in the realm of his artistic, philosophical, religious, and historical and social activities has been too great to be bridged. Some have tried to bring psychoanalysis together with other fields. Sometimes they even abandoned their former professional commitment and become practicing psychoanalytic psychotherapists. But there is another group of investigators of man's creative involvement, a group that seems in recent times to have increased in size and to have hardened its stand. It consists mainly of academically based humanists who for a variety of reasons have turned away from psychoanalysis in bitterness, scorn, and ridicule. It seems they felt the insights that we had to offer them bypassed the essence of man and of the products of his creativity and dealt only with peripheral trifles. It is to this latter group that the psychology of the self now addresses itself, primarily with the hope that it might succeed in rekindling their interest in the applicability of psychoanalytic conceptions to their fields. And what does self psychology have to offer to them? Let me turn to some concrete illustrations.

Literature

The first illustration is the most famous example of the application of psychoanalysis to literature, the interpretation of Shakespeare's immortal Hamlet. Is the classical assertion correct that Hamlet's behavior, and thus the action of the drama, is explained by the conflicts of his Oedipus complex? And, if the answer to the first question is affirmative, does the demonstration of the vicissitudes of Hamlet's infantile neurosis address itself to the most important aspect of Hamlet's personality, in particular to that aspect of it that is the most instrumental among the forces that propel the action of the play?

Francis Fergusson (1949, pp. 111–112) once objected to "psychoanalytic reductionalism" in the following terms:

> My objection to Jones's interpretation is that it reduces the motivation of the play to the emotional drives of the Oedipus complex . . . The Oedipus complex does not account for the fact that Hamlet, besides being a son, is also a deposed prince; nor that Claudius, besides being a father symbol, is also the actual ruler of the state. But the actual movement of the play—to say nothing of its ultimate meaning—depends on such objective facts and values as these.

And what is the response of the psychoanalytic self psychologist to Fergusson's in many respects cogent observations? In tune with the traditional psychoanalytic approach, I maintain that the questions to be answered with regard to the personality of Hamlet as an individual are of great importance for our understanding of Shakespeare's play, that it is indeed the unwinding coil within a specific personality, Hamlet, that provides the tension that drives the action of the drama to its conclusion. I agree with Fergusson's view that the explanations provided by Hamlet's Oedipus complex have only limited power. They clarify the content of

Hamlet's ultimate actions and the conflicts that delay their execution. But they are off the mark with regard to the essence of
Hamlet's self-belittling failures, the essence of his ultimate triumph
despite biological death, the essence of the force that lies behind
the unrolling of the tragedy in time. It is the idealized pole of
Hamlet's self that has yet to be firmed and activated, and his
bitterness and sarcastic pseudo-insanity on the way to this
achievement are no more than the outward signs of the intense
work that is going on in the depth. The ghost appears—he is still
"outside"—but not as evidence of a static failure: He expresses
the beginning of the work of integration of the self as all of
Hamlet's inner resources are mobilized. Ophelia is rejected and
abandoned to her death. This is cause for mourning and self-
reproach from the side of Hamlet's guilty self. And yet the work
must continue, whatever the cost to self and others. The selfobjects (the mother and the father figures of Claudius-Polonius)
are no help to Hamlet. They do not provide him with the idealizing figure he so desperately needs. They want social compliance and pretense of greatness and can promise only external
success and high position. Only the twinship support of Laertes
and the childhood memories of the sustaining Yorick are helpful. Hamlet must find psychological strength within himself and
go on until it is completed. The ultimate deed, the killing of the
guilty usurper of the throne of Denmark, is no more than the
external symbol for the inner achievement: the idealized pole,
weakly established because of paternal distance, has firmed the
self. Adequate, if hasty, action has realized the program. Hamlet
has found an ideal in which to believe, for which to fight. The
wrong has been put to right. Hamlet has found himself, and
now may safely die. What the tragedy protrays is the regained
ability of a self to run its course toward a fulfilled death. Great
tragedy is the portrayal of the full course of life, however condensed into a narrow span of time and fitted into traditional
scenes and acts.

On History and Literature

Now we will turn to a different challenge for the explanatory
power of psychoanalytic self psychology. We will focus on a
chapter of recent history, specifically on the terrible events that

took place in Germany in the fourth decade of our century, the rise to power of National Socialism and Hitler. These events had one thing in common with the Hamlet tragedy: the ultimate death of the protagonist. Nor is that the only similiarity between the two. Some might object that the action of Hamlet and the rise and fall of Nazi Germany cannot be compared at all because the one being moving fiction, the other hateful reality, makes them psychologically too different. My answer is that they are comparable and that they present even certain similarities, when we look upon both of them in their relationship to certain basic psychological constellations. My focus is a purely psychological one. In both cases the propelling force for the ensuing action is the attempt of an injured self to remedy the disease. Furthermore, in both cases the personal defect in the protagonist's self leads him to carry out deeds that are in harmony with the diseased self of the nation he represents.

Thanks to Hamlet, who stood in proxy for the nation and performed its psychological labors, we know what it was that was rotten in the state of Denmark, what it was that undermined the cohesion of the nation's group self: It was the idealized pole of the group self, the values of and pride in the Danish monarchy that had become defective because the idealized leader had been replaced by a usurper via a non-idealizable (a hidden and not proudly displayed) deed. Although the people did not know the actual facts, they were able, we can surmise, to sense the hollowness of Claudius' exhortations (which might be compared to the analogous experience of the American people toward Nixon's grandiloquent lies). Hamlet's self, for reasons that we can only imagine, was in an analogous state. The selfobjects of his early childhood may have responded insufficiently to his phase-appropriate needs for mirrored greatness. The mother, perhaps emotionally frustrated by an emotionally shallow husband whose mind was on the enforcement of morally buttressed rules and on the affairs of court and state, may have been seductive rather than maternal toward her son. She would thus have failed to respond to his actual developmental needs, while overstimulating him seductively in the oedipal phase with emotional expectations that were not in tune with the child's actual self that he wanted to display in order to obtain her joyous response. He, therefore, did not become securely self-assertive as an adult and could not sustain the self-confidence he needed in order to face the needs that would constitute the realization of his inner conviction that he was great and powerful.

We may also surmise that the selfobjects of Hamlet's childhood did not respond—though here the failure was less severe—to his need for merger with an idealized imago. His self was thus unable to form the firmly integrated pole of ideals capable of organizing a cohesive sector of his personality that would allow him to engage in self-realizing, idealized actions, actions in tune with a cohesive set of guiding ideals. We do not know the causal genetic circumstances and can do no more than speculate about time, e.g., by fastening on the Yorick reminiscences (only a member of the servant-class gave him the sense of participation in an adult's idealized strength) and on the personality of the father as portrayed in the ghost appearances (the father's distance, his moroseness, and the moralizing injunctions like those of Polonius, who lacks joyous pride in his son, Laertes, and does not bequeath upon him the legacy of shared ideals).

All in all, after implying that Hamlet was exposed to paternal attitudes that restricted the focus of his life increasingly to the preoccupation of guilty man, while simultaneously depriving him of the support that would have enabled him to turn to the tasks of tragic man, Shakespeare shows us how Hamlet was ultimately able to transcend the insufficient father-ideal. He rejoins the recourse of life of tragic man via the performance of courageous, masculine, assertive *actions*, or real deeds enacted in the social arena. But Shakespeare provides us also with a glimpse—an autobiographical allusion, I believe—concerning the other road to tragic life that is open to man: the road not to significant action but to significant thought, in particular the road to art. Hamlet's deeply moving warmth toward the actors (as to the presence of Yorick) attests, I feel, not just to the fact that as a child he found a degree of selfobject sustenance by turning from the royal parents to members of the socially degraded class (servants, actors); the scene in question also suggests something about Shakespeare's own life. Is it too farfetched to assume that Shakespeare is telling us in the play about his own emotional experiences with the selfobjects of his childhood in his allusions to those of Hamlet and Laertes? And could we not assume that Shakespeare, employing the armamentarium of his gifts and his education, cured his self defect via artistic creation, just as Hamlet, employing the armamentarium of his gifts and education, cured his by turning to the heroic deed?

And so, how about Hitler and Germany? In what respect can they be said to be similar to Hamlet and Denmark, and in what respect are they different? Let me, first of all, respond to those who will at this point lose interest in my argument and turn from it with the angry assertion that it is an insult to common sense to compare Shakespeare's sweet prince, one of the most attractive figures in all of literature, with Hitler, one of the most abhorrent scourges of history. I could well understand the feelings that motivate such a reaction. But I would have to insist that the comparison is justified. In fact, it is more than justified; we have hardly any options. I chose Hitler because I believe that to advance our understanding and, we hope, ultimate mastery of the historical phenomenon that he represents is the most important and worthy challenge that the depth psychologist confronts in the "applied" field. The task is a crucial one because the rise of Hitler and Nazi Germany may well be representative of similar and— *horrible dictu!*—even worse historical events, however unimaginable worse horrors may be. On the other hand, I chose Hamlet because the classical psychoanalytic interpretation of the tragedy that bears his name is not only the best known example of applied analysis, but also perhaps the most fully documented and most solidly supported one. I could have chosen less attractive characters, like Macbeth, or despicable ones, like Iago or Richard III. What is at stake for us is not whether a character, a personality, is attractive or unattractive but whether he can or cannot be the protagonist of true tragedy.

But to return to the argument, when we compare Hitler and Germany with Hamlet and Denmark one difference is immediately apparent. In the case of Hamlet-Denmark we are dealing with a work of art in which all the details, however disparate in appearance, are the products of one mind. Shaped by the creator's conscious artistic and unconscious psychological intentions, they are parts of a unitary whole. In the case of Hitler-Germany, however, we are dealing with the confluence of the effects of many disparate factors, which have produced certain fateful results united by the mind of the observer. As you can see, I am not, in the Tolstoyan mode, assigning primacy to the role of Hitler among the causes and motivations that led to the historical events in question. My attention is focused on certain aspects of the condition of the German nation. I believe that, in doing so, I am focusing on the crucial psychological condition—however diverse the influences that were responsible for the German state of mind at that time and however diverse the events that we ultimately perceive as a circumscribed chapter in history. The primary psychological cause of the historical events under scrutiny was a serious disturbance in the strength and cohesion of the German group self, which was experienced without the empathic sustaining voice of the truly creative individuals among the artists or political leaders or from the world that surrounded Germany during the 15 years between the peace of Versailles and the assumption of power by the Nazi party.

The scientific task of elaborating the preceding assertion is a gigantic one. It is not only beyond my personal powers, but also, I feel certain, beyond the powers of the depth psychologist. I can do no more than attempt to convince the historians and the political scientists of the rising generation that the psychological explanations which self psychology can offer are in essence correct. It is incumbent on historians and political scientists to deepen and broaden our insights—and to improve and correct them. The cultural, economic, political, and military situation that followed the military defeat and the effectiveness of the "blockade" led, via the pettiness and shortsightedness of the measures instituted by the victorious powers and via the empathic obtuseness vis-à-vis the diseased condition of the German group self of the artists, the intelligentsia, and the political leadership of the Weimar republic, to the situation in which a proud, gifted, moral and highly civilized nation became ready to accept the leadership of a man who offered it the instantaneous feeling of intense power and pride and the sense of action-poised idealized omnipotence with which individual Germans could merge.

What are the issues upon which the self psychologically informed historian should focus? First and foremost, he should investigate the receptive state of the German nation. He should consider the presence of Hitler as an auxiliary phenomenon—not accidental, certainly, but able to become effective only by virtue of the specific state of the nation. Still, the analysis of Hitler's personality is of the utmost importance. And I would predict that, despite the deplorable scarcity of adequate genetic data about the psychological matrix of Hitler's childhood, the undertaking will lead to important insights if it focuses on the question of the specific effectiveness of his personality vis-à-vis the weakness of the German group self and its state of fragmentation.

Much has been said about the inherent shortcomings of applied analysis. It seems to me, however, that one can also make a strong point in its defense. The most important source of significant data obtainable about the psychological depths—more reliable, I maintain, than even the data from observation of children by analysts—comes from the scrutiny of the unrolling transference in the analytic situation. Self psychology can come to the defense of analysis applied outside the clinical setting by pointing out that the scrutiny of an unrolling life if viewed as the struggles of a self to realize its basic pattern can furnish data that may be as significant and as reliable as those obtained during therapeutic analysis. Thus, to return to our specific example, a depth-psychological investigation of the structure and genesis of Hitler's charismatic powers and of his chronic narcissistic rage, which overcame all traces of morality and compassion and which propelled him into a course that led from victory to ultimate defeat, is a very worthwhile undertaking indeed.

In sketching the outline of the work that is to be done by the psychohistorian of the next generation, we should permit ourselves some license at this point—there is always time later for correction, emendation, and restrictive qualification. Let us look upon the German group self, and on the matrix of the selfobjects who influenced its condition before and after the advent of Hitler's influence, as if we were dealing with the diseased (weakened, fragmented) state of the self of an individual and on its changing matrix of selfobjects. We will then say that this group self—the sum total of those clusters of interconnected experiences of each individual that prevail in consequence of his temporary or continuous submersion into the group—can be conceived of, like the self of the individual, as being laid down and formed in the energic arc between mirrored *self*object greatness (ambitions) and admired self*object* perfection (ideals).

The group self, like that of the individual, consists of three constituents, each of which, including the specific selfobjects that belong to it, manifests itself in the clinical situation as a selfobject transference and is thus open to detailed investigation. We know, from our clinical experience, not only that these transferences occur in three forms (mirror transference, idealizing transference, alter-ego transference) but also that each, apart from its concealment by transference resistance, may be activated, roughly speaking, in two different ways: via gross identifications (the revival of an archaic state), and via those fluid processes of alternating self-strength through empathic merger and renewed self-weakness subsequent to breaks in the empathic state, which we call working-through. Applying these findings to group psychology, we can first say that group cohesion can be established and maintained via identification of the group members with the leader and with each other. The processes that create and sustain the group may be of two types: on the one hand, sudden gross, archaic, essentially unstable identifications that, for example, require the presence of the leader in order to be maintained and disappear *in toto* when he disappears (or becomes unidealizable via a failure); and, on the other hand, slowly acquired, increasingly mature internal changes, corresponding to transmuted internalizations in analysis, that will ultimately remain, even when the leader disappears, physically or psychologically.

There is an important difference between group processes in history and that of the individual in psychoanalysis. In the clinical situation it is mainly with regard to a single person—the analyst—that the transferences establish themselves and are worked through. In the arena of history, however, it is either the leader who mobilizes the transferences or a leading group that fills this role. Furthermore, archaic and unstable gross identifications in the historical field take place in relation to a single dominant figure who by his presence is able to give instant relief to the diseased group self, while the slow process of working-through that leads to a stable firming of a diseased group self requires the interpretative presence of many active and influential minds.

What moves society toward health is that of creative individuals in religion, philosophy, art, and in the sciences concerned with man (sociology, political science, history, psychology). These "leaders" are in empathic contact with the illness of the group self and, through their work and thought, mobilize the unfulfilled narcissistic needs and point the way toward vital internal change. It follows that during crisis and periods of regressive identification of the group self with pathological leaders there is an absence of creativity in religion, philosophy, art, and the sciences of man. The absence of creative experimental art during such periods is a striking phenomenon. Creativity in all fields is choked off. There is no one in empathic touch with the diseased group self. This points toward the increasingly worsening condition of the group self (corresponding to the disintegration threat of incipient psychosis in individual psychology) and leads to pathological ad hoc solutions.

To return to the example of Hitler and the Nazis: Was—and is—there a chronic weakness in the German group self? Would other nations have been able to respond to the attacks on group self structures to which the German nation was exposed in the pre-Hitler period by successfully mobilizing all their inner resources? Perhaps the case of Hamlet can be instructive here. Was Hamlet's self stronger than that of Germany's group self? Was the acute destruction of his self less severe, less widespread, than the corresponding aspects of Germany's illness? Both Hamlet and Germany had suffered external defeats. But a dispossessed prince still knows that he *is* a prince. Did the German nation lack the analogous conviction to sustain it? Was it too recently established as a unit to feel secure in being a self? Had it never successfully asserted itself and taken responsibility for its destiny? Was it still weak and relied on being told by archaic external selfobjects not only what to *believe* but also what to *be*?

Having outlined the psychohistorian's task with regard to a probably existing latent chronic weakness in the German group self that made it subject to react to injuries by becoming seriously depleted or fragmented, to regress toward archaic states, and to respond with primitive rage, we will now look, with the eye of the self psychologist, on all the well-known and often discussed factors in the realm of the narcissism of the group which have not only in retrospect been standard historical explanations for the fateful turn of events by those who took the stance of the objective observer but were indeed used even by those who were responsible for these events, at the very time when they took place, especially by their Nazi spokesmen, as justifications for their actions. Still, when seen from the perspective of the self psychologist, the blows that the German group self had to suffer during the ominous 15 years that were ushered in by the last war and by Versailles and ended with Hitler's seizure of power will be seen in a different light and take on a new, and deeper, significance.

How do the discoveries of self psychology assist the psychohistorian in this specific task? How, in particular, do the well-known facts fit into the schema that has been so helpful to us in our assessment of, approach to, and therapeutic strategy vis-à-vis the individual with self pathology? I suggest that the psychohistorian order the well-known data—and perhaps, with vision sharpened by the insights of self psychology discover additional ones—by keeping in mind (a) the fact that the self has three constituents, and (b) the thesis that two of them, at least, need to be functionally destroyed in order to cause a manifest illness of the self.

Which constituents were the ones that became so seriously impaired that they led to the manifestation of the historical disease of the German self in the form of Hitler and the Nazis and their horrible deeds? Without going into details here, it seems clear that it was not, at least not primarily, the destruction of the area of skills and talents that can be blamed. If some of the assets of Germany in the realm of industrial and scientific technology were indeed diminished at all during the period in question, it seems to me at least that a lowering of efficiency, if indeed it took place, was secondary in nature, i.e., that it was due to the persisting disease, namely, the serious destruction of large areas of the two poles of the self.

I would assume that most historians would not take issue with the foregoing statement, would even accept it as a matter of course—perhaps with the exception of those who take a Marxian point of view. (I am, however, not even sure that a Marxist orientation would necessarily lead to an opposing opinion here.) It may also not be surprising to most historians when I now add that I am interested not only in the fate of the pole of ambition, power and greatness of the German group self but also, and in certain respects even more, in the fate of the pole that is the carrier of the ideals of the nation. The professional historian may, however, be taken aback—although only initially, I believe— when I now suggest furthermore that the consciously experienced injuries of its self-esteem, such as the blow of having lost the war and of having to pay reparations, should not be considered as the psychological basis for Germany's readiness to espouse the Hitlerian remedy for its self-pathology. The Nazis clearly exploited German sensibilities in order to harness the ensuing narcissistic rage in the service of their vengeful atrocities and of a vengeful war. Nevertheless, we are not dealing here with the primary manifestations of a diseased group self but with the secondary symptoms of an underlying self-disorder. The disease itself, as would be the case with an individual patient, was silent. What the skilled psychohistorian must look for now, in retrospect, is evidence of a sense of depression, a lack of vitality, and a sense of discontinuity in time and of fragmentation in space. Behind the noisy rage was a despair that the legitimate demands for respectful "mirroring" and the legitimate needs for a merger with powerful ideals were not responded to in action and before Hitler received no effectively communicative empathic recognition through words or other symbolic means. Basing myself openly and unashamedly on the profound insights about man's self and its experiences and reactions that are obtained in individual psychoanalytic treatment of patients with self-pathology, I suggest, in other words, that the psychological illness of pre-Hitler Germany was not caused by the external adversities to which Germany was exposed at the time. Of course they mattered, especially since these adversities occurred not only in the realm of power and greatness via defeat and poverty but also in the realm of ideals. But the real issue was the absence of an empathic matrix that would have recognized and acknowledged the emotional needs of the German group self exposed to such external adversities.

I hope that the line of thought that I have been pursuing with the foregoing remarks will not again expose me to the danger of losing the good will, even the attention, of the scientific, professional historian whose interest I am trying to engage, whose skills and energies I want to direct toward the task of fleshing in the skeleton-outline that I am presenting here. I am afraid he might feel at this point that I am overstating my case and going too far in comparing the individual and the group, especially when I explain the unbalanced state of a nation with the self-pathology of a patient observed in the setting of psychoanalytic therapy. I do not believe, however, that my presentation is idiosyncratic or that my conclusions are farfetched. For it seems to me that man, as an individual and as a member of a group—perhaps even most empathically when he functions as a member of a group in history—reacts not to raw facts but to the meaning that these facts have for him, i.e., to facts embedded in an emotional matrix. The deprivations suffered through temporary unemployment of city-dwellers on relief may be minute in terms of food, shelter, and physical discomforts, when compared with the protracted deprivations suffered by soldiers who fight for a cause they believe in or consider to be a glorious adventure. But the unemployed will be depressed, devitalized, and joyless, while the soldier, suffused by heightened self-esteem, may be active, alive, and joyful. The difference lies in the different perception of the external events by the self: whether they are experienced as unempathic vis-à-vis the self and its needs and demands or whether they are experienced as sustaining—either of its need for mirrored greatness or of its need for a merger with an ideal, or both.

Let me summarize my reflections at this point. In outlining the future psychohistorian's task as he embarks on a self psychologically oriented investigation of Nazi-Germany and its actions, I posited a chronic weakness of the German group self which, when deprived of sustaining selfobject responses during the period before Germany turned to Hitler, suffered a serious acute or subacute disorder, which took the form of serious fragmentation. This was experienced as a painful loss of vitality and cohesion and manifested itself in empty pleasure-hunting and rage-proneness, on the one side, and an increasingly frantic search for a selfobject that would provide the archaic needs with relief-providing responses. The blows suffered by the German group self during the pre-Hitler period not only shattered the pole of self-confidence—the pole of mirrored greatness—via the inability of the Kaiser's armies to achieve a military victory, the absence of a powerful army after Versailles, and the widespread unemployment and poverty of the '20s and early '30s, but also wiped out the pole of ideals—the pole that had been formerly sustained by the goals, inside and outside of religion, each German had shared with the leaders of a stable hierarchy in the defunct order of Imperial Germany.

But why, to turn now squarely to my second question, was Germany unable to move toward a genuine cure of its diseased and suffering self? What was the nature of the failure, as I put it earlier, to obtain it? Again, as was the case with regard to the previously discussed specific questions concerning pre-Hitler Germany, I am more interested in establishing the principles by which the psychohistorian must be guided than in answering this specific question, except insofar as a tentative answer may illustrate the theoretical tenet I wish to state. The principle in brief is this. A healthy group self, as is the case for the healthy self of the individual, is continuously sustained in its course throughout time—during its life one can say—by ongoing psychological work that provides the cohesion and vigor of its changing yet continuous structure within a matrix of selfobjects who are in empathic contact with its changing needs. The sum total of the results of this work that must affect all layers of a people or at least the great majority of them—those minorities who are excluded are the disenfranchized, the outsiders, the true pariahs of a nation—we call "culture." In contrast to Freud, but in agreement with his translators, I would rescue the term "civilization" for the drive-psychological context of classical analysis. Thus the discontent vis-à-vis the drive-restrictions imposed by social life that Freud described in *Civilization and Its Discontents* was misnamed in the terms of my definition in the original since the title that Freud gave to his pioneering monograph is *Das Unbehagen in der Kultur*. Why, then, to return to the specific issue, did the cultural work fail to respond to the disease of the fragmented and depleted German self? What were the faulty self object responses, like erroneous interpretations in analysis, to which it was exposed— so consistently, repeatedly and unchangingly that it finally lost all confidence in obtaining a real core, regressed and went to the quack-doctor, Hitler, and his "wild analysis." Let me focus for a moment, in particular, on two areas—widely apart and yet both within the broad field of the German culture of that period— the area of art and the area of political organization, that I would especially recommend to the self-psychological psychohistorian's detailed investigation.

Art And Self Psychology

The great artists of any period are in touch with the currently preeminent psychological tasks of a culture. I call this the anticipatory function of art. The artist is thus ahead of the scientist in responding to man's unfolding needs. Through his work he leads man to a dawning conscious awareness of a preconsciously experienced psychological conflict or of an only preconsciously experienced psychic defect. The artist prepares the way for the culturally supported solution to the conflict or for healing of the defect. A large sector of Weimar Germany, including all classes and those with all levels of education, knew that they were not in touch with modern German art and felt preconsciously that German art was out of touch with them. And the Nazis knew it. They heaped endless scorn on the art of Weimar, they paraded it in large exhibits under the banner-title *Entarte Kunst* (Degenerate Art) all over the Reich. Why this display, why the bitter sarcasm, why the angry laughter? I think the Nazis accurately reflected a disappointment that they shared with a broad sector of Germany, a disappointment over the fact that their artists had failed to understand their needs and had failed to portray them with any degree of sensitivity.

The leading experimental art of the Weimar republic, of course, had switched from dealing with man's conflict to dealing with man's suffering a defective, fragmented, depleted self. But, like an inaccurately focused interpretation in therapeutic analysis, it was off center and too far away from Germany's particular experience; it was too general. Furthermore, the artists themselves were, to use Peter Gay's (1968) cogent insight and felicitous phrase, outsiders who had become insiders. Perhaps their lingering resentment made them either oblivious to the prevailing psychological needs or even contemptuous of them. I do not believe, in other words, that it was the unfamiliar formal element in the art—the blue horses of the painter, the twelve-tone scale of the musician, the noncapitalized nouns of the poet—that prevented effective communication, even though it was these formal elements which the Nazis singled out and on which they heaped their scorn. Initial formal strangeness often stands in the way of popular resonance in much of great art, but I don't believe that it can serve as an explanation here. All artistic activities of a period are interrelated. Artists closer to popular appeal will reverberate the work of the pioneers and thus gradually through their productions allow the broader public to accept the new artistic style and its language. And there are always great artists—like Kafka and Rilke in the realm of verbal art and, perhaps, Alban Berg and, on a more popular level, Weill in that of music—where the formal obstacle was not insurmountable. But their art addressed itself either to the lonely, estranged, disintegrating and depleted individual of modern times (Kafka) or to the experience of the formerly disenfranchised and estranged who had not yet formed a reliable sustaining matrix of selfobjects within German society (the Brecht-Weill operas). Somehow art needed to express the empty, devitalized, fragmented state of those who had formerly felt alive, strong, and cohesive in the symbol of a Kaiser and of a strong, disciplined army, and in the ideals of Imperial Germany, of its soldiers and civil servants, and in the ideals of German Christianity that had sprung from Luther's powerful words. That kind of art did not exist. The great works of the German past could not fill the void.

It might be replied here that the art to which the Nazis began to turn filled the void. But much of it—like *Rembrandt als Erzieher* or *Volk ohne Raum*—while in touch with certain aspects of German needs, was not art, and certainly not great art.[1] Wagner, whose preoccupations were indeed closely related to the work of building a strong German group self, was in essence out of phase with the needs of the 1920s. He was in tune with a self in the process of formation but not with a state caused by the sudden deprivation of something that had already been achieved, however insecurely. Nazi-supported art—and that includes the architecture of Hitler, the stereotyped replica of the symbols of Roman imperial power—unlike the art that would have been needed at the time, was the symptom of a pseudo-cure for a selfobject. It helped deny the persisting self-defect via sudden and wholesale identifications with symbols of strength and failed to deal with the depressive, devitalized and fragmented state of Germany. Nazi art fostered regression to archaic symbols of power and unity.

Political thought of the time also failed to provide the German group self with the needed resonance that would have encour-

---

[1] [Editor: *Rembrandt als Erzieher* by Julius Langbehn was a turgid racist tract first published in 1890. It went through 40 printings in two years and profoundly influenced the German youth movement. *Volk ohne Raum* by Hans Grimm first appeared in 1926 and was a best-seller in Weimar Germany. The book played on fears of encirclement by vengeful neighbors and inadequate living space for an expanding Volk. A sense of claustrophobia haunts the novel.]

aged development toward a new self-image. But the reasons for the obtuseness of the leading group of political thinkers is hard to determine. Polarized by the heat of political battles, inexperienced in the exercise of political power, the new leaders of Germany, in action and thought (including, above all, the press) pursued their political maneuvers, played their games, and propagandized their solutions but failed to realize the fragmentation and devitalization of the national self. They focused on the fragments of this self: on the problems of the proletariat, of the middle classes, and of the industrialists; on the problems of international relations; and on the various problems posed by the new positions of the ecclesiastical and educational systems. But political thinkers failed to grasp that the central disease was the yearning for a feeling of wholeness. It is not physical pain and deprivation that drives people to despair. It is meaningless pain and deprivation that makes them feel hopeless and lack the joyful conviction that a single experience is part of a destiny. "I can give you nothing but blood, sweat, and tears," Churchill told the English people. And they responded by feeling strong because they had a spokesman of their destiny. Could Weimar have created a German Churchill? Would a German Churchill have given meaning to German despair by placing it into time, into a course of cohesive experiences? These are good questions, I believe, but it is pointless to try to answer them. Instead I will turn to Hitler and to the genius of his preceptions and verbal responses, to the satanic catastrophe of his actions.

Hitler's genius lay not in his psychological knowledge or political shrewdness or in his rhetorical gifts but in his total resonance with the disease of the German self. In his own experience, he worked out a cure for the devitalization and fragmentation of his nuclear self by a shift, first performed in early life and then repeated and entrenched in late adolescence and early adulthood, from a traumatically failing selfobject to the archaic grandiose self. This personality organization, while infrequent, is by no means unique. The core of the self, except for one nucleus of infantile grandiosity, is lost. Thus the personality, however extensive its growth in the many layers that are acquired around the archaic core, remains cold. Having severed its relationship with a traumatically frustrating selfobject, it never acquires the capacity for modulated empathy with others. Such a personality is characterized by a near-total absence of compassion, except where total identification is concerned, when the "other" is totally experienced as part of the self. Such people—and they may well be the majority of the charismatic and messianic leaders of all nations, whether in the historical and political arena, or in religion or health cults, or as the crystallization point for cultural fads—are no longer in need of selfobjects. They have acquired self-sufficiency. Whatever the details of their personality organization may be, such people become ideal targets for those who are in desperate need of selfobjects.

What is the difference, to return to my favorite analogy, between the selfobject transference of the German group self to the leaders of Weimar and the transference they established to Hitler? Actually, that segment of the German people whose self had been most severely damaged by the First World War days formed no workable transference at all to the new Weimar insiders but, like many analysands with self disorders, responded to the presence of the potential transference targets with hostility and contempt. And just like a bad analyst, the Weimar leaders responded with counter hostility, contemptuous admonitions, moralizing interpretations, and the kind of emotional withdrawal that, in the clinical situation, leads to the silly diagnosis that the patient is unanalyzable. Only when the patient became threatening, after years of feeling secretly disappointed in the hope that his hidden suffering would be recognized, and proceeded to break off treatment, did the Weimar leaders become alarmed and offer some remedial understanding. But then, as in the analogous moments of analysis, it was too late.

And what about the Nationalists among the pre-Hitler and non-Nazi elite? What did they provide for the broken German self? Here transferences did indeed establish themselves, but like the solution Hitler provided they did not bring about remedial working-through. Like Hitler the Nationalists did not focus on the underlying depression, on the basic disease of fragmentation, acknowledging its presence, explaining that it was understandable and that it was human to feel and react that way. The Nationalists denied the presence of the depression, the devitalization, the fragmentation of the German self and failed to outline the difficult but exhilarating task of forming a new one out of the ruins of the old, followed by persistent support as the creative work moved on. The Hugenbergs and Schleichers tried, in other words, to do what Hitler later did, but they lacked Hitler's unique talents. Their personalities were uncharismatic. Their exhortations that a German self would be restored was in essence a replica of the old, lost one. Such atavism prevented the creation of a really new German self and could not do away with its fragmentation.

Everyone failed miserably, except Hitler. But it was the abysmal failure of constructive empathy in Germany and in its European surroundings that made Hitler possible. Even psychoanalysts, I cannot help but add, failed. What a ridiculous statement, it will be said. What influence could a handful of psychologists, each working with a few patients, have exerted in stemming a historical tide that moved on with such vehemence that it nearly succeeded in innundating the whole of Western civilization? On the face of it, it seems to be an utterly convincing argument, and perhaps even a correct one. But not necessarily so. What might have happened if analytic insights, filtering through the intelligentsia toward men in positions of political leadership and toward artists and journalists, had provided at least a dawning insight into the state of the broken self of individuals who were suddenly deprived of the two major constituents of their selves? We do not know. What we do know, however, in retrospect, is that analysis not only lacked the power to influence populations, but also lacked the insights then that would have given it effectiveness, that would have given it a chance, however miniscule, to support the remnants of good will and of constructive political action.

Psychoanalysis lacked, I submit, an understanding of the pathology of the self, both in the individual and in the group. Both were seen in terms of a mental apparatus that had to be helped in the task of taming the drives. Freud's applications of the drive-defense theory to history were limited in value, to say the least. It is no wonder that analysis felt helpless and that, in the final general theory of a death-instinct that remained untamable, it could do no more than offer proud resignation to the inevitable. It failed, as Christianity had failed, because in the end, after the aggressive drive had been made conscious, it could do no more than apply moral pressure and appeal for inner controls. One of the most telling anecdotes about Freud's attitude concerns his reply to a question about the source of anti-Semitism. He said, with touching openness, that here his understanding stopped; here he could only hate. In one sentence he did away with any further examination of the effect that the narcissistic injury of anti-scientific rejection had on him and declared himself simultaneously unable to explore the self of those who were inflicting these injuries. He thus deprived himself of the opportunity of recognizing the narcissistic injury that lies behind the anti-Semite's rage. It was, to be sure, not a lack of cognitive powers that blocked Freud here. He had long since toyed with the idea that anti-Semitism may be related to the fact that Jews claimed to be the chosen people and that anti-Semitic gentiles behaved as if they really believed the claim. It was an emotional obstacle, present only with regard to other areas of man's narcissism, that stood in the way of his examining this area in depth and relevant detail.

Reflections on Self Psychology

4

Forms and Transformations of Narcissism

(1966)

I

Although in theoretical discussions it will usually not be disputed that narcissism, the libidinal investment of the self,[1] is per se neither pathological nor obnoxious, there exists an understandable tendency to look at it with a negatively toned evaluation as soon as the field of theory is left. Where such a prejudice exists it is undoubtedly based on a comparison between narcissism and object love, and is justified by the assertion that it is the more primitive and the less adaptive of the two forms of libido distribution. I believe, however, that these views do not

Presented at the Sunday morning Plenary Session of the Fall Meeting of the American Psychoanalytic Association, December 5, 1965, New York. This essay was first published in the *Journal of the American Psychoanalytic Association* (1966), 14:243–272.
This essay consists of extracts from a larger study of certain aspects of narcissism, currently in preparation, which will deal more broadly and deeply not only with the topics introduced at this time, but also with a variety of other, related subject matters (with the phenomenon of narcissistic rage, for example; with the therapeutic implications of the theoretical views which are expressed here; and with their application to the investigation of some sociocultural phenomena). The completed study will contain a number of extensive references to clinical material and a review of the relevant literature which had to be omitted in the present context.

[1] For the delimitation of narcissism as "strictly defined, libidinal cathexis of the self" and its differentiation from other libido distributions (such as those employed by ego functions or in "self-interest") see Hartmann (e.g., 32, esp. p. 185; and 33, esp. p. 433).

stem primarily from an objective assessment either of the developmental position or of the adaptive value of narcissism, but that they are due to the improper instrusion of the altruistic value system of Western civilization. Whatever the reasons for them, these value judgments exert a narrowing effect on clinical practice. They tend to lead to a wish from the side of the therapist to replace the patient's narcissistic position with object love, while the often more appropriate goal of a transformed narcissism (i.e., of a redistribution of the patient's narcissistic libido, and of the integration of the primitive psychological structures into the mature personality) is neglected. On the theoretical side, too, the contribution of narcissism to health, adaptation, and achievement has not been treated extensively.[2] This predilection, however, is justifiable on heuristic grounds since the examination of the relatively silent states of narcissism in equilibrium is clearly less fruitful than the scrutiny of narcissism in states of disturbance. The disturbances of narcissistic balance to which we refer as "narcissistic injury" appear to offer a particularly promising access to the problems of narcissism, not only because of the frequency with which they occur in a broad spectrum of normal and abnormal psychological states but also because they are usually easily recognized by the painful affect of embarrassment or shame which accompanies them and by their ideational elaboration which is known as inferiority feeling or hurt pride.

In Freud's work two complementary directions can be discerned which analysts have tended to follow in their endeavor to fit the occurrence of some instances of narcissistic disequilibrium into a pre-established psychoanalytic context. On the one hand, Freud drew attention to certain functions of the ego which relate to the id, especially to the exhibitionistic aspects of the pregenital drives; i.e., he pointed to potential shame as a motive for defense (the ego's *Schamgefühl*, its sense of shame) and to the occurrence of shame with failures of the defense (14, pp. 169, 171, 178; 16, p. 242ff.; 26, pp. 99n., 106n.; furthermore, 17, p. 177f.; 18, p. 171; and 19, p. 108). On the other hand, Freud

---

[2] Federn's statements in line with his approach were conjoined to form a chapter of the volume *Ego Psychology and the Psychoses* (9). Here, too, however, as is true with so many other of Federn's fascinating insights into ego psychology, the formulations remain too close to phenomenology, i.e., to the introspected experience, and are thus hard to integrate with the established body of psychoanalytic theory (cf. 31, p. 84).

asserted that a part of the child's narcissism is transferred upon his superego, and thus narcissistic tensions occur in the ego as it strives to live up to the ego ideal. The superego, Freud said, is "the vehicle of the ego ideal by which the ego measures itself, which it emulates, and whose demands for ever greater perfection it strives to fulfil" (27, p. 64f.).

I cannot in the present context discuss the numerous contributions in the psychoanalytic and related literature which have followed Freud's lead concerning the two directions of the development of narcissism. Although in certain areas I arrived at conclusions which go beyond the outlines indicated by Freud, the general pattern of my own thought has also been determined by them.

Despite the fact that, in the present study, I shall frequently be referring to well-known phenomena on the psychological surface which can easily be translated into behavioral terms, the concepts employed here are not those of social psychology. The general definition of narcissism as the investment of the self might still be compatible with a transactional approach; but the self in the psychoanalytic sense is variable and by no means coextensive with the limits of the personality as assessed by an observer of the social field. In certain psychological states the self may expand far beyond the borders of the individual, or it may shrink and become identical with a single one of his actions or aims (cf. 43, p. 226f.). The antithesis to narcissism is not the object relation but object love. An individual's profusion of object relations, in the sense of the observer of the social field, may conceal his narcissistic experience of the object world; and a person's seeming isolation and loneliness may be the setting for a wealth of current object investments.

The concept of primary narcissism is a good case in point. Although it is extrapolated from empirical observations, it refers not to the social field but to the psychological state of the infant. It comprehends the assertion that the baby originally experiences the mother and her ministrations not as a you and its actions but within a view of the world in which the I-you differentiation has not yet been established. Thus the expected control over the mother and her ministrations is closer to the concept which a grownup has of himself and of the control which he expects over his own body and mind than to the grownup's experience of others and of his control over them.[3]

Primary narcissism, however, is not in the focus of the ensuing developmental considerations. Although there remains throughout life an important direct residue of the original position—a basic narcissistic tonus which suffuses all aspects of the personality—I shall turn our attention to two other forms into which it becomes differentiated: the *narcissistic self* and the *idealized parent imago.*

The balance of primary narcissism is disturbed by maturational pressures and painful psychic tensions which occur because the mother's ministrations are of necessity imperfect and traumatic delays cannot be prevented. The baby's psychic organization, however, attempts to deal with the disturbances by the building up of new systems of perfection. To one of them Freud (21, p. 136) referred as the "purified pleasure ego,"[4] a stage in development in which everything pleasant, good, and perfect is considered as part of a rudimentary self, while everything unpleasant, bad, and imperfect is considered as "outside." Or, in contrast to this at first attempted solution, the baby attempts to maintain the original perfection and omnipotence by imbuing the rudimentary you, the adult, with absolute perfection and power.[5]

The cathexis of the psychic representation of the *idealized parent imago* is neither adequately subsumed under the heading of narcissism nor of object love. Idealization may of course be properly described as an aspect of narcissism, i.e., of the (still undifferentiated) original bliss, power, perfection, and goodness which is projected on the parent figure during a phase when these qualities become gradually separated into perfection pertaining to pleasure, or power, or knowledge, or beauty, or morality. The intimate relationship between idealization and

[3] Bing, McLaughlin, and Marburg (3, p. 24) consider primary narcissism as a condition "in which the libido diffusely and in an undifferentiated way is invested in various parts of the organism." Their definition thus places primary narcissism as existing prior to the time when a psychological approach begins to be appropriate.

[4] The purified pleasure ego may be considered as a prestage of the structure which is referred to as *narcissistic self* in the present essay.

[5] For a discussion of the concept formed by the immature psyche of the all-powerful object and the child's relationship to it, see Ferenczi (10) and Jones (37). See also Sandler et al., who in this context speak of an "ideal object" (48, p. 156f.).

narcissism is attested to by the fact that homosexual libido is always predominantly involved even when the object is of the opposite sex. The ease, furthermore, with which the representation of the idealized object may at various stages of its development be taken back into the nexus of the self through identification is an additional piece of evidence for its narcissistic character, as Freud (23, p. 250), following Rank (46, p. 416), mentioned when he said that a "narcissistic type of object-choice" may lay the groundwork for the later pathogenic introjection of the depressed. Yet to subsume the idealized object imago under the heading of narcissism is telling only half the story. The narcissistic cathexis of the idealized object is not only amalgamated with features of true object love, the libido of the narcissistic cathexis itself has undergone a transformation, i.e., the appearance of idealizing libido may be regarded as a maturational step *sui generis* in the development of narcissistic libido and differentiated from the development of object love with its own transitional phases.

Although the idealization of the parent imago is a direct continuation of the child's original narcissism, the cognitive image of the idealized parent changes with the maturation of the child's cognitive equipment. During an important transitional period when gratification and frustration are gradually recognized as coming from an external source, the object alternatingly emerges from and resubmerges into the self. When separated from the self, however, the child's experience of the object is total at each point of development, and the seemingly objective classification into "part" and "whole" objects rests on the adult observer's value judgment.

Form and content of the psychic representation of the idealized parent thus vary with the maturational stage of the child's cognitive apparatus; they are also influenced by environmental factors that affect the choice of internalizations and their intensity.

The idealized parent imago is partly invested with objectlibidinal cathexes; and the idealized qualities are loved as a source of gratifications to which the child clings tenaciously. If the psyche is deprived, however, of a source of instinctual gratification, it will not resign itself to the loss but will change the object imago into an introject, i.e., into a structure of the psychic apparatus which takes over functions previously performed by the object.

Internalization (although part of the autonomous equipment of the psyche and occurring spontaneously) is, therefore, enhanced by object loss. In the present metapsychological context, however, object loss should be conceived broadly, ranging from the death of a parent, or his absence, or his withdrawal of affection due to physical or mental disease, to the child's unavoidable disappointment in circumscribed aspects of the parental imago, or a parent's prohibitions of unmodified instinctual demands.

I would not contradict anyone who feels that the term object loss should not be employed for the frustrations imposed by education or other demands of reality. In the context of the preconditions for the internalization of drive-regulating functions, however, the differences are only quantitative. The kindly rejection of a child's unmodified instinctual demand, even if enunciated in the form of a positive value, is still a frustration which connotes the impossibility of maintaining a specific object cathexis; it may, therefore, result in internalization, and the accretion of drive-regulating psychic structure. The unique position of the superego among the drive-regulating psychic structures is correlated to the fact that the child has to achieve a phase-specific decathexis of his infantile object representations at the very time when the cathexis had reached the peak of its intensity.

If we apply these considerations to our specific topic, we may say that during the preoedipal period there normally occurs a gradual loss of the idealized parent imago and a concomitant accretion of the drive-regulating matrix of the ego, while the massive loss during the oedipal period contributes to the formation of the superego. Every shortcoming detected in the idealized parent leads to a corresponding internal preservation of the externally lost quality of the object.[6] A child's lie remains

---

[6] A whole broad spectrum of possibilities is condensed here. Not only parental illness or death but also the parents' reactions to an illness of a young child may prematurely and traumatically shatter the idealized object imago and thus lead to phase-inappropriate, inadequate, massive internalizations which prevent the establishment of an idealized superego and lead later to vascillation between the search for external omnipotent powers with which the person wants to merge, or to a defensive reinforcement of a grandiose self concept.

Not only premature discovery of parental weakness, however, can lead to trauma in this area; a narcissistic parent's inability to permit the child the gradual discovery of his shortcomings leads to an equally traumatic result. The ultimate

undetected; and thus one aspect of the omniscient idealized object
is lost; but omniscience is introjected as a minute aspect of the
drive-controlling matrix and as a significant aspect of the all-
seeing eye, the omniscience of the superego. It is due to the phase-
specific massive introjection of the idealized qualities of the object
that, as Freud states, the superego must be regarded as the "vehicle
of the ego ideal." Or, expressed in another way: the ego ideal is
that aspect of the superego which corresponds to the phase-specific, massive introjection of the idealized qualities of the object.
The fact that the idealized parent was the carrier of the originally narcissistic perfection and omnipotence accounts now for
the omnipotence, omniscience, and perfection of the superego,
and it is due to these circumstances that the values and standards
of the superego are experienced as absolute. The fact, however,
that the original narcissism has passed through a cherished object
before its reinternalization, and that the narcissistic investment
itself had been raised to the new developmental level of idealization, accounts for the unique emotional importance of our
standards, values, and ideals in so far as they are part of the
superego. Psychologically such a value cannot be defined in terms
of its content or form. A funny story ceases to be amusing when
its content is told without regard to the specific psychological
structure of jokes. Similarly, the unique position held by those
of our values and ideals which belong to the realm of the superego is determined neither by their (variable) content (which may
consist of demands for unselfish, altruistic behavior or of demands
for prowess and success) nor by their (variable) form (i.e., whether
they are prohibitions or positive values, even including demands
for specific modes of drive discharge), but by their genesis and
psychic location. It is not its form or content but the unique quality of arousing our love and admiration while imposing the task
of drive control which characterizes the ego ideal.

Our next task is the consideration of the *narcissistic self*. Its
narcissistic cathexis, in contrast to that which is employed in the
instinctual investment of the idealized parent imago and of the
ego ideal, is retained within the nexus of the self and does not
make that specific partial step toward object love which results

---

confrontation with the parent's weakness cannot be avoided and, when it occurs,
the resulting introjection is massive and pathological.

in idealization. The ego ideal is predominantly related to drive control, while the narcissistic self is closely interwoven with the drives and their inexorable tensions. At the risk of sounding anthropomorphic, yet in reality only condensing a host of clinical impressions and genetic reconstructions, I am tempted to say that the ego experiences the influence of the ego ideal as coming from above and that of the narcissistic self as coming from below. Or I might illustrate my point by the use of imagery which pertains to the preconscious derivatives of the two structures and say that man is *led* by his ideals but *pushed* by his ambitions. And in contrast to the idealized parent imago which is gazed at in awe, admired, looked up to, and like which one wants to become, the narcissistic self wants to be looked at and admired.

The establishment of the narcissistic self must be evaluated both as a maturationally and predetermined step and as a developmental achievement, and the grandiose fantasy which is its functional correlate is phase-appropriate and adaptive just as is the overestimation of the power and perfection of the idealized object. Premature interference with the narcissistic self leads to later narcissistic vulnerability because the grandiose fantasy becomes repressed and inaccessible to modifying influences.

The narcissistic self and the ego ideal may also be distinguished by the relationship of the surface layers of the two structures to consciousness. Perception and consciousness are the psychological analogue of the sensory organs which scan the surroundings. The fact that the ego ideal has object qualities facilitates, therefore, its availability to consciousness.[7] Even the surface aspects of the narcissistic self, however, are introspectively hard to perceive since this structure has no object qualities. In a letter to Freud (June 29, 1912) Binswanger mentioned that he "had been struck by his [Freud's] enormous will to power . . . to dominate. . . . Freud replied (July 4, 1912): "I do not trust myself to contradict you in regard to the will to power but I am not aware of it. I have long surmised that not only the repressed content of the psyche, but also the . . . core of our ego [*"das Eigentliche unseres Ichs,"* i.e., the essential part of our ego] is unconscious.

---

[7] These considerations do not apply, of course, when aspects of the ego ideal have been concealed in consequence of endopsychic conflict. Corresponding to the special status of the ego ideal as an internal object, this concealment occupies a position which lies between repression and denial.

. . . I infer this from the fact that consciousness is . . . a sensory organ directed toward the outside world, so that it is always attached to a part of the ego which is self unperceived" (4, p. 57f.).

As I mentioned before, the preconscious correlates of the narcissistic self and of the ego ideal are experienced by us as our ambitions and ideals. They are at times hard to distinguish, not only because ambitions are often disguised as ideals but also because there are indeed lucky moments in our lives, or lucky periods in the lives of the very fortunate, in which ambitions and ideals coincide. Adolescent types not infrequently disguise their ideals as ambitions and, finally, certain contents of the ego ideal (demands for achievement) may mislead the observer. If the metapsychological differences, however, are kept in mind, the phenomenological distinction is greatly facilitated.

Our ideals are our internal leaders; we love them and are longing to reach them. Ideals are capable of absorbing a great deal of transformed narcissistic libido and thus of diminishing narcissistic tensions and narcissistic vulnerability. If the ego's instinctual investment of the superego remains insufficiently desexualized (or becomes resexualized), moral masochism is the result, a condition in which the ego may wallow in a state of humiliation when it fails to live up to its ideals. In general, however, the ego does not specifically experience a feeling of being narcissistically wounded when it cannot reach the ideals; rather it experiences an emotion akin to longing.

Our ambitions, too, although derived from a system of infantile grandiose fantasies may become optimally restrained, merge with the structure of the ego's goals, and achieve autonomy. Yet here too, a characteristic, genetically determined psychological flavor can be discerned. We are driven by our ambitions, we do not love them. And if we cannot realize them, narcissistic-exhibitionistic tensions remain undischarged, become dammed up, and the emotion of disappointment with the ego experiences always contains an admixture of shame. If the grandiosity of the narcissistic self, however, has been insufficiently modified because traumatic onslaughts on the child's self esteem have driven the grandiose fantasies into repression, then the adult ego will tend to vacillate between an irrational overestimation of the self and feelings of inferiority and will react with narcissistic mortification (6) to the thwarting of its ambitions.

Before we can pursue our examination of the relationship between the narcissistic self and the ego, however, we must turn our attention to two subsidiary topics: exhibitionism and the grandiose fantasy.

Let me begin with the description of a mother's interaction with her infant boy from the chapter called "Baby Worship" from Trollope's novel *Barchester Towers* (51). "Diddle, diddle . . . , dum . . . ; hasn't he got lovely legs?" said the rapturous mother. ". . . He's a . . . little . . . darling, so he is; and he has the nicest little pink legs in all the world, so he has. . . . . Well, . . . did you ever see? . . . My naughty . . . Johnny. He's pulled down all Mamma's hair . . . the naughtiest little man. . . . The child screamed with delight. . . ." The foregoing much abbreviated description of a very commonplace scene illustrates well the external surroundings correlated to two important aspects of the child's psychological equipment: his exhibitionistic propensities and his fantasies of grandeur. Exhibitionism, in a broad sense, can be regarded as a principal narcissistic dimension of all drives, as the expression of a narcissistic emphasis on the aim of the drive (upon the self as the performer) rather than on its object. The object is important only in so far as it is invited to participate in the child's narcissistic pleasure and thus to confirm it. Before psychological separateness has been established, the baby experiences the mother's pleasure in his whole body self, as part of his own psychological equipment. After psychological separation has taken place the child needs the gleam in the mother's eye in order to maintain the narcissistic libidinal suffusion which now concerns, in their sequence, the leading functions and activities of the various maturational phases. We speak thus of anal, or urethral, and of phallic exhibitionism, noting that in the girl the exhibitionism of the urethral-phallic phase is soon replaced by exhibitionism concerning her total appearance and by an interrelated exhibitionistic emphasis on morality and drive control.

The exhibitionism of the child must gradually become desexualized and subordinated to his goal-directed activities, a task which is achieved best through gradual frustrations accompanied by loving support, while the various overt and covert attitudes of rejection and overindulgence (and especially their amalgamations and rapid, unpredictable alternations) are the emotional soil for a wide range of disturbances. Although the unwholesome results vary greatly, ranging from severe hypochondria to mild forms of embarrassment, metapsychologically speaking they are all states of heightened narcissistic-exhibitionistic tension with incomplete and aberrant modes of discharge. In all these conditions the ego attempts to enlist the object's participation in the exhibitionism of the narcissistic self, but after the object's rejection the free discharge of exhibitionistic libido fails; instead of a pleasant suffusion of the body surface there is the heat of unpleasant blushing; instead of a pleasurable confirmation of the value, beauty, and lovableness of the self, there is painful shame.

Now I shall turn to an examination of the position which is held by the grandiose fantasy in the structure of the personality and of the function which it fulfills. While the exhibitionistic-narcissistic urges may be considered as the predominant drive aspect of the narcissistic self, the grandiose fantasy is its ideational content. Whether it contributes to health or disease, to the success of the individual or to his downfall, depends on the degree of its deinstinctualization and the extent of its integration into the realistic purposes of the ego. Take, for instance, Freud's statement that "a man who has been the indisputable favorite of his mother keeps for life the feeling of a conqueror, that confidence of success that often induces real success" (24, p. 26 [as transl. by E. Jones, 38, p. 5]). Here Freud obviously speaks about the results of adaptively valuable narcissistic fantasies which provide lasting support to the personality. It is evident that in these instances the early narcissistic fantasies of power and greatness had not been opposed by sudden premature experiences of traumatic disappointment but had been gradually integrated into the ego's reality-oriented organization.

We can now attempt to summarize the ultimate influence which is exerted by the two major derivatives of the original narcissism upon the mature psychological organization. Under favorable circumstances the neutralized forces emanating from the narcissistic self (the narcissistic needs of the personality and its ambitions) become gradually integrated into the web of our ego as a healthy enjoyment of our own activities and successes and as an adaptively useful sense of disappointment tinged with anger and shame over our failures and shortcomings. And, similarly, the ego ideal (the internalized image of perfection which we admire and to which we are looking up) may come to form a continuum with the ego, as a focus for our ego-syntonic values, as a healthy sense of direction and beacon for our activities and pursuits, and as an adaptively useful object of longing disappointment, when we cannot reach it. A firmly cathected, strongly idealized super-ego absorbs considerable amounts of narcissistic energy, a fact which lessens the personality's propensity toward narcissistic imbalance. Shame, on the other hand, arises when the ego is unable to provide a proper discharge for the exhibitionistic demands of the narcissistic self. Indeed, in almost all clinically significant instances of shame propensity, the personality is characterized by a defective idealization of the superego and by a concentration of the narcissistic libido upon the narcissistic self; and it is therefore the ambitious success-driven person with a poorly integrated grandiose self concept and intense exhibition-istic-narcissistic tensions who is most prone to experience shame.[8] If the pressures from the narcissistic self are intense and the ego is unable to control them, the personality will respond with shame to failures of any kind, whether its ambitions concern moral per-fection or external success (or, which is frequently the case, alternatingly the one or the other, since the personality possesses neither a firm structure of goals nor of ideals).

Under optimal circumstances, therefore, the ego ideal and the goal structure of the ego are the personality's best protection against narcissistic vulnerability and shame propensity. In the maintenance of the homeostatic narcissistic equilibrium of the personality, however, the interplay of the narcissistic self, the ego, and the superego may be depicted in the following way. The narcissistic self supplies small amounts of narcissistic-exhi-bitionistic libido which are transformed into subliminal signals of narcissistic imbalance (subliminal shame signals) as the ego tries to reach its goals, to emulate external examples and to obey external demands, or to live up to the standards and, especially, to the ideals of the superego (i.e., to the "ego ideal . . . whose

[8] E. Jacobson (36, p. 203f.), in harmony with A. Reich (47), speaks cogently of the fact that such patients often blame their high ideals for their "agonizing experiences of anxiety, shame, and inferiority" but that in reality they suffer from conflicts relating to "aggrandized, wishful self images" and "narcissistic-exhibitionistic strivings."

demands for ever greater perfection it strives to fulfil" [27]). Or, stated in a whimsical fashion: the narcissistic self attempts to exhibit its perfection to the ego or, indirectly through the mediation of the ego, to the external world or the superego and finds itself wanting; the resulting minute faulty discharge of libido, however, alerts the ego about a potential experience of painful shame.

In contrast to the metapsychological explanation of the emotion of shame presented here, Saul (49, pp. 92–94), basing himself on Alexander (1), and in harmony with the approach of cultural anthropology (2), compared guilt and shame as parallel phenomena; he suggested a differentiation between these two emotions by specifying that, unlike guilt, shame arises when people are unable to live up to their ideals. The question of the appropriateness of such structural distinctions (cf. especially Piers and Singer's comprehensive statement of his position [44]) is not germane to the present study and will not be pursued here. It was recently discussed by Hartmann and Loewenstein (34, p. 67) who maintain that it is inadvisable "to overemphasize the separateness of the ego ideal from the other parts of the superego," a theoretical procedure on which "the structural opposition of guilt and shame hinges."[9]

Sandler, Holder, and Meers (48, p. 156f.), on the other hand, retain the ego ideal within the context of the superego. Basing themselves on contributions by Jacobson (35) and A. Reich (47), however, they postulate the existence of an "ideal self" (as differentiated from the ego ideal), state that the child attempts to "avoid disappointment and frustration by living up to his ideal self," and conclude that shame arises when the individual fails "to live up to ideal standards which he accepts, whereas guilt is experienced when his ideal self differs from that which he feels to be directed by his introjects."

The interplay between the narcissistic self, the ego, and the superego determines the characteristic flavor of the personality

---

[9]See also Kohut and Seitz (39, p. 135) who stress the importance of retaining the conception of the essential "functional and genetic cohesion" of the internal moral forces which reside in the superego, despite the heuristic advantages and the convenience of a differentiation according to the phenomenology of their psychological effects.

and is thus, more than other building blocks or attributes of the personality, instinctively regarded as the touchstone of a person's individuality or identity.[10] In many outstanding personalities this inner balance appears to be dominated more by a well-integrated narcissistic self (which channels the drives) than by the ego ideal (which guides and controls them). Churchill, for example, repeated again and again, in an ever-enlarging arena, the feat of extricating himself from a situation from which there seemed to be no escape by ordinary means. (His famous escape during the Boer war is one example.) I would not be surprised if deep in his personality there was hidden the conviction that he could fly and thus get away when ordinary locomotion was barred. In the autobiographical volume *My Early Life* (5, p. 43f.) he describes the following events. During a vacation in the country he played a game in which he was being chased by a cousin and a younger brother. As he was crossing a bridge which led over a ravine he found himself entrapped by his pursuers who had divided their forces. ". . . capture seemed certain" he wrote, but "in a flash there came across me a great project." He looked at the young fir trees below and decided to leap onto one of them. He computed, he meditated. "In a second, I had plunged," he continues, "throwing out my arms to embrace the summit of the fir tree." It was three days before he regained consciousness and more than three months before he crawled out of bed. Yet although it is obvious that on this occasion the driving unconscious grandiose fantasy was not yet fully integrated, the struggle of the reasoning ego to perform the behest of the narcissistic self in a realistic way was already joined. Luckily, for him and for the forces of civilization, when he reached the peak of his responsibilities the inner balance had shifted.

II

Up to this point I have surveyed the origin, development, and functions of two major forms of narcissism and their integration

[10] It is difficult to find an appropriate place in psychoanalysis for the concept of "identity" (8) since, amphibologically, it is equally applicable in social and individual psychology. Under these circumstances an empirical approach to an area vaguely outlined by the impressionistic use of the term seems justified and, indeed, has occasionally (see, for example, Kramer [40]) led to illuminating findings, especially in the realm of psychopathology.

into the personality. Although the mutual influences between the narcissistic self, the ego, and the ego ideal were not ignored, our attention was focused predominantly on the narcissistic structures themselves and not on the ego's capacity to harness the narcissistic energies and to transform the narcissistic constellations into more highly differentiated, new psychological configurations. There exist, however, a number of acquisitions of the ego which, although genetically and dynamically related to the narcissistic drives and energized by them, are far removed from the preformed narcissistic structures of the personality, and which therefore must be evaluated not only as transformations of narcissism but even more as attainments of the ego and as attitudes and achievements of the personality.[11] Let me first enumerate those whose relationship to narcissism I shall discuss. They are: (i) man's creativity; (ii) his ability to be empathic; (iii) his capacity to contemplate his own impermanence; (iv) his sense of humor; and (v) his wisdom.

First we will briefly examine the relationship of narcissism to creativity. Like all complex human activities, artistic and scientific creativity serves many purposes, and it involves the whole personality, and thus a wide range of psychological structures and drives. It is therefore to be expected that the narcissism of the creative individual participates in his creative activity, for example, as a spur, driving him toward fame and acclaim. If there existed no further connection between narcissism and creativity, however, than the interplay between ambition and superior executive equipment, there would be no justification for discussing creativity specifically among the transformations of narcissism. It is my contention, however, that while artists and scientists may indeed be acclaim-hungry, narcissistically vulnerable individuals, and while their ambitions may be helpful in

---

[11] In his paper on poise Rangell (45) demonstrated the genetic and dynamic interrelatedness of specific drives with a whole integrative attitude of the ego. Poise, to state it in my words, rests on the desexualization of the crudely exhibitionistic cathexis of the narcissistic self and on the permeation of the neutralized libido into the whole physical and mental personality. Although poise may be nearer to the exhibitionistic drives than the various achievements of the ego to be discussed here, it too cannot be fully explained by reference to the drives which supply its fuel but must be considered as a new, broad configuration within the realm of the ego itself.

prompting them toward the appropriate communication of their work, the creative activity itself deserves to be considered among the transformations of narcissism.

The ambitions of a creative individual play an important role in his relationship to the public, i.e., to an audience of potential admirers; the transformation of narcissism, however, is a feature of the creator's relationship to his work. In creative work narcissistic energies are employed which have been changed into a form to which I referred earlier as idealizing libido, i.e., the elaboration of that specific point on the developmental road from narcissism toward object love at which an object (in the sense of social psychology) is cathected with narcissistic libido and thus included in the context of the self.

The analogy to the mother's love for the unborn fetus and for the newborn baby is inviting, and undoubtedly the singleminded devotion to the child who is taken into her expanded self, and her empathic responsiveness to him are similar to the creative person's involvement with his work. Nevertheless, I believe that the creative person's relationship to his work has less in common with the expanded narcissism of motherhood than with the still unrestricted narcissism of early childhood. Phenomenologically, too, the personality of many unusually creative individuals is more childlike than maternal. Even the experiments of some of the great in science impress the observer with their almost childlike freshness and simplicity. The behavior of Enrico Fermi, for example, while witnessing the first atomic explosion is described by his wife in the following way. He tore a piece of paper into small bits and, as soon as the blast had been set off, dropped them, one by one, watching the impact of the shock wave rise and subside (11, p. 239).

The creative individual, whether in art or science, is less psychologically separated from his surroundings than the noncreative one; the "I-you" barrier is not as clearly defined. The intensity of the creative person's awareness of the relevant aspects of his surroundings is akin to the detailed self perceptions of the schizoid and the childlike: it is nearer to a child's relationship to his excretions or to some schizophrenics' experiences of their body,[12]

[12] I treated once a gifted schizoid young woman who at one point gave me an artistically detached, beautiful description of the areolar area of one of her nip-

than to a healthy mother's feeling for her unborn child.

The indistinctness of "internal" and "external" is familiar to all of us in our relationship to the surrounding air which, as we take it in and expel it, is experienced by us as part of our selves, while we hardly perceive it as long as it forms a part of our external surroundings. Similarly, the creative individual is keenly aware of these aspects of his surroundings which are of significance to his work and he invests them with narcissistic-idealizing libido. Like the air which we breathe, they are most clearly experienced at the moment of union with the self. The traditional metaphor which is expressed by the term "inspiration" (it refers both to the taking in of air and to the fertilizing influence of an external stimulation upon the internal creative powers) and the prototypical description of creativity ("and the Lord God formed man of the dust of the ground, and breathed into his nostrils the breath of life; and man became a living soul" [Genesis 2:7]) support the assertion that there exists a close psychological proximity, on the one hand, between respiratory and creative inspiration and, on the other hand, between the coming to life of dust and the creative transformation of a narcissistically experienced material into a work of art.

Greenacre who recently discussed the nature of creative inspiration (30, p. 11f.) and who mentions the child's interest in the air as a mysterious unseen force which becomes a symbol for his dreams and thoughts, and for his dawning conscience, maintains that the future creative artist already possesses in infancy not only great sensitivity to sensory stimuli coming from the primary object, the mother, but also to those from peripheral objects which resemble the primary one. She uses the terms "collective alternates" and "love affair with the world" in describing the artist's attitude to his surroundings, and declares that it should not be considered as an expression of his narcissism but that "it partakes of an object relationship, though a collective one . . ." (29, p. 67f.).

K. R. Eissler, too, refers to the problem of the artist's relationship to reality when he speaks of "automorphic techniques" (7, p. 544), i.e., artistic activities which take place in a borderland of

---

ples, with an almost microscopic knowledge about the details and a concentrated absorption as if it were the most fascinating landscape.

autoplastic and alloplastic attitudes toward reality. A work of art, he explains, is autoplastic in so far as, like a dream or symptom, it serves the solution of an inner conflict and the fulfillment of a wish; it is simultaneously alloplastic, however, since it modifies reality by the creation of something original and new.

Greenacre and Eissler approach the problem of creativity from directions which are different from the one taken here, and arrive therefore at different conclusions. I believe, nonetheless, that their findings are consistent with the proposition that the artist invests his work with a specific form of narcissistic libido. Thus Greenacre's observation of the intensity of the future artist's early perception of the world, and of the persistence of his sensitivity during maturity, is in harmony with the contention that a leading part of the psychological equipment of creative people has been shaped through the extensive elaboration of a transitional point in libido development: idealization. In the average individual this form of the narcissistic libido survives only as the idealizing component of the state of being in love, and a surplus of idealizing libido which is not absorbed through the amalgamation with the object cathexis may account for the brief spurt of artistic activity which is not uncommon during this state. The well-established fact, furthermore, that creative people tend to alternate during periods of productivity between phases when they think extremely highly of their work and phases when they are convinced that it has no value, is a sure indication that the work is cathected with a form of narcissistic libido. The spreading of the libidinal investment upon "collective alternates" and ultimately upon "the world," which Greenacre describes, appears to me as an indication of a narcissistic experience of the world (an expanded self which includes the world) rather than as the manifestation of a "love affair' within an unqualified context of object love. The fact, too, that, as Eissler shows convincingly, the work of art is simultaneously the materialization of autoplastic and alloplastic psychic processes and that, in certain respects, the artist's attitude to his work is similar to that of the fetishist toward the fetish, lends support to the idea that, for the creator, the work is a transitional object and that it is invested with transitional narcissistic libido. The fetishist's attachment to the fetish has the intensity of an addiction, a fact which is a manifestation not of object love but of a fixation on an early object that is experienced as part of the self. Creative artists, and scientists, may be attached to their work with the intensity of an addiction, and they try to control and shape it with forces and for purposes which belong to narcissistically experienced world. They are attempting to re-create a perfection which formerly was directly an attribute of their own; during the act of creation, however, they do not relate to their work in the give-and-take mutuality which characterizes object love.

I am now turning to empathy as the second of the faculties of the ego which, though far removed from the drives and largely autonomous, are here considered in the context of the transformation of narcissism.[13]

Empathy is the mode by which one gathers psychological data about other people and, when they say what they think or feel, imagines their inner experience even though it is not open to direct observation. Through empathy we aim at discerning, in one single act of certain recognition, complex psychological configurations which we could either define only through the laborious presentation of a host of details or which it may even be beyond our ability to define.[14]

Empathy is an essential constituent of psychological observation and is, therefore, of special importance for the psychoanalyst who, as an empirical scientist, must first perceive the complex psychological configurations which are the raw data of human experience before he can attempt to explain them. The scientific use of empathy, however, is a specific achievement of the autonomous ego since, during the act of empathy, it must deliberately

[13] Although, even concerning the other subject matters discussed in this study, I am, within the present limits, often not able to adduce sufficient empirical support for my assertions, the following considerations about empathy are more speculative in essence and, for their verification, are probably in need of a psychoanalytically oriented experimental approach.

[14] The capacity to recognize complex psychological states through empathy has its analogy in the capacity to identify a face in a single act of apperception. Here, too, we do, in general, not add up details or go through complex theories of comparative judgment, and here, too, we are generally unable to define our certain recognition by adducing details. The similarity between the perceptual immediacy of the recognition of a face and the empathic grasp of another person's psychological state may not be only an incidental one; it may well be derived from the significant genetic fact that the small child's perceptual merging with the mother's face constitutes simultaneously its most important access to the mother's identity and to her emotional state (cf. 50, p. 103ff.).

suspend its predominant mode of operation which is geared to the perception of nonpsychological data in the surroundings.

The groundwork for our ability to obtain access to another person's mind is laid by the fact that in our earliest mental organization the feelings, actions, and behavior of the mother had been included in our self. This *primary empathy* with the mother prepares us for the recognition that, to a large extent, the basic inner experiences of people remain similar to our own. Our first perception of the manifestations of another person's feelings, wishes, and thoughts occurred within the framework of a narcissistic conception of the world; the capacity for empathy belongs, therefore, to the innate equipment of the human psyche and remains to some extent associated with the primary process.

Nonempathic forms of cognition, however, which are attuned to objects which are essentially dissimilar to the self become increasingly superimposed over the original empathic mode of reality perception and tend to impede its free operation. The persistence of empathic forms of observation outside psychology is, indeed, archaic and leads to a faulty, prerational, animistic conception of reality. Nonempathic modes of observation, on the other hand, are not attuned to the experiences of other people and, if they are employed in the psychological field, lead to a mechanistic and lifeless conception of psychological reality.

Nonempathic forms of cognition are dominant in the adult. Empathy must thus often be achieved speedily before nonempathic modes of observation are interposed. The approximate correctness of first impressions in the assessment of people, by contrast with subsequent evaluations, is well known and is exploited by skillful men of affairs. Empathy seems here to be able to evade interference and to complete a rapid scrutiny before other modes of observation can assert their ascendancy. The exhaustive empathic comprehension, however, which is the aim of the analyst requires the ability to use the empathic capacity for prolonged periods. His customary observational attitude ("evenly suspended attention"; avoidance of note taking; curtailment of realistic interactions; concentration on the purpose of achieving understanding rather than on the wish to cure and to help) aims at excluding psychological processes attuned to the nonpsychological perception of objects and to encourage empathic comprehension through the perception of experiential identities.

Foremost among the obstacles which interfere with the use of empathy (especially for prolonged periods) are those which stem from conflicts about relating to another person in a narcissistic mode. Since training in empathy is an important aspect of psychoanalytic education, the loosening of narcissistic positions constitutes a specific task of the training analysis, and the candidate's increasing ability to employ the transformed narcissistic cathexes in empathic observation is a sign that this goal is being reached.

Could it be that among the obstacles to the use of empathy is also the resistance against the acknowledgment of unconscious knowledge about others? Could it be that to the "I have always known it" of the analysand when an unconscious content is uncovered (20, p. 148) may correspond an "I have always recognized it" in the analyst when he and the patient arrive at a valid reconstruction, or when the patient supplies a relevant memory?

Freud pondered the question whether thought transference does occur (27, pp. 54–56) and referred to such biological and social phenomena as the means by which "the common purpose comes about in the great insect communities" and the possibility of the persistence of an "original, archaic method of communication between individuals" which "in the course of phylogenetic evolution . . . has been replaced by the better method of giving information with the help of signals," yet which may still "put itself into effect under certain conditions for instance, in passionately excited mobs" (p. 55). To these statements one could add only that an intentional curbing of the usual cognitive processes of the ego (such as is brought about in the analytic situation) may free the access to empathic communication as does the involuntary trancelike condition which occurs in those who become submerged in an excited mob[15] and that the prototype

---

[15] For a striking description of the ego's perviousness to the dominant mental tendencies of an aroused multitude, and an illuminating discussion of the propensity of the individual who is trapped in an agitated group to shed ego autonomy and to respond regressively in narcissistic-identificatory compliance, see A. Mitscherlich (42, esp. p. 202f.).

of empathic understanding must be sought not only in the pre-history of the race but also in the early life of the individual. Under favorable circumstances, however, the faculty of perceiving the psychological manifestations of the mother, achieved through the extension of narcissistic cathexes, becomes the starting point for a series of developmental steps which lead ultimately to a state in which the ego can choose between the use of empathic and nonempathic modes of observation, depending on realistic requirements and on the nature of the surroundings that it scrutinizes.

Man's capacity to acknowledge the finiteness of his existence, and to act in accordance with this painful discovery, may well be his greatest psychological achievement, despite the fact that it can often be demonstrated that a manifest acceptance of transience may go hand in hand with covert denials.

The acceptance of transience is accomplished by the ego, which performs the emotional work that precedes, accompanies, and follows separations. Without these efforts a valid conception of time, of limits, and of the impermanence of object cathexes could not be achieved. Freud discussed the emotional task which is imposed on the psyche by the impermanence of objects, be they beloved people or cherised values (22, p. 303), and gave expression to the conviction that their impermanence did not detract from their worth. On the contrary, he said, their very impermanence makes us love and admire them even more: "Transience value is scarcity value in time."

Freud's attitude is based on the relinquishment of emotional infantilism, an abandonment even of a trace of the narcissistic insistence on the omnipotence of the wish; it expresses the acceptance of realistic values. More difficult still, however, than the acknowledgment of the impermanence of object cathexes is the unqualified intellectual and emotional acceptance of the fact that we ourselves are impermanent, that the self which is cathected with narcissistic libido is finite in time. I believe that this rare feat rests not simply on a victory of autonomous reason and supreme objectivity over the claims of narcissism but on the creation of a higher form of narcissism. The great who have achieved the outlook on life to which the Romans referred as living *sub specie aeternitatis* do not display resignation and hopelessness but a quiet pride which is often coupled with mild disdain of the rabble which, without being able to delight in the variety of experiences which life has to offer, is yet afraid of death and trembles at its approach. Goethe (28) gave beautiful expression of his contempt for those who cannot accept death as an intrinsic part of life in the following stanza:

> Und so lang du das nicht hast,
> Dieses: Stirb and werde!
> Bist du nur ein trüber Gast
> Auf der dunklen Erde.[16]

Only through an acceptance of death, Goethe says here, can man reap all that is in life; without it, however, life is dim and insignificant. I do not believe that an attitude such as the one expressed by Goethe is to be understood as a beautiful denial of the fear of death. There is no undertone of anxiety in it and no excitement. Conspicuous in it, however, is a nonisolated, creative superiority which judges and admonishes with quiet assurance. I have little doubt that those who are able to achieve this ultimate attitude toward life do so on the strength of a new, expanded, transformed narcissism: a cosmic narcissism which has transcended the bounds of the individual.

Just as the child's *primary empathy* with the mother is the precursor of the adult's ability to be empathic, so his *primary identity* with her must be considered as the precursor of an expansion of the self, late in life, when the finiteness of individual existence is acknowledged. The original psychological universe, i.e., the primordial experience of the mother, is "remembered" by many people in the form of the occasionally occurring vague reverberations which are known by the term "oceanic feeling" (26, pp. 64–73). The achievement—as the certainty of eventual death is fully realized—of a shift of the narcissistic cathexes, from the self to a concept of participation in a supraindividual and timeless existence, must also be regarded as genetically predetermined by the child's primary identity with the mother. In contrast to the oceanic feeling, however, which is experienced passively

---

[16] Adapted from a translation by Ludwig Lewisohn (41):
> And till thine this deep behest:
> Die to win thy being!
> Art thou but a dreary guest
> Upon earth unseeing.

(and usually fleetingly), the genuine shift of the cathexes toward a cosmic narcissism is the enduring, creative result of the steadfast activities of an autonomous ego, and only very few are able to attain it.

It seems a long way from the acceptance of transience and the quasi-religious solemnity of a cosmic narcissism to another uniquely human acquisition: the capacity for humor. And yet, the two phenomena have much in common. It is not by accident that Freud introduces his essay on humor (25, p. 161) with a man's ability to overcome the fear of his impending death by putting himself, through humor, upon a higher plane. "When . . . a criminal who was being led out to the gallows on a Monday remarked: 'Well, the week's beginning nicely',," Freud says that "the humorous process . . . affords him . . . satisfaction." And Freud states that "humor has something liberating about it"; that it "has something of grandeur"; and that it is a "triumph of narcissism" and "the victorious assertion of . . . invulnerability" (p. 162). Metapsychologically, however, Freud explains that humor— this "triumph of narcissism"—is achieved by a person's withdrawing "the psychical accent from his ego" and "transposing it on to his super-ego" (p. 164).

Humor and cosmic narcissism are thus both transformations of narcissism which aid man in achieving ultimate mastery over the demands of the narcissistic self, i.e., to tolerate the recognition of his finiteness in principle and even of his impending end.

There is no doubt that the claim that the ego has mastered its fear of death is often not authentic. If a person is unable to be serious and employs humor excessively, or if he is unwilling to face the pains and labors of everyday living and moves along continuously with his head in the clouds, we will become suspicious of both the clown and the saint, and we will most likely be right in surmising that neither the humor nor the otherworldliness are genuine. Yet, if a man is capable of responding with humor to the recognition of those unalterable realities which oppose the assertions of the narcissistic self, and if he can truly attain that quiet, superior stance which enables him to contemplate his own end philosophically, we will assume that a transformation of his narcissism has indeed taken place (a withdrawal of the psychical accent from the "ego," as Freud put it) and will respect the person who has acieved it.

A disregard for the interests of the self, even to the point of allowing its death, may also come about during states of supreme object cathexis. Such instances (for example, as a consequence of an upsurge of extreme, personified patriotic fervor) take place in a frenzied mental condition, and the ego is paralyzed, as if in a trance. Humor and cosmic narcissism, on the other hand, which permit us to face death without having to resort to denial, are metapsychologically based not on a decathexis of the self through a frantic hypercathexis of objects but on a decathexis of the narcissistic self through a rearrangement and transformation of the narcissistic libido; and, in contrast to states of extreme object cathexis, the span of the ego is here not narrowed but the ego remains active and deliberate.

A genuine decathexis of the self can only be achieved slowly by an intact, well-functioning ego; and it is accompanied by sadness as the cathexis is transferred from the cherished self upon the supraindividual ideals and upon the world with which one identifies. The profoundest forms of humor and cosmic narcissism therefore do not present a picture of grandiosity and elation but that of a quiet inner triumph with an admixture of undenied melancholy.

We have now reached our final subject matter, the human attitude which we call wisdom, the first two can still be defined almost exclusively within the sphere of cognition itself. The term information refers to the gleaning of isolated data about the world; knowledge to the comprehension of a cohesive set of such data held together by a matrix of abstractions. Wisdom, however, goes beyond the cognitive sphere, although, of course, it includes it.

Wisdom is achieved largely through man's ability to overcome his unmodified narcissism and it rests on his acceptance of the limitations of his physical, intellectual, and emotional powers. It may be defined as an amalgamation of the higher processes of cognition with the psychological attitude which accompanies the renouncement of these narcissistic demands. Neither the possession of ideals, nor the capacity for humor, nor the acceptance of transience alone characterizes wisdom. All three have to be linked together to form a new psychological constellation which goes beyond the several emotional and cognitive attributes of which it is made up. Wisdom may thus be defined as a stable attitude of the personality toward life and the world, an attitude which is formed through the integration of the cognitive function with humor, acceptance of transience, and a firmly cathected system of values.

In the course of life the acquisition of knowledge clearly must be preceded by the gathering of information. Even from the point of view of its cognitive component, therefore, wisdom can hardly be an attribute of youth since experience and work must first have led to the acquisition of broadly based knowledge. Ideals are most strongly cathected in youth; humor is usually at its height during maturity; and an acceptance of transience may be achieved during the advanced years. Thus we can see again that the attainment of wisdom is usually reserved for the later phases of life.

The essence of this proud achievement is therefore a maximal relinquishment of narcissistic delusions, including the acceptance of the inevitability of death, without an abandonment of cognitive and emotional involvements. The ultimate act of cognition, i.e., the acknowledgment of the limits and of the finiteness of the self, is not the result of an isolated intellectual process but is the victorious outcome of the lifework of the total personality in acquiring broadly based knowledge and in transforming archaic modes of narcissism into ideals, humor, and a sense of supraindividual participation in the world.

Sarcasm occurs in consequence of the lack of idealized values and attempts to minimize the emotional significance of narcissistic limitations through the hypercathexis of a pleasure-seeking omnipotent self. The most important precondition for the feat of humor under adverse circumstances, however, and for the ability to contemplate one's impending end, is the formation and maintenance of a set of cherished values, i.e., metapsychologically, a strong idealization of the superego. Wisdom is, in addition, characterized not only by the maintenance of the libidinal cathexes of the old ideals but by their creative expansion. And in contrast to an attitude of utter seriousness and unrelieved solemnity vis-à-vis the approaching end of life, the truly wise are able in the end to transform the humor of their years of maturity into a sense of proportion, a touch of irony toward the achievements of individual existence, including even their own wisdom. The ego's ultimate mastery over the narcissistic self, the final control of the rider over the horse, may after all have been decisively assisted by the fact that the horse, too, has grown old. And, lastly, we may recognize that what has been accomplished is not so much control but the acceptance of the ultimate insight that, as concerns the supreme powers of nature, we are all "sunday riders."[17]

In concluding this presentation let me now give a brief résumé of the principal themes which I laid before you. I wanted to emphasize that there are various forms of narcissism which must be considered not only as forerunners of object love but also as independent psychological constellations, whose development and functions deserve separate examination and evaluation. In addition, I tried to demonstrate the ways by which a number of complex and autonomous achievements of the mature personality were derived from transformations of narcissism, i.e., created by the ego's capacity to tame narcissistic cathexes and to employ them for its highest aims.

I would finally like to say that I have become increasingly convinced of the value of these conceptualizations for psychoanalytic therapy. They are useful in the formulation of broad aspects of the psychopathology of the frequently encountered narcissistic personality types among our patients; they help us understand the psychological changes which tend to be induced in them; and, last but not least, they assist us in the evaluation of the therapeutic goal. In many instances, the reshaping of the narcissistic structures and their integration into the personality—the strengthening of ideals, and the achievement, even to a modest degree, of such wholesome transformations of narcissism as humor, creativity, empathy, and wisdom—must be rated as a more genuine and valid result of therapy than the patient's precarious compliance with demands for a change of his narcissism into object love.

---

[17] The German word *"Sonntagsreiter"* in the well-known joke mentioned by Freud (12, p. 275; and 15, p. 237) has been rendered as "sunday horseman" in the English translations (13, p. 258; and 16, p. 231).

5

Thoughts on Narcissism and Narcissistic Rage

(1972)

One of the gems of German literature is an essay called "On the Puppet Theatre" by the dramatist Heinrich von Kleist (1777–1811), written in 1811, not long before he ended his short life by suicide. Kleist and his work are almost unknown outside the circle of those familiar with the German language, but my fascination with his short essay—and with one of his stories—has had, as I can see in retrospect, a particular significance in my own intellectual development: it marks the first time that I felt drawn to the topic that has now absorbed my scientific interest for several years.

Ever since reading Kleist's essay during my school days I had puzzled about the mysterious impact the plain account has on the reader. A male ballet dancer, we are told, asserts in a fictitious conversation with the author that, by comparison with human dancing, the dance of puppets is nearly perfect. The puppet's center of gravity is its soul; the puppeteer need only to think himself into this point as he is moving the puppet and the movement of its limbs will attain a degree of perfection that cannot be reached by the human dancer. Since puppets are not bound down by gravity, and since their physical center and soul are one, they are never artificial or pretentious. The human dancer,

This essay was presented in an abbreviated version as the A. A. Brill Lecture of the New York Psychoanalytic Society on November 30, 1971. It was first published in *The Psychoanalytic Study of the Child* (1972), 27: 360–400. New York: Quadrangle Books.

by comparison, is self-conscious, pretentious, artificial. The author responds to the dancer by recalling how, some years ago, he had admired the grace with which his nude male companion had set his foot upon a stool. Mischievously he had asked him to repeat the motion. He blushed and tried—but became self-conscious and clumsy. ". . . beginning at this moment," Kleist writes, "a puzzling change took hold of the young man. He began to stand in front of the mirror for days; . . . [An] incomprehensible force appeared to engage . . . the play of the motility that formerly had so freely expressed his emotions" (my translation).

It is not my intention to bring our psychoanalytic knowledge to bear on this story. But the psychoanalytic reader will have no difficulty identifying the problems with which the writer of the story was preoccupied: apprehensions about the aliveness of self and body, and the repudiation of these fears by the assertion that the inanimate can be graceful, even perfect. The topics of homosexuality (see Sadger, 1909), of poise and of exhibitionism, of blushing and self-consciousness are alluded to; and so is the theme of grandiosity in the fantasy of flying—the notion of "antigravity"—and that of merger with an omnipotent environment by which one is controlled—the puppeteer. Finally, there is the description of a profound change in a young man, ushered in by the ominous symptom of gazing at himself for days in the mirror.

Of all the facets of narcissism, only one is missing in Kleist's essay: aggression as it arises from the matrix of narcissistic imbalance. It is a striking manifestation of the unity of the creative forces in the depth of the personality of a great writer that Kleist had indeed dealt with this theme a year or two earlier, in the story of *Michael Kohlhaas* (1808), a gripping description of the insatiable search for revenge after a narcissistic injury—in its field, I believe, surpassed by only one work, Melville's great *Moby Dick*. Kleist's story tells of the fate of a man who, like Captain Ahab, is in the grip of interminable narcissistic rage. It is the greatest rendition of the revenge motif in German literature, a theme that plays an important role in the national destiny of the German nation, whose thirst for revenge after the defeat of 1918 came close to destroying all of Western civilization.

In recent years I have investigated some phenomena related to the self, its cohesion and its fragmentation (Kohut, 1966, 1968,

1970, 1971). The present essay gives me the opportunity to turn from the former topic to the relationship between narcissism and aggression. I shall first deal once more with the work that lies behind, draw attention to topics that are in need of emphasis and point up areas that will provide a basis for subsequent formulations.

The Self and Its Libidinal Investment

The Influence of Parental Attitudes on the Formation of the Self

If I were asked what I consider to be the most important point to be stressed about narcissism I would answer: its independent line of development, from the primitive to the most mature, adaptive, and culturally valuable. This development has important innate determinants, but the specific interplay of the child with his environment, which furthers, or hinders, the cohesion of the self and the formation of idealized psychic structures, is well worth further detailed examination, especially with the aid of the study of the varieties of the narcissistic transferences. In this essay I shall add only one small point to the results I have previously reported, namely, that the side-by-side existence of separate developmental lines in the narcissistic and in the object-instinctual realms in the child is intertwined with the parents' attitude toward the child, i.e., that the parents sometimes relate to the child in empathic narcissistic merger and look upon the child's psychic organization as part of their own, while at other times they respond to the child as to an independent center of his own initiative, i.e., they invest him with object libido.

On the Acceptance of an Affirmative Attitude Toward Narcissism in Theory and Practice

My second retrospective point refers to a broad question. In assuming an independent line of development in the narcissistic sector of the personality, a development that leads to the acquisition of mature, adaptive, and culturally valuable attributes in the narcissistic realm, I have, of course, taken an essentially affirmative attitude toward narcissism. But while I have become convinced of the appropriateness of this affirmative outlook on narcissism, I am also aware of the fact that it may be questioned, that indeed there exist a number of arguments that can be marshaled in opposition to a consideration of narcissism as an integral, self-contained set of psychic functions rather than as a regression product; that there exist a number of obstacles that stand in the way of its acceptance as potentially adaptive and valuable rather than as necessarily ill or evil.

One aspect of classical theory (see, especially, Freud, 1914b, 1915, 1917b)—and the, in general, appropriate conservatism of analysts concerning changes in theory—may adventitiously play a role in this regard. We are used to thinking of the relation between narcissism and object love in a way corresponding to the image of the fluid levels in a U-shaped tube. If the level of fluid in one end rises, it sinks in the other. There is no love where there is toothache; there is no pain where there is passionate love. Such thought models, however, should be replaced when they cannot accommodate the data of observation. The sense of heightened self-esteem, for example, that accompanies object love demonstrates a relationship between the two forms of libidinal cathexis that does not correspond to that of the oscillations in a U-tube system. And while the behavior of the fluid levels in the U-tube, and Freud's amoeba simile (1914b, p. 75), are models that adequately illustrate the total preoccupation of the sufferer with his aching tooth and the waiting lover's obliviousness to rain and cold, these phenomena can be readily explained in terms of the distribution of attention cathexes and do not *require* the U-tube theory.

Be that as it may, more formidable than the scientific context, in which the term narcissism may have acquired a slightly pejorative connotation as a product of regression or defense, is a specific emotional climate that is unfavorable to the acceptance of narcissism as a healthy and approvable psychological constellation. The deeply ingrained value system of the Occident (pervading the religion, the philosophy, the social utopias of Western man) extols altruism and concern for others and disparages egotism and concern for one's self. Yet, just as is true with man's sexual desires, so also with his narcissistic needs: neither a contemptuous attitude toward the powerful psychological forces that assert themselves in these two dimensions of human life nor the attempt at their total eradication will lead to genuine progress in man's self-control or social adaptation. Christianity, while leaving open narcissistic fulfillment in the realm of the merger with the omnipotent selfobject, the divine figure of Christ, attempts to curb the manifestations of the grandiose self. The current materialistic rationalism in Western culture, on the other hand, while giving greater freedom to the enhancement of the self, tends to belittle or (e.g., in the sphere where a militant atheism holds sway) to forbid, the traditional forms of institutionalized relatedness to the idealized object.

In response to ostracism and suppression, the aspirations of the grandiose self may indeed seem to subside, and the yearning for a merger with the idealized selfobject will be denied. The suppressed but unmodified narcissistic structures, however, become intensified as their expression is blocked; they will break through the brittle controls and will suddenly bring about, not only in individuals, but also in whole groups, the unrestrained pursuit of grandiose aims and the resistanceless merger with omnipotent selfobjects. I need only refer to the ruthlessly pursued ambitions of Nazi Germany and of the German population's total surrender to the will of the Führer to exemplify my meaning.

During quiescent historical periods the attitude in certain layers of society toward narcissism resembles Victorian hypocrisy toward sex. Officially, the existence of the social manifestations emanating from the grandiose self and the omnipotent selfobject are denied, yet their split-off dominance everywhere is obvious. I think that the overcoming of a hypocritical attitude toward narcissism is as much required today as was the overcoming of sexual hypocrisy a hundred years ago. We should not deny our ambitions, our wish to dominate, our wish to shine, and our yearning to merge into omnipotent figures, but should instead learn to acknowledge the legitimacy of these narcissistic forces as we have learned to acknowledge the legitimacy of our object-instinctual strivings. We shall then be able, as can be observed in the systematic therapeutic analysis of narcissistic personality disturbances, to transform our archaic grandiosity and exhibitionism into realistic self-esteem and into pleasure with ourselves, and our yearning to be at one with the omnipotent selfobject into the socially useful, adaptive, and joyful capacity to be enthusiastic and to admire the great after whose lives, deeds, and personalities we can permit ourselves to model our own.

Ego Autonomy and Ego Dominance

It is in the context of assessing the value of the transformation (rather than of the suppression) of the archaic narcissistic structures for man as an active participant in human affairs—*l'homme engagé*—that I would like to mention a conceptual distinction I have found useful, namely, the demarcation of *ego dominance* from *ego autonomy* (see Kohut, 1971, p. 187). There is a place for ego autonomy; the rider *off* the horse; man as he reflects coolly and dispassionately, particularly as he scrutinizes the data of his observations. But there is also a place for ego dominance: the rider *on* the horse; man as he responds to the forces within himself, as he shapes his goals and forms his major reactions to the environment; man as an effective participant on the stage of history. In the narcissistic realm, in particular, ego dominance increases our ability to react with the full spectrum of our emotions: with disappointment and rage or with feelings of triumph, controlledly, but not necessarily restrainedly.

A Comparison of the Genetic and Dynamic Importance of Narcissistic and Object-Instinctual Factors

In my retrospective survey I shall now take up the question whether by focusing our attention on narcissism we may not run the risk of disregarding the object-instinctual forces in the psychic life of man. We must ask ourselves whether our emphasis on the genetic and dynamic importance of the vicissitudes of the formation and cohesion of the self may not lead to a de-emphasis of the crucial genetic and dynamic role played in normal and abnormal development by the object-instinctual investments of the Oedipus complex.

A short while ago, a younger colleague who has followed my work on narcissism with interest reviewed the relations between the generations in our field and, speaking for the rising generation of analysts, suggested that the anxiety of the older group was not so much "that we become grownup, but that we become different" (Terman, 1972). I thought that the clear implication of this incisive statement was that the older generation was concerned less about being endangered by the oedipal killing wish than about being deprived in the narcissistic realm—and I felt strongly inclined to agree with this opinion. But then I began to worry. Am I the Pied Piper who leads the young away from the solid ground of the object-libidinal aspects of the Oedipus complex? Are preoedipal and narcissistic factors perhaps no more than precursors and trimming? And will the preoccupation with them become a focus for the old resistances against the full acceptance of the emotional reality of the passions of the oedipal drama? Does not, behind the preconscious fear that the younger generation will be "different," lie the deeper and more powerful fear of their wish to kill, for which the narcissistic concern is only cover and disguise?

I shall not attempt to pursue this question directly. I assume that it is not going to be answered in the form in which we see it now, but that it will some day be superseded by a reformulation of the nexus of causal factors in early life. (The work of Gedo and Goldberg [1973], for example, constitutes, I believe, a significant step in this direction.) In the meantime we must, without prejudice, study all analytic data—oedipal and preoedipal, object-instinctual and narcissistic—and determine their developmental and genetic significance.

We shall therefore do well to refrain from setting up a choice between theoretical opposites concerning the question of the genetic importance of the young child's experiences in the narcissistic and in the object-instinctual realm. An examination of two topics will, however, illuminate the relative influence that these two sets of early experiences exert in later childhood and in adult life. The first topic concerns the significance of the pivotal developmental phase in which the nucleus of a cohesive self crystallizes; the second concerns the interplay of pathology of the self (narcissistic pathology) and pathology of structural conflict (oedipal pathology).

The Prototypical Significance of the Period of the Formation of the Self. Concerning the first of these two topics it must be stressed that, like the persisting influence of the vicissitudes of the Oedipus complex, the vicissitudes of the early formation of the self determine the form and the course of later psychological events that are analogous to the crucial early phase. Just as the period of pubertal drive increase, for example, or the time when a marriage partner is chosen constitute emotional situations in which a dormant Oedipus complex is prone to be reactivated, so do certain periods of transition which demand from us a reshuffling of the self, its change, and its rebuilding, constitute emotional situations that reactivate the period of the formation of the self. The replacement of one long-term self-representation by another endangers a self whose earlier, nuclear establishment was faulty; and the vicissitudes of early pathology are experienced as repeated by the new situation. Extensive changes of the self must, for example, be achieved in the transition from early childhood to latency, from latency to puberty, and from adolescence to young adulthood. But these sociobiologically prescheduled developmental processes are not the only ones that impose on us a drastic change of our self; we must also consider external shifts, such as moves from one culture to another; from private life into the army; from the small town to the big city; and the modification in the self that is necessitated when a person's social role is taking a turn—whether for better or worse, e.g., sudden financial success or sudden loss of fortune.

The psychopathological events of late adolescence described by Erikson (1956)—I would call them the vicissitudes of self-cohesion in the transitional period between adolescence and adulthood—should therefore neither be considered as occupying a uniquely significant developmental position, nor be explained primarily as due to the demands of this particular period. (The stresses constitute only the precipitating external circumstances.) But an adolescent's crumbling self experience should in each individual instance be investigated in depth—no less than in those equally frequent and important cases of self fragmentation that occur during other periods of transition which have overtaxed the solidity and resilience of the nucleus of the self. Why did the self break down in this specific adolescent? What is the mode of its fragmentation? In what form is the task of the construction of a new self—the self of young adulthood—experienced? How does the present situation repeat the early one? What traumatic interplay of parent and child (when the child began to construct a grandiose-exhibitionistic self and an omnipotent selfobject) is now being repeated for the patient, and—most importantly—how is it revived in one of the specific forms of the narcissistic transference?

To repeat: just as the object-instinctual experiences of the oedipal period become the prototype of our later object-instinctual involvements and form the basis for our specific weaknesses and strengths in this area, so do the experiences during the period of the formation of the self[1] become the prototype of the specific forms of our later vulnerability and security in the narcissistic realm: of the ups and downs in our self-esteem; of our lesser or greater need for praise, for merger into idealized figures, and for other forms of narcissistic sustenance; and of the greater or lesser cohesion of our self during periods of transition, whether in the transition to latency, in early or late adolescence, in maturity, or in old age.

Pseudonarcissistic Disorders and Pseudotransference Neuroses. The relationship between the focus of the development of the object-instinctual strivings, the Oedipus complex, and the focus of the development in the narcissistic realm, the phase of the formation of the self, will be further illuminated by comparing two paradigmatic forms of psychopathology: nuclear oedipal psychopathology that is hidden by a broad cover of narcissistic disturbance; and narcissistic disorders that are hidden by seemingly oedipal symptomatology.

Concerning the first, a brief remark will suffice. Every analyst has seen the gradual emergence of the oedipal passions and anxieties from behind a broad cover of narcissistic vulnerabilities and complaints, and he knows that the careful observation of the oedipal transference will also reveal how the narcissistic manifestations are related to the central oedipal experiences. How, for example, a sense of low self-esteem relates to phallic comparisons and a feeling of castration, how cycles of triumphant self-confidence and depression relate to fantasies of oedipal success and the discovery of being in fact excluded from the primal scene, and the like. Surely, I need not elaborate further.

Now to the second form of paradigmatic psychopathology. I have chosen to focus on a specific, somewhat complex type of narcissistic disorder, despite its comparative infrequency, because

---

[1] To be exact, one would have to call this point in development the *period of the formation of the nuclear self and selfobject.* The archaic self-object is, of course, still (experienced as) part of the self.

its examination is very instructive. (Cases, it may be added, in which the narcissistic blows suffered by the child in the oedipal phase lead to the first straightforward breakdown of the self are much more common.) I believe that, among the, in principle, analyzable disorders, it confronts the analyst with one of his most trying and difficult therapeutic tasks. These patients initially create the impression of a classical neurosis. When their apparent psychopathology is approached by interpretations, however, the immediate result is nearly catastrophic: they act out wildly, overwhelm the analyst with oedipal love demands, threaten suicide—in short, although content (of symptoms, fantasies, and manifest transference) is all triangular oedipal, the very openness of their infantile wishes, the lack of resistances to their being uncovered, are not in tune with the initial impression.

That the oedipal symptomatology in such cases (e.g., of "pseudohysteria") is not genuine is generally accepted. However, in contrast to what I believe to be the prevailing view that we are dealing with hidden psychosis or with personalities whose psychic equilibrium is threatened by severe ego weakness, I have become convinced that many of these patients suffer from a narcissistic personality disturbance, will establish one of the forms of narcissistic transference, and are thus treatable by psychoanalysis.[2]

The nuclear psychopathology of these individuals concerns the self. Being threatened in the maintenance of a cohesive self because in early life they were lacking in adequate confirming responses ("mirroring") from the environment, they turned to self-stimulation in order to retain the precarious cohesion of their experiencing and acting self. The oedipal phase, including its

[2] See in this context the differentiation of *psychosis*, i.e., premanent or protracted fragmentation of the nuclear grandiose self and the nuclear omnipotent selfobject, and *narcissistic personality disturbance*, i.e., insecure cohesion of the nuclear self and selfobject, with only fleeting fragmentation of these configurations. See, furthermore, the classification of the disorders whose essential psychopathology consists in permanent or protracted fragmentation of the self of selfobject, i.e., the psychoses. They fall into three groups, namely: the frank *psychoses* where the symptomatology openly reflects the breakup of the nuclear narcissistic structures; the *latent psychoses* or *borderline cases* where the symptomatology hides to a greater or lesser extent the fact that a breakup of the nuclear narcissistic structures has taken place; and the *schizoid personalities* where a breakup of the nuclear narcissistic structures (the development of an overt or latent psychosis) is the ever-present pathognomonic potentiality, which is, however, prevented by the patient's careful avoidance (through emotional distancing) of regression-provoking narcissistic injuries (Kohut, 1971, Ch. 1).

conflicts and anxieties, became, paradoxically, a remedial stimulant, its very intensity being used by the psyche to counteract the tendency toward the breakup of the self—just as a small child may attempt to use self-inflicted pain (head banging, for example) in order to retain a sense of aliveness and cohesion. Patients whose manifest psychopathology serves this defensive function will react to the analyst's interpretations concerning the object-instinctual aspects of their behavior with the fear of losing the stimulation that prevents their fragmentation; and they will respond with an intensification of oedipal dramatizing so long as the analyst does not address himself to the defect of the self. Only when a shift in the focus of the analyst's interpretations indicates that he is now in empathic closeness to the patient's fragmenting self does the stimulation of the self through forced oedipal experiences (dramatizing in the analytic situation, acting out) begin to diminish.

It might bear repeating at this point what I have, of course, already said in earlier contributions: that the only reliable way by which the differential diagnosis between a narcissistic personality disturbance and a classical transference neurosis can be established clinically is by the observation of the transference which emerges spontaneously in the analytic situation. In the classical transference neurosis, the vicissitudes of the triangular oedipal situation will gradually unfold. If we are dealing with a narcissistic personality disturbance, however, then we will witness the emergence of one of the forms of narcissistic transference, i.e., of a transference in which the vicissitudes of the cohesion and (fleeting and reversible) fragmentation of the self are correlated to the vicissitudes of the patient's relation to the analyst.

If we wish to state the difference between classical transference neurosis and narcissistic personality disturbance in metapsychological terms, then we must focus on the structure of the psychopathology. Concerning the two aforementioned contrasting paradigmatic disorders, for example, we can say the following. In the pseudohysterias we are dealing with patients who are attempting to maintain the cohesion of an endangered self through the stimulation that they derive from the hypercathected oedipal strivings. An overt oedipal symptomatology is used to keep hidden self pathology within bounds. In the pseudonarcissistic disorders, on the other hand, we are dealing with patients who are attempting to come to terms, not only with the object-instinctual conflicts, wishes, and emotions of the oedipal period, but also—a point deserving emphasis—with the narcissistic injuries to which their securely established self had been exposed within the context of the oedipal experience. The presence, in other words, of narcissistic features—and even their initial predominance within the total picture—does not alter the fact that the essential psychopathology is a classical psychoneurosis.

Organ Inferiority and Shame

My comments so far may be regarded as an attempt to tidy up the house before going on a trip. The work on the libidinal aspects of narcissism, in other words, is more or less done, but I wish to straighten out odds and ends before leaving it behind. The trip should lead into the rugged terrain of narcissistic rage, and, later, into the far-off region of group psychology. A glance, however, at a topic that lies in the main within the familiar area of the libidinal cathexis of the self, yet extends into the unfamiliar territory of narcissism and aggression, should serve as a bridge to the new undertaking. Let me refer to this topic by what is nowadays a somewhat discredited name:[3] "organ inferiority" (Adler, 1907).

In his "New Introductory Lectures" (1933, p.66) Freud took the writer Emil Ludwig to task—without naming him, however. Ludwig had, in one of the biographical novels (1926) that were his specialty, interpreted the personality of Emperor Wilhelm II in accordance with the theories of Alfred Adler. He had explained the Hohenzollern's readiness to take offense and to turn toward war as reactions to a sense of organ inferiority. The Emperor had been born with a withered arm. The defective limb became the sore that remained sensitive throughout his life and brought about the character formation that, according to Ludwig, was one of the important factors leading to the outbreak of the First World War.

Not so! said Freud. It was not the birth injury in itself that resulted in Emperor Wilhelm's sensitivity to narcissistic slights,

[3] Freud (1914a), however, spoke of "the valuable work he [Adler] had done on 'organ-inferiority' " (p.51).

but the rejection by his proud mother, who could not tolerate an imperfect child.

It takes little effort to add the appropriate psychodynamic refinements to Freud's genetic formulation. A mother's lack of confirming and approving "mirroring" responses to her child prevents the transformation of the archaic narcissistic cathexis of the child's body-self, which normally is achieved with the aid of the increasing selectivity of the mother's admiration and approval. The crude and intense narcissistic cathexis of the grandiose body-self (in Emperor Wilhelm's case: the withered arm) thus remains unaltered, and its archaic grandiosity and exhibitionism cannot be integrated with the remainder of the psychic organization, which gradually reaches maturity. The archaic grandiosity and exhibitionism thus become split off from the reality ego ("vertical split" in the psyche) or separated from it through repression ("horizontal split"). Deprived of the mediating function of the reality ego, they are therefore no longer modifiable by later external influences, be these ever so accepting or approving, i.e., there is no possibility for a "corrective emotional experience" (Alexander et al., 1946). On the other hand, the archaic grandiose-exhibitionistic (body-) self will from time to time assert its archaic claims, either by bypassing the repression barrier via the vertically split-off sector of the psyche or by breaking through the brittle defenses of the central sector. It will suddenly flood the reality ego with unneutralized exhibitionistic cathexis and overwhelm the neutralizing powers of the ego, which becomes paralyzed and experiences intense shame and rage.

I do not know enough about the personality of Emperor Wilhelm to judge whether the foregoing formulation does indeed apply to him. I believe, however, that I am on more solid ground when I suspect that Emil Ludwig did not take kindly to Freud's criticism. At any rate he later wrote a biography of Freud (Ludwig, 1947) which was the undisguised expression of narcissistic rage--so coarse, in fact,[4] that even those inimical to psychoanal-

---

[4] Lionel Trilling (1947), who reviewed Emil Ludwig's book *Dr. Freud,* closed his remarks about this biography with the following trenchant sentence: "We are not an age notable for fineness and precision of thought, but it is seldom indeed that we get a book as intellectually discreditable, as disingenuous and as vulgar as this."

ysis and Freud considered the crudity of Ludwig's attack an embarrassment, and disassociated themselves from it.

Be this as it may with regard to Emperor Wilhelm and his biographer, I have no doubt that the ubiquitous sensitivity about bodily defects and shortcomings can be effortlessly explained within the metapsychological framework of the vicissitudes of the libidinal cathexes of the grandiose self and, in particular, of the grandiose-exhibitionistic body-self.

The topic of the sense of inferiority of children about the small size of their genitals (in the boy, in comparison with the penis of the adult man; in the girl, in comparison with the boy's organ) may warrant a few special remarks. Children's sensitivity about their genitals is at its peak during the pivotal phallic phase of psychosexual development—later sensitivities concerning the genitals must be understood as residuals (e.g., during latency) or as revivals (e.g., during puberty) of the exhibitionism of the phallic phase. The significance of the genitals during the phallic phase is determined by the fact that at this period they temporarily constitute the *leading zone of the child's* (bodily) *narcissism*—they are not only the instruments of intense (fantasied) *object-libidinal* interactions, they also carry enormous *narcissistic* cathexes. (The narcissistic cathexis of feces during the anal phase of development and the narcissistic cathexis of certain autonomous ego functions during latency are examples of earlier and later leading zones of the child's narcissism during preceding and subsequent stages of his development.) The genitals are thus the focal point of the child's narcissistic aspirations and sensitivities during the phallic phase. If we keep these facts in mind and emphasize in addition that the exhibitionistic component of infantile narcissism is largely unneutralized, then we will also understand the much-disputed significance of infantile penis envy. This topic has aroused a great deal of unscientific and acrimonious discussion, even leading to the ludicrous spectacle of opposing scientific line-ups of men who assign the phenomenon exclusively to women, and of women who deny either its existence or its importance.

Some of the difficulties may resolve themselves if the intensity of the exhibitionistic cathexes is taken into account and particularly if we do not underestimate the importance of the *visible* genital in this context: in other words, if we keep in mind that the narcissistic demands of the phallic period are no more—but also no less!—than an important instance in the developmental series of demands for immediate mirroring responses to concretely exhibited aspects of the child's body or of his physical or mental functions. That his penis will grow is small consolation for the little boy; and that a complex but invisible apparatus will be maturing that will enable her to bear children is small consolation for the little girl within the framework of the psychology of childhood exhibitionism—notwithstanding the simultaneous existence of other sources of direct narcissistic gratification and of acceptable substitutive mirroring which enhances the acquisition of sublimations in children of both sexes.

The shame of the adult, too, when a defective body part is looked at by others—indeed, his conviction that others are staring at it![5]—is due to the pressure of the unmodified, archaic, exhibitionistic libido with which the defective organ has remained cathected. And the self-consciousness concerning the defective organ and the tendency to blush when it is being scrutinized by others are the psychological and psychophysiological correlates of the breakthrough of the unmodified exhibitionistic cathexes. (I shall return to this topic in the context of the metapsychology of narcissistic rage.)

The Motivational Role of Disturbed Narcissism in Certain Types of Self-Mutilation and Suicide

Related to the preceding formulations about "organ inferiority" are those concerning the self-mutilation of the psychotic, and certain types of suicide. With regard to both self-mutilations and suicide, one must differentiate the motive for these acts from the ability to perform them.

The motivation for the self-mutilations of psychotics emanates, I believe, in many instances not from specific conflicts—such as incest guilt leading to the self-punitive removal of an

---

[5] This quasi-delusion is, I believe, a manifestation of the archaic exhibitionistic urge which is isolated from the rest of the psychic organization and projected (with reversed aim) upon the person who is the supposedly gloating onlooker. The relation between this phenomenon and the paranoiac's delusion of being watched is obvious.

organ which symbolizes the evil penis. It is rather due to the fact that a break-up of the body-self has occurred and that the fragments of the body-self that cannot be retained within the total organization of the body-self become an unbearably painful burden and are therefore removed. The schizophrenic who (like the young man in Kleist's essay on the puppet theater) looks into the mirror for hours and days attempts to unite his fragmenting body-self with the aid of his gaze. If these and similar endeavors (e.g., stimulation of the total body-self through forced physical activity) to replace the cohesion-producing narcissistic cathexes fail, then the organ is removed.

The understanding of the motivation for self-mutilation is not, by itself, sufficient to explain the actual performance of such acts. A person may sense in himself the analogue of the Biblical command, "If thine eye offend thee, pluck it out" (Matthew 18:9), but he would still be unable to obey this order. The ability to perform an act of gross self-mutilation depends, in some instances at least, on the fact that the organ the psychotic removes has lost its narcissistic libidinal cathexis; i.e., it is no longer part of the self and can therefore be discarded as if it were a foreign body. This explanation applies to those instances in which the act of self-mutilation is performed calmly by the psychotic patient. Self-mutilations performed during stages of emotional frenzy may have different motivations, and the ability to carry them out rests on the almost total concentration of the psychotic's attention on some delusional aim. The ability to carry out the act, then, does not rest on the fragmentation of the body-self, but is based on a scotoma of the psychotic's perception—similar to those instances when soldiers during a frenzied attack on enemy lines may temporarily not be aware of the fact that they have suffered a severe physical injury.

Analogous considerations also apply to certain kinds of suicide with regard to both the motivation that leads to the act and the ability to carry it out. Such suicides are in the main based on the loss of the libidinal cathexis of the self. Analogous to certain self-mutilations, such suicide does not emanate from specific structural conflicts—it does not constitute, for example, a step taken in order to expiate oedipal guilt. Characteristically, these suicides are preceded, not by guilt feelings, but by feelings of

unbearable emptiness and deadness or by intense shame, i.e., by
the signs of profound disturbance in the realm of the libidinal
cathexis of the self.

Narcissism and Aggression

The hypothesis that a tendency to kill is deeply rooted in man's
psychobiological makeup and stems from his animal past—the
assumption, in other words, of man's inherent propensity toward
aggression (and the correlated conceptualization of aggression
as a drive) protects us against the lure of the comforting illusion
that human pugnacity could be easily abolished if only our material needs were satisfied. But these broad formulations contribute little to the understanding of aggression as a psychological
phenomenon. It is obviously not enough to say that such phenomena as warfare, intolerance, and persecution are due to man's
regression toward the undisguised expression of a drive. And
the often-heard complaint that it is the thinness of the civilized
layer of the human personality that is responsible for the evils
wrought by human aggression is appealing in its simplicity, but
misses the mark.

True, the protagonists of the most dreadful manifestation of
aggression in the history of modern Western civilization pro-
claimed loudly that their destructive acts were performed in the
service of a law of nature. The Nazis justified their warfare and
the extermination of those they considered weak and inferior by
seeing their misdeeds within the framework of a vulgarized Darwinism: the inherent right of the stronger, and the survival of
the fittest race for the good of mankind. But I do not believe
that, despite their own theories, we can come closer to understanding the Nazi phenomenon by conceiving of it as a regression toward the biologically simple, toward animal behavior—
whether such a regression be extolled, as it was by the Nazis
themselves, or condemned and despised, as it was ultimately by
the rest of the world.

It would, on the whole, be pleasant if we could do so; if we
could state—in a simplistic application of a Civilization-and-Its-
Discontents principle—that Hitler exploited the readiness of a
civilized nation to shed the thin layer of its uncomfortably carried restraints, leading to the unspeakable events of the decade

1935 to 1945. But the truth is—it must be admitted with sadness—that such events are not bestial, in the primary sense of the word, but are decidedly human. They are an intrinsic part of the human condition, a strand in the web of the complex pattern that makes up the human situation. So long as we turn away from these phenomena in terror and disgust and indignantly declare them to be a reversal to barbarism, a regression to the primitive and animal-like, so long do we deprive ourselves of the chance of increasing our understanding of human aggressivity and of our mastery over it. The psychoanalyst must therefore not shrink from the task of applying his knowledge about the individual to the field of history, particularly to the crucial role of human aggression as it has shaped the history of man. It is my conviction that we will reach tangible results by focusing our attention on human aggression as it arises out of the matrix of archaic narcissism, i.e., on the phenomenon of narcissistic rage.

Human aggression is most dangerous when it is attached to the two great absolutarian psychological constellations: the grandiose self and the archaic omnipotent object. And the most gruesome human destructiveness is encountered, not in the form of wild, regressive, and primitive behavior, but in the form of orderly and organized activities in which the perpetrators' destructiveness is alloyed with absolute conviction about their greatness and with their devotion to archaic omnipotent figures. I could support this thesis by quoting Himmler's self-pityingly boastful and idolatrous speeches to those cadres of the S.S. who were the executors of the extermination policies of the Nazis (see Bracher, 1969, p. 422–423; see also Loewenberg, 1971, p. 639)—but I know that I shall be forgiven for not displaying this evidence here.

On Narcissistic Rage

In its undisguised form, narcissistic rage is a familiar experience which is in general easily identified by the empathic observer of human behavior. But what is its dynamic essence? How should it be classified? How should we outline the concept and define the meaning of the term?

I shall first respond to the last of these interrelated questions. Strictly speaking, the term narcissistic rage refers to only one specific band in the wide spectrum of experiences that reaches from such trivial occurrences as a fleeting annoyance when someone fails to reciprocate our greeting or does not respond to our joke to such ominous derangements as the furor of the catatonic and the grudges of the paranoic. Following Freud's example (1921, p. 91), however, I shall use the term *a potiori* and refer to all points in the spectrum as narcissistic rage, since with this designation we are referring to the most characteristic or best known of a series of experiences that not only form a continuum, but, with all their differences, are essentially related to each other.

And what is it that all these different experiences, which we designate by the same term, have in common? In what psychological category do they all belong? What are their common determinants? And what is their common metapsychological substance?

It is self-evident that narcissistic rage belongs to the large psychological field of aggression, anger, and destructiveness and that it constitutes a specific circumscribed phenomenon within this great area. From the point of view of social psychology, furthermore, it is clearly analogous to the fight component of the fight-flight reaction with which biological organisms respond to attack. Stated more specifically, it is easily observed that the narcissistically vulnerable individual responds to actual (or anticipated) narcissistic injury either with shamefaced withdrawal (flight) or with narcissistic rage (fight).

Since narcissistic rage is clearly a manifestation of the human propensity for aggressive responses, some analysts believe that it requires no further explanation, once the preconscious motivational context in which it is likely to occur has been established. Alexander, for example, dealt with this important psychological phenomenon by identifying its position in a typical sequence of preconscious and conscious attitudes. He attempted to clarify the psychological significance and the metapsychological position of shame and rage, these two principal experiential and behavioral manifestations of disturbed narcissistic equilibrium, in a paper (1938) that has influenced the relevant work of a number of authors (e.g., Saul, 1947; Piers and Singer, 1953; and, with wider individual elaborations, Eidelberg, 1959, and Jacobson, 1964). In this contribution he presented the schema of a self-perpetuating cycle of psychological phenomena—an explanatory device which is appealing in its pedagogical clarity and in its similarity to formulations cogently employed in other branches of science, e.g., in physics. He described the dynamic cycle of hostility→guilt→submission→reactive aggression→ guilt, etc. He thus restricted himself to explaining narcissistic rage (in his terms: reactive aggression that follows upon a shameful submission) in the context of the motivational dynamics of (pre)conscious experiences and overt behavior without investigating this phenomenon in depth, i.e., without attempting to uncover its unconscious dimensions and its developmental roots.

Narcissistic rage occurs in many forms; they all share, however, a specific psychological flavor which gives them a distinct position within the wide realm of human aggressions. The need for revenge, for righting a wrong, for undoing a hurt by whatever means, and a deeply anchored, unrelenting compulsion in the pursuit of all these aims, which gives no rest to those who have suffered a narcissistic injury—these are the characteristic features of narcissistic rage in all its forms and which set it apart from other kinds of aggression.

And what is the specific significance of the psychological injuries (such as ridicule, contempt, and conspicuous defeat) that tend to provoke narcissistic rage; and how do these external provocations interact with the sensitized aspects of the rage- and revenge-prone personality?

The propensity for narcissistic rage in the Japanese, for example, is attributed by Ruth Benedict (1946) to their methods of child rearing through ridicule and the threat of ostracism, and to the sociocultural importance the Japanese attach to maintaining decorum. Small wonder, therefore, says Benedict, that "sometimes people explode in the most aggressive acts. They are roused to these aggressions not when their principles or their freedom is challenged . . . but when they detect an insult or a detraction" (p. 293).

The desire to turn a passive experience into an active one (Freud, 1920, p. 16), the mechanism of identification with the aggressor (A. Freud, 1936), the sadistic tensions retained by those who as children had been treated sadistically by their parents— all these factors help explain the readiness of the shame-prone individual to respond to a potentially shame-provoking situation by the employment of a simple remedy: the active (often anticipatory) inflicting on others of those narcissistic injuries which he is most afraid of suffering himself.

Mr. P., for example, who was exceedingly shame-prone and narcissistically vulnerable, was a master of a specific form of social sadism. Although he came from a conservative family, he had become very liberal in his political and social outlook. He was always eager to inform himself about the national and religious background of acquaintances and, avowedly in the spirit of rationality and lack of prejudice, embarrassed them at social gatherings by introducing the topic of their minority status into the conversation. Although he defended himself against the recognition of the significance of his malicious maneuvers by well-thought-out rationalizations, he became in time aware of the fact that he experienced an erotically tinged excitement at these moments. There was, according to his description, a brief moment of silence in the conversation in which the victim struggled for composure after public attention had been directed to his social handicap, and, although all acted as if they had not noticed the victim's embarrassment, the emotional significance of the situation was clear to everyone. Mr. P.'s increasing realization of the true nature of his sadistic attacks through the public exposure of a social defect, and his gradually deepening awareness of his own fear of exposure and ridicule, led to his recall of violent emotions of shame and rage in childhood. His mother, the daughter of a Fundamentalist minister, not only had embarrassed and shamed the boy in public, but had insisted on exposing and inspecting his genitals—as she claimed, to find out whether he had masturbated. As a child he had formed vengeful fantasies—the precursors of his current sadistic enactments—in which he would cruelly expose his mother to his own and to other people's gaze.

The heightened sadism, the adoption of a policy of preventive attack, the need for revenge, and the desire to turn a passive experience into an active one,[6] do not, however, fully account

[6] Many psychotherapists, including psychoanalysts, traumatize their patients unnecessarily by sarcastic attacks of their archaic narcissism. Despite the analyst's increasing understanding of the significance of the reactivation of the patient's archaic narcissistic demands, such tendencies are hard to overcome and the ana-

for some of the most characteristic features of narcissistic rage. In its typical forms there is utter disregard for reasonable limitations and a boundless wish to redress an injury and to obtain revenge. The irrationality of the vengeful attitude becomes even more frightening in view of the fact that—in narcissistic personalities as in the paranoiac—the reasoning capacity, while totally under the domination and in the service of the overriding emotion, is often not only intact but even sharpened. (This dangerous feature of individual psychopathology is the parallel of an equally malignant social phenomenon: the subordination of the rational class of technicians to a paranoid leader and the efficiency—and even brilliance—of their amoral cooperation in carrying out his purposes.[7])

Two Phenomena Related to Narcissistic Rage

I shall now examine two forms of anger which are related to narcissistic rage: the anger of a person who because of cerebral defect or brain injury is unable to solve certain simple problems, and the anger of a child who has suffered a minor painful injury.

The "Catastrophic Reaction" and Similar Occurences. If a person with a brain defect strives unsuccessfully to perform some task that should be easily accomplished—naming a familiar object, for example, or putting a round or square peg into the fitting hole—he may respond to his incapacity with the intense and frenzied anger that is known as "catastrophic reaction" (Goldstein, 1948).[8] His rage is due to the fact that he is suddenly not

---

lyst's inappropriate sarcasm intrudes again and again. The difficulty is, in some instances at least, due to the fact that the psychotherapist (or analyst) had himself been treated in similar fashion (by his parents and teachers, for example, and, specifically, by his training analyst). The fact that an analyst will persist, despite insight and effort, in his nontherapeutic sarcasm toward his narcissistic patients is evidence for the power of the need to turn a passive experience into an active one. In addition, we must not disregard the fact that the motivator of the deleterious attitude (i.e., the urge, which is deeply rooted in the unconscious, to inflict a narcissistic injury on others) can easily be rationalized: The therapist's attacks can be justified as being undertaken for the good of the patient and in the service of realism—or a maturity-morality.

[7] For a discussion of these events in National-Socialist Germany see Rauschning (1938). The relation of Speer, Minister for Armaments and War Production—an organizational genius—to Hitler is especially revealing in this context (see Speer, 1969).

[8] The organic defect itself undoubtedly contributes to the diminution of the capacity to control emotions and impulses. Yet, many patients who respond with

in control of his own thought processes, of a function people consider to be most intimately their own—i.e., as a part of the self. "It must not be! It cannot be!" the aphasic feels when he is unable to name a familiar object such as a pencil: and his furious refusal to accept the unpleasant truth that his incapacity is a reality is heightened by the fact that his spontaneous speech may be comparatively undisturbed and that his sensorium is clear.

We take our thought processes as belonging to the core of our self, and we refuse to admit that we may not be in control of them. To be deprived of the capacity to name a familiar object or to solve a simple problem is experienced as even more incredible than the loss of a limb. We can see our own body and, since perception is primarily directed toward the outside world, it is easier to think of our body in objective terms. The unseeable thought processes, however, we consider inseparable from, or coinciding with, our very self. The loss of a limb can therefore be mourned, like the loss of a love object;[9] a defect in the realm of our mental functions, however, is experienced as loss of self.

An attenuated variant of the catastrophic reaction is familiar to all: the annoyance when we cannot recall a word or name. And our patients, especially early in analysis, experience slips of the tongue and other manifestations of the unconscious as narcissistic blows. They are enraged about the sudden exposure of their lack of omnipotence in the area of their own mind—not about having disclosed a specific unconscious wish or fantasy. ". . . the trace of affect which follows the revelation of the slip," Freud says, "is clearly in the nature of shame" (1901, p. 83).

It is instructive to observe our own behavior after we have made a slip of the tongue, especially under circumstances such as a lecture in which our exhibitionism is mobilized. The victim's reaction to the amusement of the audience is very specific: he either pretends that the revelation had been intentional or he claims that he understands the meaning of the slip and can interpret it himself. Our immediate tendency is thus to deny our loss of control rather than to obliterate the unconscious content.

the catastrophic reaction under comparatively bland conditions (e.g., in the harmless test situation) will not react with equal intensity under different circumstances which might arouse anger (e.g., when they are being teased or otherwise annoyed).

[9] Tolstoy's description of Anatole Kurágin's farewell to his amputated leg is a deeply moving illustration of this process (1866, Book 10, Ch. 7, pp. 907–908).

Or, expressed differently: our defensive activity is motivated primarily by our shame concerning a defect in the realm of the omnipotent and omniscient grandiose self, not by guilt over the unconscious forbidden sexual or aggressive impulse that was revealed.

The excessive preoccupation with a situation in which one has suffered a shameful narcissistic injury (e.g., a social *faux pas*) must similarly be understood as an enraged attempt to eradicate the reality of the incident by magical means, even to the point of wishing to do away with oneself in order to wipe out the tormenting memory.

The Child's Reaction to Painful Injuries. The other phenomenon that illuminates the significance of narcissistic rage is the emotional reaction of children to slight injuries. When a child has stubbed his toe or pinched his finger, his response expresses a number of feelings. We might say with Freud (1926) that in the child's feelings "certain things seem to be joined together . . . which will later on be separated out" (p. 169). The child gives voice not only to his physical pain and fear, but also to his wounded narcissism. "How can it be? How can it happen?" his outraged cries seem to ask. And it is instructive to observe how he may veer back and forth between enraged protests at the imperfection of his grandiose self and angry reproaches against the omnipotent selfobject for having permitted the insult.[10]

The Experiential Content of Narcissistic Rage

The various forms of narcissistic rage, the catastrophic reaction of the brain-damaged, and the child's outrage at being suddenly exposed to a painful injury are experiences that are far apart in their psychological impact and social consequences. Yet, underlying all these emotional states is the uncompromising insistence on the perfection of the idealized selfobject and on the limitlessness of the power and knowledge of a grandiose self which must remain the equivalent of "purified pleasure" (Freud,

---

[10] When the archaic selfobject does not provide the needed narcissistic sustenance or does not prevent or dispel the child's discomfort, it is held to be sadistic by the child because it is experienced as all-powerful and all-knowing, and thus the consequences of its actions and omissions are always viewed by the child as having been brought about intentionally.

1915, p. 136). The fanaticism of the need for revenge and the
unending compulsion of having to square the account after an
offense are therefore not the attributes of an aggressivity that is
integrated with the mature purposes of the ego—on the contrary, such bedevilment indicates that the aggression was mobilized in the service of an archaic grandiose self and that it is
deployed within the framework of an archaic perception of reality. The shame-prone individual who is ready to experience set-
backs as narcissistic injuries and to respond to them with insatiable
rage does not recognize his opponent as a center of independent
initiative with whom he happens to be at cross-purposes.
Aggressions employed in the pursuit of maturely experienced
causes are not limitless. However vigorously mobilized, their aim
is definite: the defeat of the enemy who blocks the way to a cherished goal. The narcissistically injured, on the other hand, cannot rest until he has blotted out a vaguely experienced offender
who dared to oppose him, to disagree with him, or to outshine
him. "Mirror, mirror, on the wall, who is the fairest of them all?"
the grandiose-exhibitionistic self is asking. And when it is told
that there is someone fairer, cleverer, or stronger, then, like the
evil stepmother in "Snow White," it can never find rest because
it can never wipe out the evidence that has contradicted its conviction that it is unique and perfect.

The opponent who is the target of our mature aggressions is
experienced as separate from ourselves, whether we attack him
because he blocks us in reaching our object-libidinal goals or hate
him because he interferes with the fulfillment of our reality-inte-
grated narcissistic wishes. The enemy who calls forth the archaic
rage of the narcissistically vulnerable, however, is seen by him
not as an autonomous source of impulsions, but as a *flaw in a
narcissistically perceived reality*. The enemy is a recalcitrant part of
an expanded self over which the narcissistically vulnerable person had expected to exercise full control. The mere fact, in other
words, that the other person is independent or different is experienced as offensive by those with intense narcissistic needs.

It has now become clear that narcissistic rage arises when self
or object fail to live up to the expectations directed at their function—whether by the child who more or less phase-appro-
priately insists on the grandiosity and omnipotence of the self

and the selfobject or by the narcissistically fixated adult whose archaic narcissistic structures have remained unmodified because they became isolated from the rest of the growing psyche after the phase-appropriate narcissistic demands of childhood had been traumatically frustrated. Or, describing the psychodynamic pattern in different words, we can say: although everybody tends to react to narcissistic injuries with embarrassment and anger, the most intense experiences of shame and the most violent forms of narcissistic rage arise in those individuals for whom a sense of absolute control over an archaic environment is indispensable because the maintenance of self-esteem—and indeed of the self—depends on the unconditional availability of the approving-mirroring selfobject or of the merger-permitting idealized one.

However different their manifestations, all instances of narcissistic rage have certain features in common because they all arise from the matrix of a narcissistic or prenarcissistic view of the world. The archaic mode of experience explains why those who are in the grip of narcissistic rage show total lack of empathy toward the offender. It explains the unmodifiable wish to blot out the offense that was perpetrated against the grandiose self and the unforgiving fury that arises when the control over the mirroring selfobject is lost or when the omnipotent selfobject is unavailable. And the empathic observer will understand the deeper significance of the often seemingly minor irritant that has provoked an attack of narcissistic rage and will not be taken aback by the seemingly disproportionate severity of the reaction.

These considerations are, of course, also valid within the context of the psychoanalytic situation. Everybody tends to react to psychoanalysis as a narcissistic injury because it gives the lie to our conviction that we are in full control of our mind (Freud, 1917b). The most severe narcissistic resistances against analysis, however, will arise in those patients whose archaic need to claim omniscience and total control had remained comparatively unaltered because they had been too rapidly, or phase-inappropriately deprived of an omniscient selfobject or had received inadequate confirmation of the phase-appropriate conviction of the perfection of the self.

Can Ego Dominance Over Narcissistic Rage Be Achieved Through Psychoanalysis?

Can narcissistic rage be tamed, i.e., can it come under the dominance of the ego? The answer to this question is affirmative—but the "yes" must be qualified and defined.

When, during the analysis of a narcissistic personality disturbance, a defensive wall of apparent tranquility that had been maintained with the aid of social isolation, detachment, and fantasied superiority begins to give way, then one has the right to regard the emergence of narcissistic rage, of sudden attacks of fury at narcissistic injuries, as a sign of the loosening of a rigid personality structure and thus of analytic progress. These developments must therefore neither be censured by the analyst, nor hastily identified as a part of an archaic psychological world, but must for some time be accepted with implicit approval. Yet, whether present from the beginning of the analysis in the narcissistic analysand, or arising after a therapeutic loosening of his personality, such rage must not be confused with mature aggression. Narcissistic rage enslaves the ego and allows it to function only as its tool and rationalizer. Mature aggression is under the control of the ego, and the degree of its neutralization is regulated by the ego in conformance with the purposes for which it is employed. The mobilization of narcissistic rage is therefore not an end point in analysis, but the beginning of a new phase— a phase of working through which is concluded when ego dominance in this sector of the personality has been established. The transformation of narcissistic rage is not achieved directly—e.g., via appeals to the ego to increase its control over the angry impulses—but is brought about indirectly, secondary to the gradual transformation of the matrix of narcissism from which the rage arose. The analysand's archaic exhibitionism and grandiosity must be gradually transformed into aim-inhibited self-esteem and realistic ambitions; and his desire to merge into an archaic omnipotent selfobject has to be replaced by attitudes that are under the control of the ego, e.g., by his enthusiasm for meaningful ideals and by his devotion to them. Concomitantly with these changes the narcissistic rage will gradually subside and the analysand's maturely modulated aggressions will be employed in the service of a securely established self and in the service of cherished values.

The relinquishment of narcissistic claims—the precondition for the subsidence of narcissistic rage—is, however, not absolute. (See in this context Tausk, 1913.) In accepting the existence of an unconscious psychic life, for example, we analysts are not unconditionally renouncing a narcissistic position that has sustained the cohesion of the self, but we are shifting the focus of our narcissism to different ideational contents and are modulating the neutralization of the narcissistic cathexes. Instead of sustaining our sense of self-assurance through the belief in the all-encompassing scope of our consciousness, we now gain a new self-respect from such derivatives of the relationship with the omniscient and omnipotent selfobject as the joy in the super-ego's approval of our stamina in tolerating unpleasant aspects of reality or the joy of having lived up to the example of an admired teacher-figure, Freud.

My emphasis on the fact that narcissism need not be destroyed, but that it can be transformed is in tune with my support of a nonhypocritical attitude toward narcissism as a psychological force *sui generis,* which has its own line of development and which neither should—nor indeed could—be relinquished. In the psychoanalytic situation, too, the analyst's nonhypocritical attitude toward narcissism, his familiarity with the forms and transformations of this psychic constellation, and his uncensorious recognition of its biological and sociocultural value will diminish the analysand's narcissistic resistance and rage against the analytic procedure. The analyst's accepting objectivity toward the patient's narcissism cannot, of course, do away with all narcissistic resistance and rage, but it will reduce the nonspecific initial resistance against a procedure in which another person may know something about one's thoughts and wishes before one knows them oneself. Through the diminution of the *nonspecific* narcissistic resistances, moreover, recognition of the significance of *specific* narcissistic resistances as repetition and transference is facilitated.

The analyst must therefore at first not ally himself unqualifiedly with the patient's reality ego when it rejects the claims of the unmodified grandiose self or when it tries to deny the persisting infantile need for full control over the narcissistically invested selfobject.[11] On the contrary, he must even be understandingly tolerant of the rage that emerges in the patient when his narcissistic needs are not totally and immediately fulfilled. If the analyst maintains his empathic attitude toward the patient's needs and toward his anger, and if, in response to the analyst's attitude, the patient's reality ego, too, learns to be understandingly accepting of the demands of the grandiose self and of its propensity for rage, then there will be a diminution of those nonspecific resistances in which the patient who feels treated like a naughty child begins indeed to act like a misunderstood naughty child. Only then will the specific resistances against the uncovering of specific repressed needs, wishes, and attitudes be brought into play. The nonspecific narcissistic resistances are in general accompanied by a great deal of rage; the specific resistances, however, are usually characterized by the presence of hypochondria and of other vague fears. The transference reactivation of the original need for approval through mirroring, and for the merger with an idealized archaic object, increases narcissistic tension and leads to hypochondria; and it creates the vague dread of having again to suffer the old traumatic rejection from the side of an environment that will not respond empathically to the rekindled narcissistic needs of childhood.

The Transformation of Narcissistic Rage into Mature Aggression. It is often more revealing to examine transitional phenomena that the extremes of a spectrum of contrasting manifestations; and it is often more instructive to study intermediate points in a developmental sequence than to compare its beginning with its end. This maxim holds true for the study of the transformation of narcissistic rage into mature aggression: the way stations of this development and the remaining imperfections deserve our attention.

Patient A.'s insufficiently idealized superego could not provide him with an adequate internal supply of narcissistic sustenance (see the discussion of this case in Kohut, 1971, pp. 57–

---

[11] This advice is valid not only when the grandiosity is on the whole in repression (horizontal split in the psyche), but also where archaic narcissistic claims are by-passing the reality ego (vertical split), i.e., where the ego is disavowing the presence or significance of the narcissistic claims and enactments (see Kohut, 1971, pp. 183–186).

73), and he needed external approbation in order to maintain his narcissistic balance. He therefore became inordinately dependent on idealized figures in his environment whose praise he craved. Every time they remained unresponsive because they failed to sense his need, he became enraged and criticized them with bitterness and sarcasm during the analytic sessions. When, however, as a result of the extensive working through of his idealizing transference, his structural defect became ameliorated, his rage changed. He continued to complain about the current stand-ins for the archaic idealized figure (his father who had disappointed him in his early life), but his attacks became less bitter and sarcastic, acquired an admixture of humor, and were more in tune with the real shortcomings of those whom he criticized. And there was another remarkable change: while he had formerly nourished his grudges in isolation (even in the analytic sessions his complaints were predominantly soliloquy, not message), he now banded together with his fellow workers and was able to savor, in enjoyable comradeship with them, the pleasure, of prolonged bull sessions in which the bosses were taken apart. In still later stages of his analysis when the patient had already mastered a large part of his psychological difficulties, and especially when certain homosexual fantasies of which he was very ashamed had disappeared, some anger at idealized figures for withholding their approval continued to be in evidence—but now there was not only benign humor instead of sarcasm, and companionship instead of isolation, but also the ability to see some positive features in those he criticized, side by side with their defects.

Another clinical example: patient P., whose attitude toward his eight-year-old son was very revealing.[12] He was in general on excellent terms with the boy and spent a good deal of time with him in enjoyably shared activities. He could, however, become suddenly outraged about minor transgressions, and would then

[12] I examined another, though not unrelated, aspect of this patient's behavior earlier in this presentation. (He is also referred to, but in a clearly different context, in Kohut, 1971, pp. 321–324.) At a meeting of the Chicago Psychoanalytic Society (September 25, 1962), in discussing a presentation on psychosomatic disturbances, I described a transient speech disorder of the then three-and-a-half-year-old son of Mr. P. I interpreted the child's stammer as a reaction to his father's narcissistic involvement with him and to his father's insistence on absolute control over him.

punish the child severely. Slowly, as the analysis proceeded, he became aware of his narcissistic vulnerability and realized that he tended to respond with violent anger when he felt frustrated by narcissistically cathected objects. Yet, he was at first unable to recognize the often seemingly unmistakable fact that he reacted to the trauma of a narcissistic injury by becoming unduly harsh toward his son. He remained convinced that his severity was objectively justified, was adamant in the defense of his behavior, and claimed that consistency and unbending justice were better for his son than ill-placed kindness and unprincipled tolerance. His rationalizations seemed foolproof for a long time, and no headway was made in the analysis. His moralistic punitiveness finally began to subside and was replaced by his growing empathy for his son after the memory of certain childhood scenes was recovered in the analysis and after their dynamic significance was understood. His mother had always reacted with severe, morally buttressed punishments when he attempted to extricate himself from her narcissistic universe. He now did likewise when he felt that an alter ego tried to withdraw from him—either the analyst through activities (such as a temporary interruption of the treatment) that upset the balance of the narcissistic transference, or the son through activities that demonstrated his growing independence from him. It had usually been one of the latter moves—such as the son's stepping over to the neighbor's garden without having asked the father's permission; or his returning home late even by one or two minutes—that the patient had considered a serious misdeed and had punished severely.

In both of the preceding examples I restricted myself to presenting a sequence of clinical events demonstrating how narcissistic rage subsides (and is gradually replaced by aggressions that are under the control of the ego) in consequence of the analytically achieved transformation of the narcissistic matrix from which it arises. The first example (Mr. A.) illustrates how the patient's sarcastic rage gradually became tamed and how his empathy for the targets of his rage increased as his neediness vis-à-vis the idealized object diminished. The second example (Mr. P.) illustrates how the patient's moralistic punitiveness gradually became tamed and how his empathy with the victim of his rage increased as he began to master his narcissistic involvement with alter-ego figures and grasped the fact that he was repeating a crucial situation from his own childhood.

Therapeutic Implications. I have now reached a point at which the convergence of clinical experience and theoretical reflection permits me to summarize and to restate certain conclusions. Our therapeutic aim with regard to narcissistic rage is neither the direct transformation of the rage into constructive aggression nor the direct establishment of controls over the rage by the autonomous ego. Our principal goal is the gradual transformation of the narcissistic matrix from which the rage arises. If this objective is reached, the aggressions in the narcissistic sector of the personality will be employed in the service of the realistic ambitions and purposes of a securely established self and in the service of the cherished ideals and goals of a superego that has taken over the function of the archaic omnipotent object and has become independent from it.

It must be admitted that in practice, e.g., at the end of a generally successful analysis of a narcissistic personality disturbance, it is not always easy to assess to what extent the propensity for narcissistic rage has been overcome, not always easy to know whether the aggressions are now the activities of a mature self and are under the dominance of the ego. But, as is true in general with regard to the completion of the analytic task in other sectors of the personality, so also here: we must make no excessive demands on our patients or on ourselves. On the contrary, the patient should openly face the fact that there exists in him a residual propensity to be temporarily under the sway of narcissistic rage when his archaic narcissistic expectations are frustrated and that he must be alert to the possibility that he might be overtaken by a tantrum. Such squarely faced awareness of the existence of residual psychopathology will stand the patient in good stead when after the termination of the analysis he has to tend his psychological household without the aid of the analyst.[13]

[13]I am here advocating the taking of an attitude of tolerance vis-à-vis a relationship between ego and id that is neither one of ego autonomy nor of ego dominance—i.e., that is less than optimal. The comparative evaluation implied in this context warrants a metapsychological elucidation. Ego autonomy is achieved when the ego can function without being disturbed by pressures from the depth.

The persistence of some subtle and seemingly peripheral manifestations of psychic malfunctioning is sometimes more dependable evidence of the incompleteness of the analytic work than the occasional recurrence of gross behavioral disturbance under stress. In the area of our scrutiny, in particular, we can say that the subtle manifestations of the persistence of a patient's inability to mobilize even a modicum of empathy and compassion for the person who is the target of his anger, and his arrogant and rigid refusal even to try to consider the other's position or motivations, are a more reliable indication that the analytic work in the narcissistic sector is unfinished than the conspicuous manifestations of his propensity to react occasionally—and under unusual stress—with the flare-up of the kind of rage which, before the analysis, had occurred frequently and in response to minor provocations. Patient P.'s unfeeling moralism toward his son, and the immovable dogmatism of his conviction that he was acting appropriately when meting out the punishments, demonstrated more clearly that his behavior was in essence motivated by narcissistic rage than did the severity of the penalties he imposed on the child. True enough, the penalties were disproportionate. (Unsurprisingly, they consisted mainly in the vindictive re-establishment of his narcissistic control in the form of the prolonged withdrawal from his son of such privileges as leaving the house, or in the boy's being banished to his room.) They were never inflicted, however, in an uncontrolled or in a sadistic manner.

Ego dominance is achieved when the archaic forces have become integrated with the ego and when their power can be employed in accordance with the ego's purposes. When I speak acceptingly of a former patient's postanalytic attitude of alertness with regard to the possibility that he might be overtaken by an attack of narcissistic rage, I am endorsing a condition that is, according to strict definition of these terms, neither ego autonomy nor ego dominance (although it is closer to the former than to the latter state). I am here referring to the ego's surveillance of untamed archaic forces: of the ego's handling or manipulating them. Such a relationship between ego and id may be considered a tolerable imperfection if it concerns a narrow sector of the psyche, i.e., if, on the whole, a broad transformation in the area of the relevant psychopathology has taken place.

An analogy from another field may illustrate my meaning concerning the type of imperfection I have in mind. I once knew a man who had so many muscular tics and spasms (probably on an organic basis) that his volitional motility was severely interfered with. He had, however, learned to wait for an appropriate tic movement that he could exploit for the action he wanted to perform.

A *Metapsychological Formulation of Narcissistic Rage*

The scrutiny of aggression as it is interrelated with the area of narcissism has, up to this point, been focused on the phenomenology of narcissistic rage and on the explanation of the matrix of archaic narcissism from which it arises. As my final task I shall now attempt to explain narcissistic rage in metapsychological terms—even though I know that metapsychology has fallen into disrepute and is considered by some to be hardly more than a sterile thought exercise.

In previous contributions (Kohut, 1966, 1968, 1971) I provided a metapsychological formulation of the emotion of shame. I said that it develops under the following conditions. Exhibitionistic libido is mobilized and deployed for discharge in expectation of mirroring and approving responses either from the environment or—I spoke in this context of "shame *signals*"—from the idealized superego, i.e., from the internal structure that took over the approving functions from the archaic environment. If the expected response is not forthcoming, then the flow of the exhibitionistic libido becomes disturbed. Instead of a smooth suffusion of self and body-self with a warm glow of approval and echoed exhibitionistic libido, the discharge and deployment processes disintegrate. The unexpected noncooperation of the mirroring object creates a psychoeconomic imbalance which disrupts the ego's capacity to regulate the outpouring of the exhibitionistic cathexes. In consequence of its temporary paralysis, the ego, on the one hand, yields to the pressure of the exhibitionistic urge, while, on the other hand, it strives desperately to stop the flow. The exhibitionistic surface of the body-self, the skin, therefore shows, not the pleasant warmth of successful exhibitionism, but heat and blushing side by side with pallor.[14] It is this disorga-

---

[14] I am grateful to Dr. Milton Malev for bringing my attention to the following passage from the Babylonian Talmud (Epstein, 1962, p. 58B): "He who makes *pale* the face of his companion in public [i.e., embarrasses his companion], it is as if he had *spilled his blood*" (my italics). This statement not only predicates the intense painfulness of narcissistic injuries, it also appears to take for granted that the physiological correlate of the painful experience is a derangement of the distribution of blood (pallor and blushing: "makes pale the face" and "spilled his blood") in the exhibitionistic surface of the body, especially in the skin of the face.

nized mixture of massive discharge (tension decrease) and blockage (tension increase) in the area of exhibitionistic libido that is experienced as shame.

Similar considerations apply to the experience of narcissistic rage. But while the essential disturbance underlying the experience of shame concerns the boundless *exhibitionism* of the grandiose self, the essential disturbance underlying rage relates to the *omnipotence* of this narcissistic structure. The grandiose self expects absolute control over a narcissistically experienced archaic environment. The appropriate mechanisms—they belong to the aggression-control-power sector of the personality—are set in motion, in expectation of total dominance over the selfobject. When the environment fails to comply—be it the unempathic mother who does not respond to the child's wishes or the table leg that noncompliantly is in the way of the child's toe or an analogous unempathic archaic object in the world of a narcissistically fixated adult—then the formerly smoothly deployed forces become deranged. Paralleling the processes described with regard to shame, we see discharge and inhibition side by side or in rapid succession, except that here, as stated before, the underlying force is not the grandiose self's boundless exhibitionism, i.e., its insistence on being admired, but its omnipotence, i.e., its insistence on the exercise of total control. It is the disorganized mixture of massive discharge (tension decrease) and blockage (tension increase) in the area of unneutralized aggression, arising after the noncompliance of the archaic selfobject, that is the metapsychological substratum of the manifestations and the experience of narcissistic rage.

Chronic Narcissistic Rage

If the rage does not subside, it may be added here, then the secondary processes tend to be pulled increasingly into the domain of the archaic aggressions seeking to re-establish control over a narcissistically experienced world. Conscious and preconscious ideation, particularly as it concerns the aims and goals of the personality, becomes more and more subservient to the pervasive rage. The ego, furthermore, increasingly surrenders its reasoning capacity to the task of rationalizing the persisting insistence on the limitlessness of the power of the grandiose self: it does not acknowledge the inherent limitations of the power of the self, but attributes its failures and weaknesses to the malevolence and corruption of the uncooperative archaic object. We are thus witnessing the gradual establishment of *chronic narcissistic rage,* one of the most pernicious afflictions of the human psyche—either in its still endogenous and preliminary form as grudge and spite, or, externalized and acted out in disconnected vengeful acts or in a cunningly plotted vendetta.[15]

Concluding Remarks

A number of the topics discussed in this essay, especially those taken up in the retrospective survey of my earlier work (i.e., on the libidinal investment of the self), were of necessity only sketchily formulated and need elaboration. But what I regret even more than the shortcomings of this condensed presentation is that I was unable to demonstrate the application of my older formulations about narcissism and of the preceding considerations about narcissistic rage to group psychology, to the behavior of man in history.

I hope very much that further efforts in this area will prove to be fruitful. But this is for the future, and I would like to mention only this much. I have begun work proceeding in two directions. First, regarding the contribution which the understanding of narcissism can make to the understanding of the formation and cohesion of groups: particularly the fact that group cohesion is brought about and maintained not only by an ego ideal held in common by the members of the group (Freud, 1921) but also by their shared subject-bound grandiosity, i.e., by a shared grandiose self. Indeed, there are groups that are characterized

---

[15] The relation between acute and chronic narcissistic rage in the area of the omnipotence of the grandiose self is paralleled by the relation between acute shame and chronic feelings of inferiority in the area of the exhibitionism of this narcissistic structure.

For completeness' sake it should also be mentioned here that narcissistic rage, especially in its chronic form, when it is blocked from being directed toward the selfobject (which is experienced as being outside the self or body-self), may shift its focus and aim at the self or at the body-self. The result in the first instance is self-destructive depression; the consequence in the second instance may be psychosomatic illness. It should be noted in this context that patient P. suffered not only from the manifestations of acute and chronic narcissistic rage, but also from a severe degree of hypertension.

by the fact that they are held together by this latter bond—crudely stated, by their shared ambitions rather than by their shared ideals. Secondly, the psychic life of groups, like that of individuals, shows regressive transformations in the narcissistic realm. When the deployment of higher forms of narcissism is interfered with (such as in the area of the grandiose self, through the blocking of acceptable outlets for national prestige; and in the area of the idealized parent imago, through the destruction of group values, e.g., religious values), then the narcissism of groups regresses, with deleterious consequences in the realm of group behavior. Such regressions become manifest particularly with regard to group aggression, which then takes on, overtly and covertly, the flavor of narcissistic rage in either its acute or, even more ominously, in its chronic form.

But this is work that still needs to be completed, even in its preliminary form, and I must resist the temptation of saying more about it at this point.

6

The Self in History

(1975)

[The Symposium began with a paper by Ernest Wolf, "The Self in History: Introductory Notes on the Psychology of the Self," analyzing and summarizing the key ideas of Kohut's theory of narcissism. The discussion published here begins with Kohut's extemporaneous response (as recorded at the time) to Dr. Wolf's paper.]

H.K.: I am very grateful to Dr. Wolf for this fine summary of my work of the last ten years or so. It is strange for me to hear it presented as if it were well-established shared knowledge. Until very recently it was shared only between me and myself, late at night, and hesitatingly put on paper. I am lucky to have received the kind of response to my ideas and to my work that so many of my colleagues and students have given me.

I have, since my school days, always been very interested in history. I can even say that my intellectual development was strongly influenced by a historian, a high school teacher—I can

A Symposium sponsored by the Group for the Use of Psychology in History and the Center for Psychosocial Studies was held in connection with the Convention of the American Historical Association, December 29, 1974. Panel: Professor John Demos of Brandeis University and Acting Director of the Center for Psychosocial Studies (Chairman); Dr. Heinz Kohut of the Chicago Institute for Psychoanalysis; Dr. Ernest Wolf of the Chicago Institute for Psychoanalysis and Associate Director of the Center for Psychosocial Studies.

This transcript of the Symposium discussion, edited by C. B. Strozier, appeared in the *Newsletter of the Group for the Use of Psychology in History* (1975), vol. 3, no. 4, pp. 3–10.

still see him in front of me—whose mode of thinking struck some kind of chord in me that never stopped vibrating from the days I sat spellbound and listened to him. I remember vividly how he began to explain the absolutist regime of the late Bourbons in France by talking about the way the parks were laid out. I was impressed by his ability to demonstrate the essential unitariness of seemingly diverse phenomena of a culture, a period in history. He didn't write, he didn't grade, he was not a feared professor, and he was a very low man on the totem pole among the teachers I had. Yet, to me, he remained an unforgotten inspiration.

The first thing I ever wrote concerning the findings and theories of which Dr. Wolf spoke to you today was a short paragraph in which I said that the importance that the discovery of the remainders of the early object love and object hate had for adult psychopathology and for adult individual life would be matched by discoveries about the remainders of childhood narcissism for group behavior and for the behavior of man within groups. I was at that time president of our national association and had been puzzling about the dissensions within our group and particularly about the fact that now and then people who seemed to have been friends suddenly turned and became enemies. I learned to recognize that almost certainly, if one only looked hard, one could always find some small but nevertheless important narcissistic injury at the pivotal moment that determined the later inimical attitude of such an individual. I have since then found that the scientist's insights had been anticipated by the artists and great writers. Not long ago I was reading *Anna Karenina*. To my great delight I encountered, toward the end, a short episode describing a man who had written a scientific treatise and was now anxiously waiting for the reviews. Finally the first review came; it gave the book a tremendous panning, but cleverly and wittily, although everything was subtly distorted. The author wondered why in the world this man used his considerable intelligence and wit to distort so cleverly what he had written, in order to pan him. And then he remembered that two years ago he had met the man in a social gathering and had corrected *one* word the man had used. Now everything became clear to him. He had shamed this man in public by correcting him; and now, two years later, the opportunity for revenge arose and the man used it with glee. He knew there was nothing to be done.

In the setting of history, thwarted narcissistic aspirations, hurts to one's pride, injuries to one's prestige needs, interferences with conscious, preconscious, or unconscious fantasies concerning one's greatness, power, and specialness, or concerning the greatness, power, and specialness of the group that one identifies with are important motivations for group behavior. The refined study of these motivations will add a new dimension to the other data which historians utilize in describing historical events. I don't mean to say that hunger and the search for areas of expansion and a variety of other forces are not important. But I think that if the narcissistic dimension of these already in themselves substantial motivations is taken into account, then their explanatory power will increase greatly—they will go much further in explaining why people behave as they do, why they sometimes would rather die than live with a narcissistic injury.

The question is what do depth-psychologists and historians have in common? It strikes me that we would recognize that we have a great deal in common if we could only drop what I have recently called the tool-and-method pride or the tool-and-method snobbishness of the scientist. We all tend to see our specialness, our *raison d'être*, in the particular methodological and conceptual instruments we have learned to use, which we have made our own and with which we communicate with our friends and professional colleagues. I know that the more I ponder the relationship between depth-psychology and history, the more I realize that the important issue at the present time is to build a bridge between history and psychoanalysis on the basis of a broader awareness of the purpose of our work.

Most of us have intentionally put on blinders and narrowed our sights in consequence of our commitment to our professions. We want to understand our craft, and to work in it, as best we can, and beyond that we don't want to look. But I don't believe it is possible to maintain this attitude toward our work. Scientists subscribe to the idea that the more knowledge we acquire the better. This is our inheritance from the freeing of the individual in the Renaissance, I believe, and it reached its peak in the great scientific successes of the nineteenth and early twentieth centuries. But knowledge has a purpose. Knowledge has a purpose that we do not need to be ashamed of. Knowledge is an intermediary step toward man's over-all goal to achieve increasing mastery over his destiny. Knowledge leads in the biological and physical sciences to the curing of illness, to man's mastery of the physical surroundings; knowledge in the psychological and social sciences should lead to man's increasing mastery over his historical, political, and social fate. In this sense it seems to me that the depth-psychologist and the historian are working on the same team, that they must work together and learn from one another.

Not only our goals, our working methods, too, have much in common. In both of our fields we are looking at complicated sets of data which would remain hopelessly unintelligible were it not for the fact that the observer and what is being observed have some inner similarity. It would be impossible to understand historical events were it not for the' fact that history is made by people and that we can obtain meaningful data—from which we can then secondarily derive explanatory formulations—about the behavior and the motivations of these people, even if they differ greatly from us. Similar considerations also apply with regard to depth psychology.

History and psychoanalysis should be the most important sciences of the future. They are important because humanity has reached a point in which populations will sooner or later have to become stabilized. This will have a profound influence on the psychological outlook of people in the future. It will be necessary for us to direct our resources toward the refinement of various individual activities. If humans are to survive in a way that has any similarity to what we have prized up till now as being the essence of human life, the narcissistic motivations, I believe, must come into the ascendancy. Each individual must refine and work out a new kind of psychological life, a new kind of meaningful existence, by expanding his inner skills and his inner powers. Can historians, can psychologists help man here? No historian, so far as I know, has claimed yet that his insights have influenced the course of history. Nor can we say that any particular insights of a psychological nature have made any real dent beyond their influence—I am thinking especially of the psychotherapeutic setting here—on the life of the individual. But must we resign ourselves to the conclusion that this restriction will forever prevail?

Insights gradually filtering into the population at large, and particularly into the intelligentsia and the elite groups, may indeed have some kind of influence, although it cannot be neatly discerned. I do not find it ludicrous, for example, to consider it possible that the fact that we have been living now for the better part of a century with the idea of an Oedipus complex, with an increased understanding of the child's involvement with the parental figures, has been a factor in the diminution of the generation gap that we are witnessing. The fact, for instance, that students are sitting in on faculty committees now, unheard of in previous eras, is clearly not the direct result of Freud's having described the Oedipus complex. But our increased familiarity with the child's experiences vis-à-vis his parents might very well be a factor in the general loosening of the stiffness and reserve that existed between the generations, of the diminution of the mutual suspiciousness that in turn has all kinds of political and social ramifications. In the same way, I believe it possible that the understanding of the intensity and meaning of narcissistic rage, what a narcissistic injury means for individuals and populations, as it filters through universities to science writers to newspapers and the popular media, might in the long run, and maybe not even in the all-too-long run, assert some kind of beneficial effect on our capacity to tolerate narcissistic injuries without having to fly into a killing rage, without having to be forever unable to make compromises.

CHAIRMAN: Thank you very much. Now let me just invite questions and comments in whatever order they may come up.

_Q:_ I wonder if Dr. Kohut could explain to us why so few women have been idealized figures in society.

_H.K.:_ I don't know the answer to this question. Classical analysis would have answered by pointing out that the absence of a visible genital in the little girl is of crucial importance in psychic development and leads to such a severe wound in self-esteem that later self-confidence remains low and idealizability therefore lessened. Now, I do not see, at least not from my own clinical experience, that the narcissistic injury that undoubtedly is connected with the absence of the visible genital in little girls is, in essence, different from the narcissistic injury to the little boy who discovers that his penis is very small as compared with the penis of a grown man. I believe, however, that a child is much more significantly influenced by the empathic attitude of the grownups around him or her than by the givens of organic equipment. A mother's and father's admiration of a little girl as a little girl, in her sweetness, in her future bearing of children, in whatever potentials of her femininity she displays, will provide her ultimately when she becomes a woman with the same degree of security and idealizability that the man has—if *he* was accepted by his admiring and happy and glad parents when he was a little boy, even though his penis was small. The importance of the matrix of empathy in which we grow up cannot be overestimated.

It is interesting that Freud in his last technical paper (1937b), "Analysis Terminable and Interminable"—a great paper in many respects—closed with a statement of ultimate pessimism. He concluded that analysis can go up to a certain point but not beyond it. It cannot persuade a man to accept his passivity toward another man, and it cannot persuade a woman to accept the absence of the penis. Here, he says, it has reached biological bedrock. Now it would seem to me that it is up to the historian to undertake a comparative study of the attitude of adults toward children at different periods in history, in order to throw some further light on the conditions that Freud tried to explain biologically. Why, he should ask, for example, was the little girl not as welcome as the little boy? Was the little boy in early times more highly esteemed because he would later be a powerful protector and helper, as a warrior, as a tiller of the soil? I admit that I do not have answers to these questions, that I am batting the ball back to the historians. Still, I would stress that I am convinced that the research of the historian would be enriched by the insights that psychoanalysis can provide for him as he gets ready for his work, and as he carries it out.

Q: I understand that, according to psychoanalytic theory, fixations on childhood attitudes come about in consequence of excess gratification. Can you explain the frequency of such fixations in view of the fact that the *absence* of the mother and *insufficiency* of mothering are well-established historical facts, especially in nineteenth-century Europe?

H.K.: A thought-provoking question. There is in the question, however, couched a bias for which I cannot blame the questioner because it is a generally accepted bias. The bias rests in the word "mothering," and it rests in the word that is even more important behind the word mothering—namely "mother." I don't believe that these terms do justice to the complexity and the variety of relationships that can constitute a psychologically good or bad environment for the child. I have come more and more to abstain from using these terms when, in the course of my work, I discuss psychic development, and I speak instead of the "empathic responsive matrix" which the child needs for psychological survival and growth. It may not make any difference whether it is the child's biological mother who is the provider. It may not even make a crucial difference whether one or several people are involved in the mothering, as you would say, or in the empathic environment of the child, as I would say.

An interesting study, relevant to our topic, about an experiment in nature, so to speak, was written by Anna Freud and Sophie Dann about twenty years ago (1951). They reported on a group of six children who had survived the concentration camp. In the course of their three years in the camp they were taken care of by ever-changing successive sets of mothers. The children survived, but the young women who were delivered into the concentration camp were all exterminated, to be replaced by a new group of young women who, until their death, took care of the children in their turn. Now, these children were surely disturbed, no doubt—but they were not schizophrenic. These children had a reasonably cohesive self; they had had a reasonable sense of being accepted in this world. The only conclusion one can draw is that the young women, as the end of their life was approaching, fastened on the next generation with a kind of empathy, with a kind of affection, with a kind of responsiveness that gave these children a sense of the continuity and reality of their self that allowed them to become viable individuals.

I used this example to show the complexity of the psychological substance that lies behind the simple term "mother." Many times you find that the children of disturbed mothers are in comparatively good psychological health, while children of not so obviously disturbed mothers are disturbed. I have long puzzled over this matter and have come to the following conclusion:

If the mothers are grossly disturbed, other adults will jump into the breach and respond to the children. But if the mothers are what we call latently schizophrenic, borderline cases, hiding their schizophrenia behind bridge cards, then such children are exposed to an emotionally empty, nonsustaining environment without being able to turn to others, without enlisting others to their cause.

I gave you a complex answer; but I think you will understand what I was aiming at. One must think not simply in terms of "mothering" and "mother," but in terms of the total complexity of an environment and whether it is positive or negative. During the era preceding our own, the overstimulating closeness with the adults to which the child was exposed led later in adult life to the hostilities and inhibitions which, as I said earlier, Freud's explanations may have ultimately helped us to overcome to a degree. Now we may see the results of a deadening distance to which children are exposed, leading in adulthood to a different kind of psychopathology, the disorders of the self, and leading also, we hope to a new set of explanations which in the long run will help us to overcome the leading psychic disturbances of our time.

Q: I have a historical question—it's a bit of turning the tables— concerning the evolution of depth-psychological thought. Please explain why the development in psychoanalysis that is represented by your ideas is taking place at this point in history when works of art and literature are being created—Pirandello, for example, on whom I am doing some research—which cannot be understood without the use of concepts like Sartre's in philosophy or like yours in psychology.

H.K.: As you can imagine, I have thought about this question before. The theory I have formed is that the greatest pioneering artists of any period are dealing with the leading psychological problems of tomorrow; that art is one day, as it were—whatever a day means in the historical sense here—ahead of science in this respect. The great artists of yesterday dealt with the experiences of people in the world of interpersonal love and hate and with the experiences of people in the sphere of the swings of narcissism to which a firmly cohesive, relatively strong self is exposed: the loves and hates, the triumphs and defeats of basically strong people were their subject matter. But now a good many artists have begun to deal with a new set of issues. This set of issues, to speak of it in the most gross terms, is the falling apart of the self and of the world and the task of reconstituting the self and the world. Among the artists who deal with this problem by verbal means is Kafka. In his stories he describes that there is nobody around to whom one can turn. One searches for a place one never gets to in *The Castle.* One searches hopelessly for a person who will at least define one's guilt, but one is killed meaninglessly in *The Trial.* One wakes up in the morning and finds with horror that one's self has become dreadfully changed and estranged in *Metamorphosis.* Perhaps the greatest expression of the central anxieties of our time was achieved by Eugene O'Neill. I don't know how many of you are familiar with *The Great God Brown,* but in this interesting play none of the personages know exactly who they are. The characters in *The Great God Brown* wonder whether they are themselves or somebody else when they put on a mask. They are always either putting on masks and becoming someone else or taking off these masks and becoming—preconsciously—themselves again. They are clearly not aware or sure of who they are. But the clearest expression of modern man's leading problem is contained in a statement by Brown who says, shortly before his death: "Man is born broken. He lives by mending. The grace of God is glue." O'Neill expressed here in Brown's words not only the sickness of modern times but also his own individual sickness. Later he told the personal story extensively in *A Long Day's Journey into Night:* about the addicted mother, the self-absorbed, vain father, and the resulting fragmentation of the selves of the sons, in particular the fragmentation-proneness of his own self. The damage suffered by his self led him, on the one hand, toward alcoholism, but also, on the other hand, through the power of his genius which enabled him to escape the addiction and to glue the fragments of his broken self, to the creation of works of art. The broken self is mended via the creation of the cohesive artistic product. These are the problems that lie in the center of the preoccupations of the artists of our time, problems that are indeed different from those with which the artists of the past had been struggling, the problems, let us say, portrayed by Ibsen's or Shakespeare's plays. But why the change?

The only answer I have is that in former times the involvement between the parents and their children was overly intense. The children were emotionally overtaxed by their proximity to adults—be they the parents or nursemaids or others. They were stimulated, touched, cajoled; and they developed all kinds of conflicts as they responded to the stimulation to which the protracted emotional interplay with the adults exposed them. In that sense we might say that the Oedipus complex, while not an artifact, was yet artificially intensified by this overcloseness between adults and children.

But now we seem to be dealing with the opposite problem. There is not enough touching, not enough genuine parental responsiveness; there exists an atmosphere of emotional flatness and sterility. Is this change to some extent due to the increasing overpopulation on earth? Is the parental self-absorption related to the need to curb the growth of the population? I don't know. But I do know that man must achieve a new psychological balance now as he learns to adapt to stable frontiers and a life without numerous children. How can he find this new balance, and what kind of inner and outer adjustment should he strive for? Here, it seems to me, lies again an area in which historians and depth psychologists should cooperate and try, via scientifically posed questions, to provide scientifically valid solutions for these crucial problems.

7

Creativeness, Charisma,
Group Psychology

Reflections on the Self-Analysis of Freud (1976)

The Psychoanalyst and His Image of Freud

We are faced by uncertainties and difficulties when we investigate Freud's self-analysis: first, by those which in all areas of applied analysis arise because we are not participating in a living clinical situation; second, by those that arise because we might not be objective about Freud, who is for us a transference figure par excellence—we are prone to establish an idealizing transference toward him or to defend ourselves against it by reaction formation; and third, by those that arise because Freud's self-analysis is a unique event in the history of human thought.

This is not the place for an examination of the goals and methodological problems of applied analysis, but I will discuss two issues: the general difficulties we confront when we undertake the study of Freud (aspects of his personality, his biography, his significance), and the additional difficulties we face when we attempt to interpret the meaning and to evaluate the significance of Freud's self-analysis. These difficulties arise because we are here dealing with a psychological situation that—as the first scientifically orderly introspective effort to scrutinize complex

First published in *Freud: The Fusion of Science and Humanism* (1976), ed. J. E. Gedo and G. H. Pollock. *Psychological Issues*, Monogr. 34 / 35. New York: International Universities Press, pp. 379–425.

psychological states—is without recorded precedent in the history of human thought.[1]

It is always hard to achieve an objective evaluation of a great man, whether the evaluation be by the average biographer, the historian, or the depth psychologist (R. and E. Sterbas' *Beethoven and His Nephew* [1954, pp. 12–17] contains an illuminating discussion of these problems). The great man is prone to become a transference figure for the beholder—usually, of course, a father figure—and the childhood ambivalences of the investigator may intrude to falsify results. Even more widespread is another pitfall: the biographer's apparently falling in love with his subject. When examined more closely, I believe it turns out that true object love is not involved here, but the establishment of a bond of identification. The choice of the subject is frequently determined by the investigator's identificatory predilections (dictated perhaps by needs emanating from structural defects or weaknesses of the biographer who is in search of identifications) and the long preoccupation with the life of the investigated is prone to reinforce the identificatory bonds even further. Still, one might expect that the pitfalls of such a scientific enterprise would prove to be least dangerous for the psychoanalyst. The analyst is after all specifically trained to observe and control his own reactions, and he should be able either to set aside his childhood loves and hates and his narcissistic (e.g., identificatory) needs during his

[1] Here two points may need to be emphasized. I am not claiming priority for Freud's self-analysis (and, by extension, for the science of psychoanalysis) simply because Freud used the introspective approach to the complexities of inner life—this approach to the broad field of inner experience has been used from time immemorial by poets and mystical philosophers—but because he did so in a scientifically orderly, systematic way and recorded and formulated the results of his observations in terms of a more or less experience-distant theory. Nor am I claiming uniqueness for Freud's self-analysis (and, by extension, for the science of psychoanalysis) simply because he used the introspective approach in order to obtain scientifically valid psychological data—this claim could also be made for the self-observations of experimental psychology—but because his subject matter was the whole of psychic life in all its breadth and depth. It is the fact Freud used the introspective approach in a systematic, scientific way without narrowing the scope of his subject matter (and that, by extension, psychoanalysis has continued to employ the introspective-empathic approach in the same fashion) which justifies the assertion that the introduction of the psychoanalytic method constituted a revolutionary step in the history of science. (For further remarks on this important topic see Kohut, 1959, especially pp. 205–211; 1970c, especially p. 593n; 1973, especially pp. 528–529.)

clinical and scientific work or at least disqualify himself when he senses his inability to do so.

In general it would be justified to make such demands on the analyst, and, on the whole, we may assume that there is at least a fair chance that he may be able to live up to these standards. As regards the figure of Freud, however, the analyst's task is vastly increased, and objectivity is hard for him to attain. In the following I shall discuss the two major obstacles standing in the analyst's way when he attempts to be objective about Freud.

The first obstacle stems from the fact that analysts usually become acquainted with Freud during the crucial formative years in which their professional selves as analysts take shape. This fact alone is weighty enough. But there is, in addition, a peculiar circumstance that must not be underestimated. While he is a student at a psychoanalytic institute, the future analyst does not primarily study Freud's life and his opinions, but is forced to identify with Freud from the inside, as it were; that is, he is asked to think himself into the most intimate and detailed activities of Freud's mental processes. Each student of psychoanalysis reads and rereads "The Interpretation of Dreams" (1900a). As he undertakes the study of this fundamental volume he undergoes over and over again the peculiar experience of moving from the manifest content of one of Freud's dreams toward Freud's unconscious dream wishes, and thus he participates in the workings of the most intimate recesses of Freud's mind: Freud's preconscious and unconscious libidinal and aggressive strivings in the object instinctual and narcissistic sectors of his personality over and over again become the student's own, and so do Freud's resistances, conflicts, and anxieties. If the student of analysis does not want to deprive himself of the full, enriching experience of obtaining his basic knowledge from the genuine source of the report of the discoverer, given at the time when the discovery was still a recent, immediate, fresh experience, he is forced to identify with the deepest layers of Freud's personality. Such empathic closeness with total sectors of another person's mind, extending from conscious to unconscious levels, is not available to us in our day-to-day relationships, not even with those we are closest to—the members of our family and our friends. True, once we are in the daily practice of clinical analysis, such contact with the inner life of others does indeed fill our working day; but this contact is diluted by the simple fact that we do not experience our empathic trial identifications with only *one* patient, but participate in the inner life of an increasing number of them. The convergence of the facts that Freud is the great father figure and teacher of our science, that we are studying him from the inside, as it were, and that this study constitutes our first, or at least a very early and basic, experience of identification with the unconscious of someone else—combine to produce in analysts a specific attitude toward Freud, i.e., an attitude of firmly established identification with an idealized figure (or, in reaction formation, of rebelliousness against this identification). The idealization of great teacher figures is undoubtedly encountered in other branches of science, too. However, in general, these idealizations constitute simply a new psychological content which temporarily attaches itself to the permanent unconscious idealized images of the superego; they are by no means analogous to the deeply anchored, lasting identifications that develop in the analyst with regard to Freud.[2]

Although the pull toward establishing a gross and uncontrolled identification with Freud is strong, I believe that with the aid of increasing self-understanding (e.g., as acquired during the training analysis) the student should be able to resist it. And I believe that insight would help dissolve even an already established identification with Freud—unless it is the symptomatic result of a persisting, unanalyzed, structural defect—if the causative factors that I have so far mentioned were the only ones responsible. Another factor exists, however, whose influence weighs even more heavily in the balance.

The most important obstacle the analyst faces when he tries to

[2] Some psychoanalytic educators might draw the conclusion that a simple curricular remedy is alluded to here—namely, the postponement of the study of Freud's "The Interpretation of Dreams" until later in the analyst's career and its replacement by the study of secondary writers and of more up-to-date approaches. Such a conclusion is unwarranted. The analyst must not attempt to sidestep psychological tasks by avoidance; on the contrary, the identificatory pull should be faced openly through increased awareness of its existence, of the psychological defect that tends to submit to it, and of the psychological assets that can be mobilized against it. (In this context see the discussion of the crucial difference between gross and wholesale identifications, on the one hand, and the result of the process of *transmuting internalization* on the other [Kohut, 1971, pp. 45–50, 165–167].)

achieve an attitude of objectivity toward Freud is that the idealized figure of Freud plays a currently active role in the dynamics
of the psychoanalytic community, i.e., that body of psychoanalytic practitioners, scholars, and researchers, which in the past
was sometimes—unfortunately, and, I think, largely erroneously—referred to as "the psychoanalytic movement" (see
Freud, 1914a). I would like to suggest that the idealization of
Freud by the individual members of the psychoanalytic community has played an important role—usually a positive one, but
not always—in maintaining both the psychic equilibrium of the
individual analyst and group cohesion in the analytic community. It exerts its influence particularly by virtue of the fact that,
on the individual level, it tends to forestall the development of
certain exquisitely painful experiences of narcissistic imbalance
in the analyst (such as the pangs of jealousy and envy) and, on
the group level, it is a counterforce to the rash and indiscrimi-
nate formation of splinter groups which tend to arise in response
to the ill-controlled narcissistic demands of certain of its creative
members (such as the tendency for new discoveries to stimulate
secessionist movements instead of becoming integrated into the
previously accumulated body of knowledge). There is no need
to expand on these formulations since they are fully in harmony
wihh certain basic psychoanalytic tenets concerning group psychology. Ever since Freud's relevant pioneering contribution
(1921), we have taken for granted that group cohesion is mainly
established and safeguarded with the aid of the imago of the
leader who, as the ego ideal held in common by the members of
the group, becomes that point to which all individuals look up,
and to whose greatness they all submit in shared admiration and
submission.

A detailed and comprehensive study of the advantages and
disadvantages for the science of psychoanalysis which are related
to the fact that psychoanalysts are held together by a shared ego
ideal, the idealized imago of Freud, should some day be undertaken—this task, however, is beyond the scope of the present
essay. Here I would only point out one of the advantages accru-
ing to analysis from the fact that psychoanalysts are held together
by powerful emotional bonds. The essential continuity of a group,
its essential sameness along the time axis despite the changes
brought about by growth and development, is a precondition for

the healthy productivity of the group, just as is the analogous continuity of the self-experience, despite the analogous changes within the confines of a single life span, for the healthy productivity of the individual. To state it differently: a firm group self[3] supports the productivity of the group just as a firm individual self supports the productivity of the individual. Applying this maxim to psychoanalysis and stating it in the negative, we can say: if—even on the basis of legitimate reforms in theory and practice—psychoanalysis should change so abruptly and to such an extent that the sense of the continuity of the science were lost, then the individual analyst would receive no further stimulation from his participation in the scientific community of analysts, would lose his sense of belonging to a living, developing body of scientific knowledge to whose growth he can contribute, and his productivity would cease.[4]

---

[3] The concept of a "group self" will be discussed later in the present essay.

[4] In harmony with my emphasis on the importance of a sense of historical continuity for the psychoanalyst, I continue to be an advocate of historically oriented presentations in the curricula of psychoanalytic educational institutions. Although I realize that the systematic rather than the historical presentation of psychoanalytic theory and technique would have some advantages for the learner, I still believe that there ought to be a minimum of courses that acquaint the student from the beginning of his studies with the germinal thoughts of Freud and of his early pupils. The familiarity with "The Interpretation of Dreams" and with Freud's great case histories is of particular value in this respect. The study of these works is not only a splendid and, I believe, still irreplaceable exercise in a difficult new mode of thinking (i.e., in terms of the symbolic notations of metapsychology), it also sets up a historical baseline for the future analyst from which he can trace the development that led to the modern theories and clinical methods. The advantages of retaining a minimum of historically oriented teaching are immeasurable and, to my mind, outweigh the advantages of a totally nonhistorical systematic orientation. To follow the unbroken line of development from the original discoveries in their original form through the various changes of the early formulations to their present state will allow the student to experience the development of psychoanalysis in the course of his psychoanalytic education and will provide the psychoanalyst with that firm sense of the cohesion and continuity of analysis which forms the secure basis of all future creative developments. Nor should the cognitive advantages of a historical orientation be underestimated. Only by studying the origins and the way stations can the present theories be fully understood. And only by realizing how analysts have in the past struggled unceasingly to formulate newly discovered data with the aid of new concepts will psychoanalysis continue to fulfill its potential for further growth. I am convinced that the vitality of psychoanalysis as a growing science is far from exhausted. It has so far hardly scratched the surface of the human mind, and it will deepen its investigations for a long time to come,

Among the disadvantages arising for psychoanalysis because analysts form strong bonds of idealization to an internalized imago of Freud, let me briefly speak of two. The first—it seems to me to be the less deleterious one—is a tendency toward conformity. New thought, in other words, is in danger of being viewed with suspicion because it is experienced as potentially disruptive. Many analysts may thus tend to be overcautious with regard to new ideas, while others, owing to the presence of a preconscious rebelliousness against the encompassing presence of an unchanging ideal, will welcome new ideas not so much because they have convinced themselves of their validity as because they have experienced them as a liberation from a dimly felt internal bondage. The second unfavorable consequence of Freud's imago having served as a stimulus for the mobilization of idealizing cathexes seems to me to be of even greater importance than the first. The channeling of the flow of a large part of the individual psychoanalyst's narcissistic energies toward the group ego ideal creates psychological conditions unfavorable to creative activities that emanate from the grandiose self. To describe the situation in experiential terms: the ambitious strivings and the cognate self-expanding urge toward new discoveries—in the physical world, to move into new territories, i.e., a derivative of archaic flying fantasies—are not sufficiently engaged and will therefore not stimulate the growth and refinement of correlated new sublimatory structures, i.e., of ego functions (talents) that would perform in accordance with the pressures emanating from the grandiose self. The potentially creative narcissistic strivings of the individual psychoanalyst may, in other words, be committed in too large a proportion to idealized goals. No doubt all creative and productive work depends on the employment of both grandiose *and* idealizing narcissistic energies, but I think that truly original thought, i.e., creativity, is energized predominantly from the grandiose self, while the work of more tradition-bound sci-

---

if—and indeed here lies a grave danger—historical and political developments do not stifle its activities from the outside. The recognition of this danger—perhaps in the form of the ascendancy of an antipsychological, totalitarian, mass society—should, in addition to the detached desire to expand the frontiers of psychological knowledge, prompt the analyst to investigate the field of history with the hope of increasing man's mastery over his historical destiny.

entific and artistic activities, i.e., productivity,[5] is performed with idealizing cathexes.

But we must leave these general and speculative considerations and return to the more narrowly circumscribed area of our present concern. We are dealing with the question of how the analyst employs his nonobjective, idealizing attitude toward Freud in the service of protecting himself against a disturbance of his narcissistic equilibrium. The answer to this question will, of course, secondarily explain certain resistances against discarding the idealization of Freud, i.e., resistances that are an outgrowth of the analyst's wish that his narcissistic equilibrium remain undisturbed.

I believe the idealization of Freud protects each analyst in two ways against the experience of painful narcissistic tensions. (1) Genuine, i.e., nondefensive idealization in any form and with any content (it is most effective in the form of a strongly idealized superego, i.e., in the form of meaningful, high ideals) is always an important and valuable safeguard against the development of narcissistic tensions (e.g., shame propensity) because a substantial amount of a person's narcissistic energies will be absorbed by his ideals. (2) The idealization of a group model protects the individual member of the group against certain states of narcissistic disequilibrium which are experienced as envy, jealousy, and rage. If these narcissistic tensions remain undischarged, they are exquisitely painful; if, however, they are discharged (through actions, especially actions motivated by narcissistic rage), then they are socially dangerous. If the present-day psychoanalyst can maintain that everything of importance in psychoanalysis has already been said by Freud, if, furthermore, the imago of Freud has been securely included in the analyst's idealized superego and has thus become a part of the self, then he can disregard contemporary competitors, they are not a threat to his own narcissistic security, and he can avoid suffering the painful narcissistic injuries that the comparison with the actual rivals for the goals of his narcissistic strivings might inflict on him. Small wonder then that the *de*idealization of the Freud imago creates strong uneasiness in the analyst and mobi-

[5] I first encountered the felicitous comparative juxtaposition of the terms "creativity" and "productivity" in a letter (February 5, 1968) to me from K. R. Eissler.

lizes strong resistances against taking an objective, realistic attitude toward Freud, i.e., an attitude in which Freud is seen as a fellow human being with his assets and defects, his achievements and his limitations. True, as I stated before, tearing down the image of Freud is a not infrequent occurrence in the history of analysis. One may assume such events to be largely defensive: in many instances, at least, they testify to a persistent, unmitigated idealization of Freud in the detractor's unconscious.

Readers inimical to psychoanalysis may well gloat over the preceding statements and may feel justified in their criticism of psychoanalysis as an unscientific, semireligious enterprise. But I will leave aside the comparatively easy task of formulating an anticipatory rebuttal to such potential abuse of my considerations and instead propose that, in true psychoanalytic tradition, we should regard these insights, if indeed they are in essence valid, as a challenge to expand the domain of our awareness. Specifically, I would say they challenge us to deepen and broaden our training analyses in the narcissistic sector of our candidates' personalities. We must be particularly watchful concerning the detrimental possibility that the unconscious grandiose-exhibitionistic strivings of our candidates will escape from becoming sufficiently engaged in the psychoanalytic situation, and that, in consequence of this evasion, they will not become gradually sublimated and integrated into the reality ego of the future psychoanalyst. The incompleteness of the mobilization of the candidate's narcissism (and / or the incompleteness of the working-through process in the narcissistic sector) may be caused in a variety of ways involving the entire spectrum of resistances in the candidate and a motley array of blind spots, countertransferences, and theoretically buttressed attitudes in the training analyst. One specific mode in which the narcissistic pressures in the candidate may be shunted aside and escape analysis is via the implicit or explicit agreement between analysand and training analyst that the potentially disturbing narcissistic cathexes of the candidate are to be committed to an idealized imago of Freud. To end a training analysis on the high-minded note of a shared admiration for Freud is, because of its emphasis on fraternal and communal feelings, not only a socially acceptable step of great respectability, it can also be a moving experience for the candidate, which soothes his pain at the parting and sweetens the inevitable bitterness of having to accept the reality of his frustrations in the object-instinctual and the narcissistic realms. It cannot be denied, nevertheless, that such a termination may in some instances tend to close off certain postanalytic potentialities for the future analyst. In particular, the commitment of his still uncommitted narcissistic cathexes to the imago of Freud may deprive him of the emotional pressure to search for individually valid solutions and may increase his structural conflicts (his guilt feelings) if he, in independent assertiveness, should try to express the pattern of his own self. The clinical issues concerning this whole problem area are too complex to be dealt with in the present context, and I will add only one statement in order to give an appropriately balanced outlook: a training analysand's spontaneously arrived at, realistic, nondefensive capacity to admire Freud as one of the great minds of the Western world and as a model of scientific rigor and moral courage by no means indicates that the narcissistic sector has not been successfully dealt with in the analysis. On the contrary, it may sometimes even be considered a sign of analytic success, especially in personalities who were formerly unable to mobilize any enthusiasm for greatness, whether encountered in the form of admirable ideas or of admirable personalities.

Freud's Self-Analysis: The Transference of Creativity

After this cautionary discussion of some of the personal, social, and methodological problems posed for the psychoanalytic investigator by an examination of Freud's personal life and scientific activities, I now turn to the hub of the present inquiry: an evaluation of Freud's self-analysis during the years preceding the publication of his decisive scientific contribution and greatest work, "The Interpretation of Dreams."

The initial question to which I shall address myself is whether Freud's self-analysis should predominantly be considered analogous to all other analyses or whether its essential significance is to be sought elsewhere.

There is no doubt that the insights Freud obtained were of benefit to his emotional health in the ordinary psychoanalytic sense of the word, i.e., his self-analysis lifted repressions, dissolved psychoneurotic symptoms and inhibitions, and thus secondarily put instinctual forces that had formerly been bound up in structural conflicts at the disposal of his ego. Seen from this, the traditional viewpoint, we will say that the success of Freud's self-analysis was the precondition for his creativity. We may furthermore say not only that the inner freedom obtained by his self-analysis liberated the nameless creative forces which served as the instinctual fuel for his achievements, but that he was in addition, on the strength of his unique endowment, able to turn each personal insight into a suprapersonal scientifically valid psychological discovery.[6]

If we look at the relationship Freud established with Wilhelm Fliess during the period of his self-analysis we will quite naturally assume that, lacking an analyst (who would become the focal point of the transference, i.e., the target of the object-directed and narcissistic, libidinal, and aggressive strivings from the unconscious), Freud would almost as a matter of course search for a suitable person in his environment who could play this role for him. Indeed, we must admire the cleverness of Freud's choice of Fliess, with whom he was not in direct contact most of the time—the behind-the-couch distance and invisibility of the ordinary analyst was here replaced by the distance between Vienna and Berlin, which likewise kept the disturbing reality input at a minimum. It is in tune, it must be stressed, with Freud's psycho-

---

[6] Here, the objection might be raised that each analysis is simultaneously therapy and research. I would have no quarrel with such an opinion if the term research in this context is meant to refer broadly to a specific mental attitude (taken by analyst and analysand) of openness to the unexpected and the unknown. In this sense, analysis may indeed be looked upon as a form of research—especially by comparison with the therapeutic processes of medicine in which known remedies are applied to cure known illnesses. True research, however, aims at the discovery of data and relationships that have not been seen before, while in the usual therapeutic analysis the open-minded attitude is directed toward the recognition—the rediscovery—of already previously discovered configurations. True research requires, in addition, the intention—whether consciously acknowledged or not—of formulating the newly seen configurations in more or less experience-distant terms and of communicating the findings and theories to the broader scientific group. My claim that Freud's self-analysis was unique by being a combination of therapy and research therefore rests on the fact that here a therapeutic endeavor was not just combined with the rediscovery of what was already known but also with the creative discovery of configurations that had never been recognized before, and with the courageous intention of communicating the findings to the appropriate representatives of society, the community of scientists and scholars.

logical genius that he did not—as so many of our patients and training analysands are wont to do even though an analyst is in fact at their disposal—live out his transferences with his friends and family or, what must have been most tempting, with his patients through the formation of countertransferences. In summary, then, we will understand why Freud's analysis has been primarily taken as a specific variant of an ordinary therapeutic one and why it was thought that no other hypothesis is needed in addition to the assumption that Fliess was called upon to fill the void of the empty chair behind the symbolic couch on which Freud struggled along his way toward insight and mastery.

Freud's self-analysis was not the first analysis ever conducted. Freud and Breuer had already approached the problems of many patients through the application of the psychoanalytic method. Yet in certain respects—particularly if we consider the breadth of Freud's aim and the persistence of his investigative effort as he conducted his self-analysis—this analysis was indeed something new, even if we disregard the absence of an analyst. It was the first specimen of the type of analysis that the modern analyst is in essence still practicing, i.e., it was an analysis that aimed at the depth-psychological comprehension of the total personality and was not narrowly focused on a pathological symptom or syndrome. It was—and indeed continued to be almost to the very end of Freud's life—the first specimen of "analysis interminable."

Even though Freud's self-analysis was the pioneering precursor of the broadly conceived analyses of today, not all of its features are equivalent to those with which we have become familiar in our usual therapeutic work. It is the specific historical position of Freud's self-analysis, not the fact that analysand and analyst were the same person, that accounted for those elements—especially the meaning of the central transference—which set it apart. I now turn to a discussion of these distinguishing features of Freud's analysis in order to offer an alternative—or to be more exact, a complement—to the traditional hypothesis about the significance of Freud's transference to Wilhelm Fliess.

At the height of the transference neurosis of the usual therapeutic analysis, the analysand's extra-analytic activities and his capacity for full emotional responsiveness outside the analytic situation are commonly impoverished; creativeness, too, is generally curtailed and tends to appear only in the final stage of the analysis, after the insightful resolution of certain specific sectors of the transference has been achieved. During the time of his self-analysis, however, Freud was not only capable of responding to his environment with strong, deep, varied, and appropriate emotions, as can be ascertained by a perusal of his correspondence, but he was arriving at the most original insights, discoveries, and formulations of his life, as is attested by the great work which was the crowning result of the labors of this period.

If Freud's self-analysis had been primarily an act of self-healing through insight, one would have expected it to end, parallel to the termination of the analysis of the usual transference neurosis, with the discovery of the meaning of the transference and, simultaneously, its resolution. In Freud's case, however, there seems to have occurred a dissolution of the transference bondage without corresponding insight, i.e., Freud's understanding of the full meaning of transference came only gradually, much later, and was derived from his clinical work. Freud's transference to Fliess must therefore be viewed as a phenomenon accompanying creative work: Freud's self-analysis was a creative spell which was simultaneously worked through analytically.

This phenomenon is outside the realm of pathology,[7] although it is distantly related to the clinically observable fact that a modicum of empathic contact with the analyst is necessary for the maintenance of a newly acquired capacity for artistic sublimation on the part of certain analytic patients.

Mr. E.,[8] for example, was suffering from a severe narcissistic personality disturbance with regressive swings that had the appearance of fleeting psychotic episodes. As a result of the systematic working through of his analysis, he gradually acquired the ability to channel certain formerly pathologically employed narcissistic cathexes into emotionally absorbing and fulfilling artistic activities. Both the leading symptom of his psychopathology (a voyeuristic perversion) and his newly acquired artistic sublimation were off-shoots of his lifelong intense concentration on the maintenance of visual contact with the world. Already in his earliest years he seems to have shifted the focus of his contact needs from his frustrated oral, tactile, and olfactory demands

---

[7] Ellenberger (1970), however, uses the term "creative illness" for such events.

[8] This patient is frequently referred to in Kohut (1971).

toward his vision, as could be reconstructed on the basis of transference fears lest his intense gaze overburden and destroy the (mother-)analyst. (Throughout the patient's childhood the patient's mother had been ill with malignant hypertension—she was frequently very tired, never picked him up when he was a baby, and was unable to give to the child the self-confirming emotional sustenance he needed. She died during the patient's late adolescence.) The significance of the patient's voyeuristic perversion—he was irresistibly driven by the dangerous urge to look at male genitals—can be gleaned from the details of the situation in which it made its first appearance. During the patient's early adolescence the boy and his mother were at a country fair. He had enjoyed himself alone on a high swing (undoubtedly in a preconscious elaboration of archaic flying fantasies) and, pleased with his skill and prowess, asked his mother to watch him perform. When the mother, who was tired and depressed, did not respond to his wish, he suddenly felt bereft of the buoyancy he had just experienced, and felt drained and empty. It was at that moment that he turned away from his mother and walked to a public toilet, driven by the irresistible wish to gaze at a powerful penis (see Kohut, 1971, pp. 158–159).

In the present context there is no need to spell out the metapsychological substance of the patient's perversion beyond the minimum necessary for understanding the relation between the patient's narcissistic transference bond, which had established itself in his analysis, and his ability to maintain a newly cathected artistic sublimation. The essence of the perversion could be gleaned from childhood memories (such as the episode at the country fair) and was confirmed over and over again as the transference was being worked through. The patient's developing self had been badly deprived of cohesion-maintaining narcissistic cathexes because of the dearth of appropriate responses (mirroring) to his narcissistic (-exhibitionistic) needs. His craving to fill an inner void, to obtain a sense of aliveness, therefore became intense; furthermore, there is little doubt that—because of innate endowment and accidental circumstances (e.g., the fact that he was deprived of tactile contact)—these needs became concentrated in the visual sphere. Deprived as it was, and severe as his regression might be, his self would never permanently disintegrate; he never quite gave up the hope that he would ultimately obtain the needed confirming-approving-mirroring response from the narcissistic object. As he offered himself (visually) to his mother (e.g., in the country fair) so, did he within the context of the analysis in the transference.

It is instructive to compare an early, beautifully elaborated attempt by the patient to channel the analysis and its insights into the visual-artistic area with the episode late in the analysis which we are contemplating here. At that time, too, it was a separation from the analyst that was the trauma to which the patient reacted. But then, under the impact of this trauma, he erected a rudimentary structure of artistic expression which was still directly related to the self-object analyst (see Kohut, 1971, pp. 130–132). It was an emergency step into art—the artistic product was crude and ephemeral. In the present episode, by contrast, the patient responded to the same trauma not with a crude forward move but with the temporary disintegration of the advanced structures of artistic expression—the artistic product was now completely unrelated to the needed selfobject—that he had in the meantime, in the course of the analysis, acquired via innumerable microinternalizations in response to microtraumata. And he was able now, with the aid of insight and on the basis of the different solidity of the newly acquired structures, to re-establish his interest in the artistic product, which was now elaborated and constituted an abiding discussion of his self. Still, the analytic work was not completed. Even now, the maintenance of the artistic sector of his personality depended to some extent on the presence of the analyst. Whenever the hope for an empathic mirroring response was disappointed, a regression took place, and instead of persisting in his demands and renewing his attempts to obtain narcissistic gratification on the level of "mirroring," he turned to the sexualized attempt to achieve his needed narcissistic sustenance through a visual merger with the symbol of powerful maleness with which he could thus identify.

It would be tempting to enter into a discussion of the meaning of the patient's perversion at this point, but—even in its briefest form—such an enterprise would lead us too far afield.[9] In our

---

[9] Those familiar with my studies of narcissism will have no problem recognizing that here again (as I first pointed out in my discussion of Patient A. [Kohut, 1971, see especially pp. 69ff.]) we can see that the perversion is not caused by the existing pregenital sexual fixations, but that it is a manifestation of the need

present context, however, we can say that in the transference the patient experienced over and over the following specific sequence of events: (1) he offered himself—or later his artistic product, i.e., the extension of his grandiose self—to the narcissistic object (the analyst in the mirror transference); (2) he was disappointed because of an empathic failure from the side of the analyst—or because of other narcissistic blows from him; (3) then followed a regression leading to the intensification of the voyeuristic perversion; (4) the analyst responded with an empathic interpretation of this reaction; (5) the perverse urge now subsided, and the patient renewed his attempt to obtain mirroring admiration. It was the working through of the repeated experience of this sequence that gradually increased the patient's mastery over the regressive trends and that buttressed his ability to persist in his creative efforts despite disappointments.

An episode that occurred after several years of analysis, when the patient had already made considerable progress, is of particular significance in illuminating the role the narcissistic object is called upon to play in support of the more or less precariously maintained ability to carry on creative activities. Mr. E.'s general condition had much improved by that time, and his whole life was now more satisfying and on a higher level. His homosexual voyeurism had nearly disappeared, and he was not only deriving considerable inner satisfaction from his art, but, since luckily he did indeed possess considerable talent, he was also receiving sufficient external acclaim to satisfy some of his needs for approving, accepting, and (self-)confirming responses. The patient was now able to weather the usual week-end separations from the analyst without feeling endangered by the pull of his voyeurism—clearly an indication of the considerable progress he had already made. On this occasion, however, he not only had to confront the tension created by the time gap between the last appointment of the present and the first appointment of the following week, he also had to confront the feeling of an increasing separation from the analyst in space. During this weekend it became necessary for him to undertake a trip to a city about two

---

to fill a structural defect. The visual merger with the powerful penis (including the accompanying unconscious or preconscious fellatio fantasy) constitutes the attempt to obtain needed narcissistic sustenance (to fill a structural void) and to escape from a sense of emptiness and depression.

hundred miles from Chicago because of some artistic work he had been commissioned to do there. As he left Chicago by train, he was not only still in high spirits, but his mind was creatively preoccupied with the work he was going to do upon his arrival. As mile after mile went by, however—specifically (as he reported in the Monday session), as mile after mile of distance interposed itself between him and the analyst whom, as he now began to realize, he had always fantasized as sitting in his analytic chair during the weekends, waiting for him to come back, the patient experienced again the old feeling he had thought he had overcome: a sense of depression, a painful lowering of self-esteem, a sense of inner emptiness, and a need to be filled up. As the train took him further and further away from Chicago, the sense of emptiness increased, and, simultaneously, his interest in the artistic task, which had formerly been so stimulating to him, declined. Finally, about halfway between Chicago and his destination, he suddenly felt the urge to follow a sailor into the toilet. It was at this moment that he was able to make use of the analytic insights he had acquired. He grasped the essence of what was going on in him, resisted the temptation, went through with his trip and his assignment (though not as zestfully and creatively as he had anticipated), and returned to Chicago. On the trip back he could observe in himself that his self-esteem began to rise, that the sense of inner emptiness diminished, and that his creative and artistic interests began to intensify again as the distance to the narcissistic object decreased.

I shall now return to Freud and his quasi analyst in order to examine the significance which the imago of Fliess may have had for Freud as narcissistic support with regard to the creative (nontherapeutic) aspects of his analysis. I am not overlooking the vast difference separating Freud's transference experience from that of Patient E.[10] As I said before, the phenomenon under

[10] I am not alluding here to the fact that Patient E.'s sublimatory activities were sustained by a *mirror* transference while Freud in the lonesome uneasiness of his voyage of discovery into the depth of the mind turned toward an omnipotent idealized figure, i.e., may be said to have established a relationship which is akin to an *idealizing* transference. These are small differences, no more than variations on a basic theme, which we may disregard in the present context. People whose self is in need of sustenance, whether because of the energic drain and anxiety during a creative spell or for other reasons, will tend to establish narcissistic relationships to archaic selfobjects—whether in the form of one of the varieties of a mirror transference or through a merger with an idealized imago.

consideration is outside the realm of psychopathology and is only distantly related to such occurrences as those illustrated by Mr. E.'s trip. Nevertheless, if we shift the focus of our attention from the specific focus of the narcissistic transference in psychopathology and examine instead the general psychological significance—whether in illness or in health—which the relationship to selfobjects may have for people, then the previous clinical material will serve as an acceptable background for the following constructions.

It is my main thesis that during periods of intense creativity (especially during its early stages) certain creative persons require a specific relationship with another person—a transference of creativity—which is similar to what establishes itself during the psychoanalytic treatment of one major group of narcissistic personality disorders.

In the treatment situation, the endopsychic substance of this relationship is the analysand's idealizing transference to the psychoanalyst. This transference is the manifestation of a phase of normal development, which, in consequence of the regression induced by the treatment situation, has been revived in a distorted form. During the normal phase of development that corresponds to the idealizing transference, the caretaking empathic adult is held to be omnipotent by the child, who obtains a sense of narcissistic well-being (of being whole and powerful, for example) when he is able to experience himself as part of the idealized selfobject. Under favorable conditions the adult's empathic response to the child sets up a situation in which the child's phase-appropriate need for a merger with an onipotent object is sufficiently fulfilled to prevent traumatization. This basic fulfillment of the need, however, is the precondition for the subsequent developmental task, which involves the child's gradual recognition that the adult is not omnipotent and that he, the child, is not a part of him but a separate person. In consequence of this gradual and phase-appropriate disillusionment, the idealizing cathexes are withdrawn from the archaic object and set up within the psychic apparatus (e.g., idealizing the values of the superego). In other words, an archaic selfobject imago has been transmuted into psychological structure. If this developmental task is not completed, however, then the personality will be lacking in sufficiently idealized psychological structures. In consequence of this defect, the person is deprived of one major endopsychic method by which he could maintain his self-esteem: the self's merging into the idealized superego by living up to the values harbored by this psychic structure. Yearning to find a substitute for the missing (or insufficiently developed) psychic structure, such persons are forever seeking, with addictionlike intensity and often through sexual means (the clinical picture may be that of perversion), to establish a relationsip to people who serve as stand-ins for the omnipotent idealized selfobject, i.e., to the archaic precursor of the missing inner structure. In everyday life and in the analytic transference the self-esteem of such persons is therefore upheld by their relations to archaic selfobjects.

Although I believe that the transference of creativity is a phenomenon akin to the idealizing transference, I do not claim that creative people are of necessity suffering from structural defects that drive them to seek archaic merger experiences. I suspect, however, that the psychic organization of some creative people is characterized by a fluidity of the basic narcissistic configurations,[11] i.e., that periods of narcissistic equilibrium (stable self-

---

[11] The metapsychological explanation of the processes of scientific and artistic creativity suggested here within the framework of the theory of narcissism (i.e., the theory of the two major narcissistic configurations and of their cathexes) should be compared with the important formulations offered by previous workers (in particular Sachs and Kris) within the frame of reference provided by the structural model of the mind.

Sachs (1942; see especially pp. 48–49) believes, in harmony with Freud (1908b), that the creative poet initially "uses his fantasy as a means of gaining narcissistic gratification for his own person." His guilt feelings, however, force him to shift his "narcissism" away from himself and onto his creation. The poet thus gives up more of his narcissism than average people, "but his work wins back immeasurably more of it than others can hope for."

Kris's relevant statements (1952b, pp. 59–62) about the sequence of "inspiration and elaboration" in the process of artistic creation are not only psychoanalytically sophisticated behavioral descriptions, they also provide us with an account of the processes of creation in metapsychological terms. Kris sees the creative process, as does Sachs, within the metapsychological context of the functions of the structural model of the mind. In contrast to Sachs' emphasis, Kris does not stress the motivational importance of the superego conflict, i.e., the motivational importance of guilt feelings, but the interplay of ego and id during the collaboration of two structures in the creative activity. To put Kris's formulation in a nutshell: during the phase of inspiration; the id holds sway, while during the phrase of elaboration, the ego predominates.

esteem and securely idealized internal values: steady, persevering work characterized by attention to details) are followed by (precreative) periods of emptiness and restlessness (decathexis of values and low self-esteem; addictive or perverse yearnings: no work), and that these, in turn, are followed by creative periods (the unattached narcissistic cathexes which had been withdrawn from the ideals and from the self are now employed in the service of the creative activity: original thought; intense, passionate work). Translating these metapsychological formulations into behavioral terms, one might say that a phase of frantic creativity (original thought) is followed by a phase of quiet work (the original ideas of the preceding phase are checked, ordered, and put into a communicative form, e.g., written down), and that this phase of quiet work is in turn interrupted by a fallow period of precreative narcissistic tension, which ushers in a phase of renewed creativity, and so on.

I am not prepared to say whether this three-phase schema applies to the vicissitudes of Freud's work and creativity, but I can furnish some evidence in support of the idea that this is so. There is no doubt, for example, that Freud had an enormous capacity for prolonged and concentrated attention to details in the service of the completion and perfection of his work (phase two of the three-phase schema) and that he possessed high, strongly cathected, internalized values. Furthermore, one might hypothesize that his intense oral-respiratory cravings (e.g., his increasing, unbreakable bondage to cigar smoking)[12] were related to a depressionlike state of precreative inner emptiness, which was the manifestation of the decathexis of the self as the narcissistic energies detached themselves and became available for the creative task.[13] Freud did indeed report that a certain distur-

---

[12] Freud himself believed that there was a connection between his addiction to cigars and his capacity to work. He wrote (in a letter to Fliess of June 12, 1895): "I have again begun to smoke, because I never stopped missing it (after fourteen months of abstinence) and because I have to spoil that psychic rascal in me, or else he won't do me any work" (my translation; cf. Schur, 1972, p. 86).

[13] The feeling of estrangement the creative person often experiences vis-à-vis the product of his creativity, his work, is in many instances not the result of structural conflicts (e.g., guilt about having produced something beautiful or discovered something important) but the direct expression of the fact that at the very moment of creativity the self is depleted, because the narcissistic cathexes have been shifted from the self to the work. In the productive activities of non-

bance of his well-being was a necessary precondition for his creativeness (Jones, 1953, pp. 345–346). Was Freud here describing the unpleasant feeling of tension that accompanies the precreative regression of narcissistic libido (i.e., an autoerotic tension state)? Did he at such times feel empty and depressed, and was there an addictionlike intensification of oral-respiratory intaking needs—all as manifestations of the decathexis of the narcissistic structures in consequence of the fact that the narcissistic energies had to remain in uncommitted suspension, waiting to be absorbed by the creative activity? I cannot do more here than to raise these questions. If these hypotheses could be confirmed, they would lend support to my interpretation of one aspect of Freud's relation to Fliess as a regression to the idealization of an archaic omnipotent figure.

In the foregoing, I supported the hypothesis that one aspect of Freud's relationship to Fliess should be understood as the expression of his regressively activated need for an idealized archaic omnipotent figure by demonstrating that this explanation fits meaningfully into the broader framework of a conception of creativeness in terms of the dynamics of narcissism. In the following, I will show that my interpretation is not only supported by its congruence with the aforementioned broader theory but also by empirical evidence gathered within the framework of (pre-)conscious motivations.

During creative periods, the self is at the mercy of powerful forces it cannot control; and its sense of enfeeblement is increased because it feels itself helplessly exposed to extreme mood swings which range from severe precreative depression to dangerous hypomanic overstimulation, the latter occurring at the moment when the creative mind stands at the threshold of creative activity. (For a summary of Freud's vivid description of his emotional state during creative periods, see Jones, 1953, pp. 343–345.) And when his discoveries lead the creative mind into lonely areas that

---

creative persons and in the phase of quiet work of creative minds the narcissistic cathexes are distributed between the self and the work, with the result that the self is experienced (and later remembered) as the active initiator, the source, the shaper of the product. During the phase of frantic creativity, however, the self is depleted because the narcissistic cathexes are concentrated on the work, with the result that the self is not experienced (and is later not remembered) as the initiator, source, or shaper of the product.

had not previously been explored by others, then a situation is brought about in which the genius feels a deep sense of isolation. These are frightening experiences, which repeat those over-whelmingly anxious moments of early life when the child felt alone, abandoned, unsupported.[14] Freud put it bitterly when he said (March 16, 1896), "I . . . live in such isolation that one might suppose I had discovered the greatest truths" (1887–1902, p. 161)—a statement to which one can add only that here a sense of humor aided Freud in confronting the fact that he had indeed discovered truths that could not but cause him to stand alone in the newly opened territory, alone until a few courageous pupils began to follow him. Small wonder, then, that creative artists and scientists—the latter at times in striking contrast to their fierce rationality in the central area of their creative pursuits—often attempt to protect their creative activity by surrounding it with superstitions and rituals. But while one creative mind will have to protect himself with "a pair of tall wax candles in silver hold-ers at the head of his manuscript" (the description of the novelist Aschenbach in Thomas Mann's *Death in Venice*) and while another (Schiller) had to work on a desk from the drawer of which the smell of rotten apples emanated (see Eckermann 1836–1848, *Conversations with Goethe,* Part 3; October 7, 1827), there are still others—among them, I believe, was Freud—who during the period of their most daring creativity will choose a person in the environment whom they can see as all-powerful, a figure with whom they can temporarily blend.

The transferences established by creative minds during periods of intense creativity are therefore much more closely related to the transferences that occur during the analysis of narcissistic personalities than to those that occur in the analysis of transfer-ence neuroses. In other words, we are dealing with either (a) the wish of a self which feels enfeebled during a period of creativity to retain its cohesion by expanding temporarily into the psychic structure of others, by finding itself in others, or to be confirmed by the admiration of others (resembling one of the varieties of a mirror transference) or (b) the need to obtain strength from an idealized object (resembling an idealizing transference). Thus,

[14] See in this context Székely's perceptive contributions (1967, 1970) concern-ing the fear of the new and unknown in scientists. For clinical material illustrat-ing such emotional states, see Gedo (1980).

relationships established during creative periods do not predominantly involve the revival of a figure from the (oedipal) past, which derives its transference significance primarily from the fact that it is still the target of the love and hate of the creative person's childhood.

It would be fascinating to pursue the investigation of the varieties of the narcissistic relationships (and of the details of the narcissistic bonds by which they are maintained) that creative people establish, especially during their creative periods. In the area of the grandiose self, for example, some evidence has already been accumulated in support of the assumption that the twin-ship relation to an alter ego may provide the necessary confirmation of the reality of the self during creative periods. Mary Gedo's studies (1980) show convincingly that under these conditions Picasso was in need of self-cohesion-providing relationships to alter-ego figures (e.g., to the painter Georges Braque). The presence of an alter ego and the narcissistic relationship to it, one might speculate, protected the self of the artist from the danger of irreversible fragmentation to which it felt exposed while it was drained of narcissistic energies during periods when the genius-artist allowed the visual universe to break into meaningless pieces before he reassembled them and, in so doing, gave Western man a new perception of the visible world.

Undoubtedly, the large areas of the relation between homosexuality and creativity, first explored by Freud (1910a, p. 59), will also be illuminated when we investigate it by taking into account the vicissitudes of the narcissistic cathexes. Although I am not able to present empirical data obtained through the systematic psychoanalytic investigation of a great creative artist or scientist, I will offer a substitute: the literary testimony of a great writer. The value of this evidence is enhanced by the fact that there is good reason to assume that the relevant insights contained in the artistic document under consideration were in essence derived from the writer's own experiences, in particular with regard to the vicissitudes of his own creativity. The examination of Thomas Mann's *Death in Venice* (Kohut, 1957) reveals that the essence of this beautiful novella is an almost scientifically exact portrayal of the disintegration of artistic sublimation. The artist Aschenbach, Mann's protagonist, had throughout his long creative life been able to channel the available free narcissistic

cathexes toward his artistic productions.[15] While in his childhood he must still have been in severe jeopardy—his childhood
self had been insufficiently sustained by his environment and
had been in danger of fragmentation—he had later become
capable of providing himself with the needed experience of psychological perfection and wholeness—i.e., the experience of basic
self-esteem—through the creation of works of art. Extensions or
duplications of the self were now available which he could invest
with narcissistic libido: he could give them formal perfection.
But, as the story begins, this ability is being lost. The artist is
aging, and his power to create replicas of the perfect self is wan-
ing. On the way to total disintegration, however—and here lies
the focus of the novella—we see the revival of the sexualized
precursor of the artistic product: the beautiful boy (though frail
and already marked for destruction) who is the symbolic stand-
in for the core of the still unaltered childhood self which craves
love and admiration. As "the cultural structure of a lifetime . . .
[is] . . . destroyed," i.e., as the writer's ability to deploy the narcissistic cathexes return from the work of art to the imago of the
fragmenting childhood self. There they rest briefly, delaying the
ultimate destruction of the personality for one more moment.

The deployment of the fluid narcissistic cathexes of creative
persons toward idealized imagoes seems to be even more common than their search for replicas or expansions of the grandiose self—as exemplified by the case of Aschenbach. At any rate,
man's need for the merger with a supporting idealized figure is
more easily observable.

But to return to Freud's self-analysis. If we accept that in its
essence Freud's self-analysis was not a self-therapeutic experience but rather the crowning achievement of his creative genius,
then we will understand why he did not discover the clinical
transference at that time. The end of Freud's self-analysis was
not analogous to the termination of the usual therapeutic analysis, i.e., it did not occur in consequence of the fact that the analysand (Freud) had recognized the transference, i.e., the illusory
aspects of his relationship with the analyst (Fliess), and that the
transference had been worked through. It was rather the opposite: the transference—an idealizing transference of creativity—

---

[15] I am in these remarks expressing the conclusions reached in an early investigation (1957b) in the terms of my more recent findings.

became superfluous and came to an end when the creative work done with the aid of the self-analysis had been consummated. In other words, for Freud during his most important creative spell, Fliess was the embodiment of idealized power; and Freud was able to dispense with the illusory sense of Fliess's greatness and thus with the narcissistic relationship—in contradistinction to a resolution of transference by insight—after he had completed his great creative task.

Charismatic and Messianic Personalities

One subsidiary question with regard to the transference of creativity still to be confronted concerns the problem of the specificity of the choice of the narcissistically cathected selfobject.

In the usual clinical circumstances, given the appropriately neutral attitude of the analyst and his noninterference with the unrolling of the endopsychic process elicited by the psychoanalytic situation, the transference will develop in accordance with preanalytically established endopsychic factors. The transference will portray the objects of the analysand's childhood, in particular as he loved and hated them in the context of the crucial events which formed his personality, especially its neurotic aspects. True, some actual features of the analyst's personality and of his actions will become temporarily amalgamated during the analysis with imagoes stemming from the analysand's childhood. But these details of the clinical transference, while of considerable tactical importance in clinical psychoanalysis, do not constitute its essence: their relation to the core of the transference, i.e., to the genetic center of the psychopathology, is the same as the relation between the day's residue and the unconscious dream-wish from childhood in dream psychology.

In the transference of creativity, on the other hand, the opposite may be held to be true. Here, it is a current situation that is central, a situation in which an enfeebled self, drained of its cohesion-maintaining cathexis and engaged in the daring exploration of the moon landscapes of the unknown, will seek the temporary aid that comes to it from the relation with an archaic selfobject, particularly with an idealized parent imago. True enough, the transference of creativity repeats an archaic childhood situation: it is a reversion to that phase of development in which the self in formation had not yet separated itself from the figures in its environment—had not separated itself, in other words, from the imagoes which for the social-psychological observer are the "objects" of the child. But the child still experienced these figures in the early environment as belonging to the self, they were still "selfobjects." Now, if in the analysis of a narcissistic personality disturbance the psychoanalytic situation is established appropriately, then a narcissistic transference will develop spontaneously, and it will take on the predetermined form—or the predetermined sequence or mixture of forms— that is the outgrowth of the analysand's childhood history and of the correlated fixation points in his development. These conditions, however, must not be expected to prevail in the creative personality—at least, they are not essential.[16]

The essential ingredients of the usual clinical transference are therefore preanalytically established, and the personality of the analyst and other reality factors concerning him must in the main be taken into account only on the basis of the question whether they might *interfere* with the unfolding, the maintenance, and the working through of the transference. This maxim does not hold true with regard to the transference of creativity, however—whether a twinship is sought (in which the alter ego must fit its role, i.e., it must *in fact* resemble the needy personality of the creative person) or whether it is the archaic idealized omnipotent object that is required (which must then *in fact* have certain features that make it suitable for the role the creative person assigns to it).

And what are the characteristic features of the person who is especially suitable to become the admired omnipotent selfobject for the creative person during the period when he makes his

---

[16]Creativity may be embedded in a great variety of personality make-ups, ranging from normal to psychotic. There are undoubtedly many creative persons who, if scrutinized with an eye to classifying them in terms of psychopathology, would have to be counted among the narcissistic personality disorders. While, on the one hand, the fluidity of the narcissistic cathexes in the creative mind creates vulnerabilities similar to those to which (noncreative) narcissistic personalities are exposed, and, on the other hand, the favorable outcome of the psychoanalytic treatment of narcissistic personality disorders is not infrequently due to the fact that the patient succeeds in channeling some of the formerly pathogenic narcissistic energies toward creative pursuits, spontaneous creativity is, in its essence, not related to the narcissistic personality disorders.

decisive steps into new territory? Certain types of narcissistically fixated persons (even bordering on the paranoid)—they display an apparently unshakable self-confidence and voice their opinions with absolute certainty—are specifically suitable to be the objects of the idealizing needs of the creative person's temporarily enfeebled self during a creative spell. Those who fall into this psychological category are obviously not likely to offer themselves to the scrutiny of the psychoanalyst. They do not feel ill, and their self-esteem is high. What makes them specifically able to play the role of the idealized archaic object for those who are in need of it, and what makes them ready to fill it, is the fact that the maintenance of their self-esteem depends on the incessant use of certain mental functions: they are continually judging others—usually pointing up the moral flaws in other people's personalities and behavior[17]—and, without shame or hesitation, they set themselves up as the guides and leaders and gods of those who are in need of guidance, of leadership, and of a target for their reverence. In many instances it appears that such charismatic and messianic personalities have fully identified themselves with either their grandiose self or their idealized superego. For most of us, the herd of common mortals, the ideals[18] we harbor are direction-setting symbols of perfection. They provide us with narcissistic pleasure when we come near to the target they have set for us, and they deprive us of narcissistic sustenance when we fall short of it by too wide a margin. The messianic leader figure, however, is done with the task of measuring himself against the ideals of his superego: his self and the idealized structure have become one.

Certainly, the endopsychic arrangements that support the self-esteem of the charismatic or messianic person deprive his personality of elasticity. Mobility and the reliance on several different sources of self-esteem are in the long run safer ways of

[17] The role that the function of judgment plays for most people in the psychic economy of narcissism must not be underestimated. I am not speaking here primarily of the mechanism of projection, with the aim of which our faults are assigned to others, but of the innumerable nonspecific acts of judgment with regard to the behavior, the morality, the personalities of others. For example, the pleasant glow experienced by participants in judgmental bull sessions in which those not present are taken apart is, in my opinion, due not so much to the discharge of sublimated sadism but rather to the enhanced self-esteem supplied by the act of judging and the comparison with those who are being judged.

[18] I am here, for the moment, disregarding the grandiose self.

psychological survival than the maintenance of a rigid narcissistic equilibrium through the employment of a single set of restricted functions. Indeed, the endopsychic equilibrium of the charismatic leader or of the messiah seems to be of the all-or-nothing type: there are no survival potentialities between the extremes of utter firmness and strength, on the one hand, and utter destruction (psychosis; suicide) on the other. I would nevertheless like to stress that, in reflecting about the messianic or charismatic leader figure, the depth psychologist should not too quickly abandon his objective stance and espouse an attitude of moral judgment. Charismatic and messianic personalities come in all shades and degrees. Some among them are no doubt close to psychosis. These are dogmatic persons who lack all empathy with the inner life of others—with the notable exception of their keen grasp of even the subtlest reactions in other people that are related to their own narcissistic requirements. There are other messianic persons, however, in whom the coalescence between self and idealized superego, while chronic, is only partial, i.e., where the nonmessianic sectors of the self, although in harmony with the messianic substance of the personality, may at times even retain the freedom of displaying a sense of quite nonmessianic humor. It must be stressed, in addition, that the social effects of messianic and charismatic personalities are not necessarily deleterious. A figure of the kind required in times of grave crisis cannot be of the more modest, self-relativistic personality type to which those chosen to positions of leadership during quiescent historical periods generally belong. In a moment of crisis and profound anxiety, the nation will turn to the messianic or charismatic personality—not primarily because it has recognized his skills and his efficiency, but because it realizes that he will satisfy its need to identify with his unquestioned righteousness or with his firmness and security.

The relation between the British people and Winston Churchill before, during, and after the greatest danger ever faced by England (and the Western world) is a good example in this context. Churchill (a leader, by the way, whose mystique emanated, I believe, predominantly from the grandiose self, not from the idealized superego), who was unacceptable before the crisis, filled his role to perfection during the crisis and was the unquestioned leader of the nation. Yet he was discarded after the crisis had subsided. The British people identified themselves with him and with his unshakable belief in his and, by extension, the nation's strength so long as their selves felt weak in the face of the serious danger; as soon as victory had been attained, however, the need for a merger with an omnipotent figure subsided, and they were able to turn from him to other (noncharismatic) leaders.[19] It takes little effort to discern the parallel between the temporary needs of the enfeebled self of the creative person and the temporary needs of an endangered nation in times of crisis; in both instances the idealization of the leader, the narcissistic transference to him, is abandoned when the need for it has come to an end.

In contrast to the endopsychic conditions prevailing in the messianic and charismatic personality, the ego of the average person, of the man who has attained that state we might refer to as average mental health, attempts to fulfill two tasks. On the one hand, it responds to the pressure of the grandiose self in the depth of the psyche; but, when it strives for the enhancement of self-esteem through activities that fulfill the ambitions nourished by the demands of the grandiose self, it does so in a realistic way. In particular, it takes into account the needs and feelings of others, of the fellow man with whom it is in empathic contact. On the other hand, as its second task, the normal ego attempts to exert its initiative and control in order to bring about behavior approaching that demanded by the idealized standards of the superego. In so doing, it will compare the performance of the actual self with that demanded by the idealized standards and will acknowledge the fact that perfection cannot become reality. In consequence of this recognition, however, its sense of narcissistic pleasure when the self comes close to living up to the ideals

[19]Two relevant topics would be worthy of study by the psychoanalytic historian and sociologist: The first is the examination of the political genius of a people, i.e., its skills, its political savvy, as manifested in its capacity to choose the right kind of leader in various historical situations. The second concerns the specific relation between leader and followers, in particular whether (1) the leader is apt to be idealized (in this case I would designate him as a messianic personality, indicating by this term that his self has largely merged with the idealized superego); (2) the leader is apt to become the target, in the main nonidealized, for an identification with an omnipotent object (in this case I would designate him as a charismatic personality, indicating by this term that his self has largely become the carrier of the grandiose self); or (3) the leader is apt to be simply the executor of certain ego functions of those who have chosen him (in this case he is neither a messianic nor a charismatic personality).

will be a limited one. And, in particular, there will again be empathic contact with others, which will prevent the development of a sense of absolute moral superiority over the fellow man. When comparing his own performance with the performance of others, the judgment of the nonmessianic person will be influenced by his empathic understanding of the fact that the others, too, experience limited failures and successes in the moral sphere, and thus no unrealistic feeling develops that the self is perfect and that the selves of other people are in essence corrupt.

But what is it that enables charismatic personalities to maintain their sense of power (as if their real self and the archaic grandiose self were one), and what bestows on messianic personalities their sense of absolute moral righteousness (as if their real self and the idealized selfobject were one) that makes them so irresistibly attractive to those who need to merge with self-assured leaders and self-righteous messiahs?

Some of these personalities appear to belong to the group to which Freud first referred, in a somewhat different context, as "the exceptions" (1916a, pp. 311–315). Freud thought that some people can allow themselves immoral actions all their lives because they feel they have suffered an unjust punishment in childhood and have therefore, ahead of time, expiated their later misdeeds, which they can now commit with inner impunity.[20]

Although, as stated earlier, messianic and charismatic persons are not likely to become willing subjects of the psychoanalyst's clinical scrutiny, I have encountered a number of patients in my psychoanalytic and psychotherapeutic practice who were close to the character type I have in mind. My clinical experience with such patients allows me to draw some tentative conclusions about the type of personality structure that may manifest charismatic and messianic features and especially about the genetic matrix that seems to favor the development of such personalities.

These persons appear to have no dynamically effective guilt feelings and never suffer any pangs of conscience about what

---

[20] Freud describes the psychological state of Shakespeare's King Richard III through the medium of an imaginary soliloquy about the consequences of being congenitally deformed: "I have the right to be an exception, to disregard the scruples by which others let themselves be held back. I may do wrong myself, since wrong has been done to me" (1916a, pp. 314–315).

they are doing. They are sensitive to injustices done to them, quick to accuse others—and very persuasive in the expression of their accusations—and thus are able to evoke guilt feelings in others, who tend to respond by becoming submissive to them and by allowing themselves to be treated tyrannically by them. As far as I could discern, however, these persons do not primarily maintain the conviction of having already in childhood expiated their present evilness. The dynamic essence of their current behavior appears to me to lie in a stunting of their empathic capacity: they understand neither the wishes nor the frustrations and disappointments of other people. At the same time, their sense of the legitimacy of their own wishes and their sensitivity to their own frustrations are intense. Genetically important is the fact, as formulated in gross approximation, that these persons suffered early severe narcissistic injuries mainly because of the unreliability and unpredictability of the empathic responses to them from the side of either the echoing-mirroring or idealized selfobject. To be more specific: intense feelings of self-confidence obtained through echoing-mirroring responses (e.g., the empathic mother's proud smile) and intense feelings of security obtained through the merger with the omnipotent selfobject (e.g., being held and carried empathically by the adult) seem in the childhood of these persons to have been followed by abrupt and unpredictable frustrations. As the result of this trauma, the developmental process of the gradual integration and neutralization of the archaic narcissistic structures was interrupted, and the child, perhaps with the aid of certain unusually strong congenital abilities in the realm of the maintenance of self esteem (we might here speak with Hartmann [1939] of the primary autonomy of these functions), took over prematurely and in toto the functions that the archaic selfobjects should still have performed for him. We are thus not dealing with persons who have escaped guilt by prior expiation. These persons do not live in accordance with the standards of an inner world regulated by guilt feelings—rather, they live in an archaic world, which, as they experience it, has inflicted the ultimate narcissistic injury on them, i.e., in a world that has withdrawn its empathic content from them after having first, as if to tease them, given them a taste of its security and delights. They responded to this injury by becoming superempathic with themselves and with their own needs, and they have remained enraged about a world that has tried to take from them something they consider to be rightfully their own: the response of the selfobject, i.e., a part of the archaic self. Self-righteously, they are themselves performing functions the selfobject was supposed to perform; they assert their own perfection, and they demand full control over the other person, whom they need as regulator of their self-esteem, without regard for his rights as an independent person. In other words, the prior injustice they suffered was the abrupt withdrawal of narcissistic sustenance, and what the world judges to be their present misdeeds is to them the expression of justified narcissistic demands.

Since mixed cases may well be encountered most frequently, I venture the opinion, at the risk of being overschematic, that those personalities who manifest charismatic strength and self-certainty (often coupled with self-righteously expressed self-pitying and hypochondriacal complaints) have suffered a traumatic withdrawal of empathy from the side of the selfobjects who were expected to respond to the child's mirroring needs, while those with messianic features have suffered analogous disappointments from the side of the archaic idealized object. Furthermore, if we consider the effect of these traumata from the developmental point of view of social psychology, we can say that in both instances the withdrawal of the selfobject led to a severe reduction of the educational power of the environment. If the needed narcissistic sustenance is self-righteously and angrily demanded, rather than having to be earned, then the object loses his leverage as an educational factor. It can no longer exert its influence in leading the child toward the gradual modification of its narcissistic demands in the spheres of both the grandiose self and the archaic precursor of the internalized ideals.

Group Psychology and the Historical Process

The elucidation of the personality of the charismatic and messianic person and of the psychological basis of the intense relationship the followers of such a person establish with him is an important task for the depth psychologist who, with the tools of psychoanalysis, attempts to investigate group processes and their effect on the dynamics of history. Although, within the confines

of the present essay, I do not illuminate the details of the interplay between the personality of a specific leader, the response of
his followers, and the dynamics of the course of the correlated
specific historical events, the psychoanalytic historian will have
no trouble finding promising subjects for study in this area. Two
brief examples here will clarify my meaning. One of them, Daniel Schreber, a historically insignificant figure, is surely better
known to the psychoanalyst than to the student of general history, since he was the father of a man whom Freud described in
one of his great case histories; by contrast, the other one, Adolf
Hitler, needs no introduction, since he is known to everyone as
one of the most fateful historical personalities of modern times.

Daniel Gottlob Moritz Schreber, the father of the *Senatspräsi-
dent* with dementia paranoides, was the leader of a very popular
health cult. Like most leaders of cults and sects, he had absolute
convictions within the area of his mission—in his case, convictions within the area of health morality, i.e., of the importance
of physical exercise, good posture, clean living, etc.—and his
teachings received an enthusiastic response not only in Germany
but also in other countries, e.g., in England. So far as I know,
the dynamics of his influence on the numerous devoted followers of his cult have not been investigated, but (thanks to the
research done by Baumeyer, 1956, Niederland, 1951, 1959a,
1959b, 1960, 1963; and others) we have a good deal of information about his empathic and tyrannical treatment of his children, which seems to have constituted a decisive genetic factor
in the development of his son's famous psychosis. And there is
Hitler, still essentially enigmatic in his personality and in his
seemingly irresistible effect on Germany. His convictions were
absolute and, in certain areas, could not be questioned or modified. After a lonesome, hypochondriacal, self-doubting period
as a young adult, he emerged with a new rigid nucleus of
immovable opinions which from that time on remained
untouchable whatever his changes and vacillations might be. He
knew with complete certainty what was evil and had to be eradicated in this world of ours, and what was good and worth preserving. His utter certainty that the Jews were an evil and
destructive element which had infected the clean and healthy
body of the godlike German race was from then on the center
of his being and not only insured the maintenance of his own

heightened self-esteem, but invited the participation of the German nation in this blissful self-image through the merger with him.

Schreber's father and Hitler—and perhaps in some more or less distantly related way personalities like Wilhelm Fliess—different as they are, what do they have in common? They seem to combine an absolute certainty concerning the power of their selves and an absolute conviction concerning the validity of their ideals with an equally absolute lack of empathic understanding for large segments of feelings, needs, and rights of other human beings and for the values cherished by them. They understand the environment in which they live only as an extension of their own narcissistic universe. They understand others only insofar—but here with the keenest empathy!—as they can serve as tools toward their own narcissistic ends or insofar as they interfere with their own purposes. It is not likely that depth psychology will find effective means to influence such persons, at least not those who present themselves in the arena of history. But the historian-analyst and the analyst-historian may well be able to make contributions that will not only increase our psychological grasp of such personalities, but will also provide answers to two interrelated questions: How do the characteristic psychological features of the messianic and charismatic person dovetail with the widespread yearning for archaic omnipotent figures? And what are the specific historical circumstances that tend to increase this yearning?

To repeat: there may well be a wide gap separating the personality of such a nearly unique historical figure as Hitler from that of a not atypical founder of a common health cult such as Daniel G. M. Schreber. And an even wider gap may well separate personalities of the type of Schreber's father from those of the type of Wilhelm Fliess. Future investigations of the personalities of these and other notable figures who, in some historically significant setting, exerted their attraction on others—whether on whole nations, or on smaller groups, or on single susceptible individuals in times of crisis—may well be able to demonstrate what they have in common. Were there similar psychological features that made all of them so irresistible? Similar traits that were the secret of their adamant strength, their apparently all-knowing certainty? And did the effect they had on others lead to similar or analogous consequences? How did those fare—their followers, their children—who could not extricate themselves from the bonds to the charismatic or messianic figure who was their leader, their father? These and related questions will surely prove to be a worthy challenge for the psychoanalytic historian.

Let us then return to one of the central themes touched upon over and over in the preceding pages: the relation of Freud to Fliess during the period when Freud's self was enfeebled while it undertook a daring exploratory venture. Is this need, which arose in Freud during his courageous voyage into the unknown, related, if ever so distantly, to the need felt by populations who follow a charismatic leader, or even to the need of a hypochondriac who swears by the teachings of a health messiah? I think there might well be a similar set of psychological factors active in all these relationships and that the time will come when we will be able to turn toward their exploration in depth, not only with regard to Freud's relation to Fliess but perhaps also with regard to our own relation to the figure of Freud.

I am keenly aware that the preceding presentation is tentative and speculative to an unusual degree. Instead of adducing a sufficient number of specific data—data, for example, concerning Freud's experiences during his self-analysis, or data that would illuminate the personality of Wilhelm Fliess—I have relied largely on the internal logic and consistency of my ideas and on the indirect evidence of clinical phenomena analogous to those for which I gave no direct empirical support. This shortcoming is regrettable and needs to be justified.

What was the essence of the task to which I addressed myself? Why did it have to be approached so tentatively? And what is the reason for the fact that it was carried out so incompletely?

The task is to apply psychoanalytic knowledge to the investigation of group psychology with the specific aim of making a contribution to the explanation of historical events, of the course— or, expressed more courageously, the process—of history. I suspect that the seemingly most expedient application of analysis in this area, the investigation of the personalities of individuals who have exerted a decisive influence on the course of historical events, can make only a limited contribution to a scientifically valid explanation of history within the framework of depth psychology. I think rather that psychoanalysis must find novel approaches if it is to provide us with more comprehensive explanations of historical phenomena that will increase man's mastery over his historical destiny. To be specific: in addition to the study of historical figures, the psychoanalytic historian must also undertake the study of historical processes, of the dynamics of historical events.

If the study of historical sequences is to be pursued successfully, however, it will have to be coordinated with a number of basic investigations of the social field. What I have in mind here is the psychoanalytic study of (more or less large) groups: their formation, cohesion, fragmentation; or, stated in more specific terms, the circumstances that favor their formation, the nature of the psychological cement that holds them together, the psychological conditions under which they begin to manifest regressive behavior and begin to crumble, etc. It will have become obvious to those who are familiar with my recent work that I am suggesting, as a potentially fruitful approach to a complex problem, that we posit the existence of a certain psychological configuration with regard to the group—let us call it the "group self"[21]—

[21] I believe that here we will find a depth-psychological approach to the scientific illumination of such currently ill-defined, impressionistic concepts as national character, and the like. The notion of a nationally, ethnically, or culturally determined "identity"—a "group identity"—must also be differentiated from the concept of a "group self." The considerations which apply to the differentiation of the analogous concepts in individual psychology are also valid in the present context (see Kohut 1970a, pp. 578–580, and Kohut 1972b, pp. 623–624, the comparison between the "psychopathological events of late adolescence described by Erikson" and the vicissitudes of the self). The sense of a person's identity, whether he views himself as an individual or as belonging to a particular group, pertains to his conscious or preconscious awareness of the manifestations of a psychological surface configuration—it concerns a self-representation that relates to the conscious and preconscious goals and purposes of his ego and to the conscious and preconscious idealized values of his superego. The psychoanalytic concept of a self, however—whether it refers to the self of an individual or to the self of a person as a member of a group or, as a "group self," to the self of a stable association of people—concerns a structure that dips into the deepest reaches of the psyche. Indeed, I have become convinced that the pattern of an unconscious nuclear self (the central unconscious ambitions of the grandiose self and the central unconscious values of the internalized idealized parent imago) is of crucial importance with regard to the overriding sense of fulfillment or failure that characterizes a person's outlook on his life, to some extent independent of the presence or absence of neurotic conflict, suffering, symptom, or inhibition. And I am now suggesting that these considerations concerning the influence of the basic unconscious narcissistic configurations in individual existence are valid also with regard to the life of the group, i.e., that the basic patterns of a nuclear

which is analogous to the self of the individual. We are then in a position to observe the group self as it is formed, as it is held together, as it oscillates between fragmentation and reintegration, as it shows regressive behavior when it moves toward fragmentation, etc.—all in analogy to phenomena of individual psychology to which we have comparatively easy access in the clinical (psychoanalytic) situation.

It is too early to say how successful this approach will be, but not too early to suggest that it should be tried. The difficulties are great, since the relevant depth-psychological data about the group self have to be obtained with the aid of a specific instrument of observation: introspection and empathy. It is with regard to the problem concerning the accessibility of such data that I return to the psychoanalytic group. (With renewed reluctance, I am reminded once more of the concept of a "psychoanalytic movement," but I must not shrink from it in the present none-valuative context.) The history of the psychoanalytic movement—its formation, the crystallization and sequestration of dissident groups, it continuity despite changes—should, in a certain sense, constitute an excellent study topic for the psychoanalyst who pursues the investigation of group processes. Potentially at least—and I say this in full awareness that my suggestion will undoubtedly be greeted with humor or sarcasm—this is the group with the greatest insight about itself. It is the group, in other words, that should be expected to supply the researcher with the maximum number of useful data relevant to the study of the nature of group cohesion and of the causes of group disintegration. Furthermore, there is no need to be defensive about the fact that the psychoanalytic community offers to the observer a rich field for the investigation of behavioral phenomena (including the whole spectrum of the manifestations of narcissistic rage—the aggressions of the members of the group against each other) that accompany group regressions.

There are, of course, many obstacles standing in the way of an objective assessment of the psychoanalytic community by psychoanalysts. Such a self-study is a difficult but by no means impossible task. I rather think it likely that despite the obvious

---

group-self (the group's central ambitions and ideals) not only account for the continuity and the cohesion of the group, but also determine its most important actions.

difficulties (or, perhaps, because the difficulties are obvious) the self-investigation of the psychoanalytic community by analysts is more promising than analogous studies which could be undertaken by other groups.

When I speak here of the self-analysis of the psychoanalytic community, I am, of course, not contemplating a group enterprise. The psychological revelations that grow out of the matrix created by group meetings are obtained in consequence of the psychological regression imposed on the individual by immersion into the group. Group pressure diminishes individuality; it leads to a primitivization of the mental processes, in particular to a partial paralysis of the ego and to a lowering of resistances. The diminution of the influence of the ego is then followed by the cathartic expression of archaic (or at any rate undisguised) impulses, emotions, and ideation, i.e., by the revelation of material not accessible in normal circumstances. The insights I have in mind cannot be obtained in a regressive atmosphere. The valid self-analysis of the psychoanalytic group—or of any group—must not only rest on the clear, nonregressive perception of archaic psychological experiences that arise within the group; it also requires the intellectual and emotional mastery of this material. The validity of the insights obtained will be demonstrated by the fact that the pressure to act out (especially to act out angrily, the principal symptom of group psychopathology) will be diminished within the group. The individual who wishes to make decisive steps toward new depth-psychological insights concerning the group must therefore be able to remain deeply and directly involved in the group processes—but instead of acting them out, he must be able to tolerate the tension of seeming passivity: all his energies must be withdrawn from participating action and concentrated on participating thought. Only if he can maintain full emotional participation with the group processes of his own group, yet channel all his energies toward his cognitive functions (specifically the gathering of data through empathic observation and the subsequent explanation of the observed data)—only then will he be able to make those decisive discoveries and obtain those crucial new insights which will deepen our understanding of the behavior of the group and its members.

Group processes are largely activated by narcissistic motives. We may therefore hope that the fact that training analysts are now paying increasing attention to the narcissistic dimensions of the personality of analytic candidates will have favorable results in the area under discussion. The strengthened ego dominance over the narcissistic sector of their personalities which future generations of analysts will obtain may, in particular, be expected to facilitate the investigation of group processes within the psychoanalytic community. And we may also assume that one or another gifted psychoanalyst will be aided in his investigations concerning the influence of narcissistic motives on the behavior of the psychoanalytic community by the insights given him by his training analysis with regard to his own narcissistic strivings.

Among the various areas that will have to be studied within the context of the psychological self-scrutiny of the psychoanalytic community, the (changing) significance of the figure of Freud for the group will prove to occupy a place of paramount importance. But the time is not quite ripe for such an undertaking. Conscious hesitations dictated by considerations of tact and decorum, as well as unconscious inhibitions, still interfere too strongly with our ability to maintain the degree of objectivity required if we wish through the creative act of the group's self-analysis to make a valid contribution to psychoanalytic group psychology and to the psychology of the historical process. But I also think that, measured by the yardstick of history, the time is not far off when psychoanalysts will indeed be able to undertake such studies with the hope of reaching objectively valid conclusions.

I am therefore justifying the presentation of this speculative and tentative essay by saying that it should be regarded as a blueprint for the future. Clearly, I believe that my suggestions concerning the meaning of Freud's self-analysis and the significance Fliess had for Freud during his self-analysis will be corroborated by the detailed work of the future analytic historian, who will look upon "the origins of psychoanalysis" with a fresh eye. Although his task will remain a difficult one—i.e., he will have to reconstruct complex psychological situations across a wide gap of time on the basis of data culled from written documents[22]— his inner readiness for it will be greater than ours, and the emo-

[22] The collection of historical material concerning the history of psychoanalysis undertaken by the Sigmund Freud Archives will be of inestimable value for future researchers in many of the areas referred to in this essay.

tional atmosphere of the social circumstances in which he will perform it will be more propitious than that in which we live. The assessment of Freud's psychological state at the peak of his creative life, the scrutiny of Fliess's personality, and, above all, the investigation of the role played by the figure of Freud in shaping the history of the psychoanalytic community (and thus in shaping the development of the science of psychoanalysis): these are tasks that must be undertaken by future generations of analysts—perhaps even by the next one—with that favorable mixture of empathic closeness and scientific detachment not yet available to the psychoanalyst of our day.

In view of the fact that I have contemplated the possibility that the community of psychoanalytic scholars might someday, in a not-too-distant tomorrow, undertake through the work of some of its creative thinkers the task of a self-scrutiny in depth of the psychoanalytic community itself, it seems appropriate to close with a few remarks on the nature of scientific progress in psychoanalysis.

Decisive progress in man's knowledge of himself is, in my opinion, not primarily a cognitive feat, but achieved mainly as a consequence of what, expressed in everyday language, must be called an act of courage. Pioneering discoveries in depth psychology require not only a keen intellect but also characterological strength, because they are in essence based on the relinquishment of infantile wishes (see Freud, 1932) and on discarding illusions that have protected us against anxiety. I have little doubt that, even in fields outside of the investigation of complex psychological states, pioneering discoveries require an analogous measure of courage.[23] But I would assume that his cognitive detachment toward the physical universe he investi-

[23] These views are in harmony with Freud's opinion (1917a) that the discoveries of Copernicus and Darwin, like his own, constituted severe blows to the narcissism of man. These discoveries, I will add, rested first and foremost on the courageous overcoming of inner resistances, because the discoverers had to deprive themselves of an illusion which had protected them against coming face to face with the painful recognition of the relative smallness and insignificance of their selves. It must not be forgotten, furthermore, that attacks on grandiose fantasies elicit dangerous narcissistic rage against the offender (see Kohut, 1972b). In addition to their inner strength, therefore, the three great discoverers had to be able to muster considerable social courage when they communicated their findings to their contemporaries, whose wrath, as they undoubtedly anticipated at least preconsciously, they would now have to face.

gates protects a physicist, for example, or an astronomer, from the kind of fear the depth psychologist experiences when he, alone, is face to face with unpleasant psychological reality. I would at least claim that this assumption is valid in our day, when scientific findings in the physical and biological sciences are no longer effectively opposed on moral grounds.

But be that as it may in these other branches of human knowledge, I am certain that decisive progress in the area of depth psychology is tied to personal acts of courage by the investigator who not only suffers anxiety but tends to be maligned and ostracized. It is therefore not an accident that one of the greatest steps of individual psychology, a gigantic advance toward the scientific understanding of the inner life of the individual, was made as the result of the victorious outcome of the grueling process of one man's inner struggles, Freud's creative self-analysis. Could it be that the analogous step in group psychology, the decisive advance toward a valid depth-psychological understanding of the experiences and actions of the group, will be the result of a similarly courageous self-scrutiny of the psychoanalytic community by itself? I know that the future cannot be predicted with any degree of reliability by analogy with the past, that the success of Freud's genius in the field of individual psychology may not be repeatable with regard to the field of group psychology, despite the intense efforts of future analysts. But of one thing I am convinced: should any group ever be able to overcome its inner resistances and thus make a decisive step toward the understanding of the dynamics of its behavior, the nature and development of its group self, and the genetics of its conflicts and of the oscillations of its self—should a group ever be able to succeed in these tasks, it will have laid the foundations for a valid psychological understanding of history.

Conversations
With Heinz Kohut

8

The Psychoanalyst and The Historian

(*January 29, 1981*)

STROZIER: Do you see a parallel between the activities of the historian and the psychoanalyst?

KOHUT: Yes, of course. The psychoanalytic historian looks at his material in a way that is similar to the way an analyst listens to his patient, except that there is no active free association from the observed field. You don't tell historical data, "Never mind whether it's embarrassing or seems unimportant, say what you feel." But the listening or the looking process is the same; that's why it's beyond the bound of the basic rule.

STROZIER: You have suggested that self psychology introduces something special in the way the analyst watches the unfolding transference in the clinical setting and the way the historian scrutinizes the struggle of a self to realize its basic patterns in history. What is special about self psychology?

KOHUT: One of the many differences between classical analysis and self psychology is the attention it pays to the time axis. Traditional psychoanalysis ignores or at any rate certainly underemphasizes this factor. The metaphor or the aphorism I use to explain this difference is that classical analysis discovered the depression of the child in the adult and self psychology discovered the depression of the adult in the depths of the child. Now, this is not just a nice juggling of words—it is that too; it happens to be a nice phrase—but what I meant of course is that the depression of a lonely child is based in the dim realization that the future will not be fulfilled. The entire life cycle is implied as the self's nuclear program is laid down in an individual. The nonfulfillment of that program is evoked in anticipation by the hopeless and depressed child, who then turns to pleasure gain rather than to the fulfillment of the program. Pathological and pathogenic drive phenomena are a turning away from the self. Isolated drive takes over. Classical concepts assume that the drive activity is the normal beginning, and that only gradually drives get tamed and organized. My feeling is that what seems to be primitive is in fact fully organized, only in a different way. I think this idea parallels what is true in the concepts of modern anthropology that does not like—so far as I understand—the idea of treating primitive cultures as archaic and different. They're different, certainly, but they are also perfect in their own way; so also is the newborn baby perfect in its own way. It is not a bundle of disconnected drives but an assertive unit that has a purpose and a future. In history, too, we must think in terms of destiny. It's a much abused word. But, you know, so much pathology is a misunderstood and slanted perception of something that is really there. I think nations or peoples or groups have their program too.

STROZIER: Do you think there has been a historical change in the meanings of time, that there is something new in the post-modern understanding of what the future means?

KOHUT: But it wouldn't be a change in history that you are talking about but a change in the attitude of historians. I'm interested in that. I don't believe the actual facts have changed, at least not in these broadest of all terms. In *The Restoration of the Self* (1977) I compared the Freudian past with the Proustian past and found that they were essentially different. One is a search for an enclave of disturbance that once found can be, as it were, removed and functioning improved. It is a physicalistic model, like abscess draining, and it has its own psychological history via hypnosis. The use of hypnosis by the early analysts, then, was a decisive step. Its aim was not to change manifest behavior but to get the patient to remember the past under pressure. The pathogenic enclave that was unconscious and overlayered by healthy tissue could be drained and then the healthy tissue could function better, since it was no longer plagued by the pus of the pathogenic repressed. Psychoanalysis was only interested in the past in order to understand better the present.

Later the emphasis shifted to overcoming of the resistances, for with that the whole psychological tissue in its depth changed. That is the outlook of modern psychoanalysis, including ego psychology. I would think the predominant attitude of the historian when he examines a bit of history is of that same type. It tries to explain the present with reference to the past, which is parallel to the quest of classical psychoanalysis. The Proustian search for the past is something else. It is initiated by the searcher's need to establish a developmental continuity of his self. There is a break. The self is fragmented along the time axis. The Proustian search is to heal this break and cure the self by feeling whole and historically continuous. I once supervised a case where the analyst introduced one of her interpretations by saying something like, "As you said two weeks ago . . ." The patient felt marvelous. He didn't even listen to the explanation itself, to the content, but the mere fact that in the selfobject's mind a continuity of his was present, that he was there in the past. In that sense he began for a moment to grow together.

STROZIER: Is the role of the historian therefore like that of the analyst?

KOHUT: Yes, absolutely. A selfobject is an object, at least in a sociological sense it is an object, and yet is experienced by the person as performing functions that are normally performed by himself. It seems to me the historian may indeed be a cultural selfobject for people. The idea that history is only a science of data collection and meant only for other historians is utter nonsense. The historian, like the artist, is an extremely important selfobject for mankind, for each nation, for each group, because he gives each group and each individual who feels a part of the group a sense of continuity in time. The meaning, however, of the sense of the continuity in time is different as perceived by self psychology. Each point in organic development, in the Eriksonian layering, let us say, is meaningful only when seen as the unrolling program. There seems to be something very basic about such an unrolling program of birth, peak, and death. We don't know about the total universe, but even there they are searching for theories that have a beginning, there is clearly an end to it, etc.

There is something very frightening as an adult—and we know the most about late middle age—when there is a sense of not fulfilling one's basic program. We realize there is a nuclear program in an individual—a tension arc between early ambitions and early ideals via a matrix of particular skills—that points into the future and points to a particular fulfillment. Once the program is in place, then something clicks and we have a degree of autonomy; this degree of autonomy we call the self. It becomes a center of independent initiative that points to a future and has a destiny. It also has its own natural, unfeared decline and end.

When we go back into the past in analysis we are attempting to recognize the program that was laid down—we call that the nuclear self. And did it gel completely? Were the means of fulfillment interfered with early? Was it too weak? Was it too disharmonious? Was it too fragmented and never completely gelled? Those are the questions we ask. Those are the things that Proust tried to do by his own efforts. It is all very different from the attempted cure of a classical neurosis. The analogue in history is to think in terms of group self. There is a basic self that at one time or another gels. It then points into the future and has its own unrolling destiny.

STROZIER: But when does the group self begin? What is your sense of how it fits on the time axis? When you reflect on the issues of the group self, do you think in terms of decades or centuries or whatever? Or do you think that tying it to a time axis limits the flexibility of the idea?

KOHUT: What I am trying to provide here, it seems to me, is a framework for the search, rather than answers to particular research problems. All I will say is that it is easiest to define a group self in the investigation of national groups. When you look, for example, at the Iranian national group with its own highly specific individuality, it seems to follow particular rules and point in very specific directions. At some point it must have once gelled. But you know the beginnings of the individual self are also not so easily determined. The newborn baby has an individual self. However, it is only within the matrix of the selfobjects that this self takes shape. The exact timing is quite indistinct.

How that is with national groups is another story. But I would think that each group surrounds itself with selfobjects to which it naturally assigns this role: artists, political seers, prophets, historians. The idea of the group self is no more than a vantage point from which to examine historical phenomena. The study of the past must locate its ambitions and ideals.

STROZIER: Can the examination of the group self be objective and scientific?

KOHUT: Scientific objectivity, as it was envisioned in the 19th century, cannot be maintained. That is clear. It is certainly not my insight, but it is perfectly clear. Modern physicists, for example, when investigating small particles, realize there is no way one can observe small particles and see how they behave. You can only see how they behave under the scrutiny of a particular type of instrumentation. Instrumentation and behavior belong together as one unit. There is no unobserved behavior in principle. Clinical work with a patient corresponds to small particle observation. The mere fact that you are listened to attentively by somebody for prolonged periods of time is part of the field. There is no behavior outside of this field. This is one of the major points in the "Charisma" paper [see this book, p. 171 ff]. Freud introduced Fliess into his life as a supportive selfobject and dropped him when he didn't need him anymore. He interpreted it differently, which has influenced analysts for generations. They thought he needed a transference object, a father on whom to project his ambivalence. But I feel this was a transference of creativity. You need somebody to support you during difficult investigative steps and you need to create this matrix of security in which you can then undertake this task. Now in history, under normal circumstances, it all seems quite different at first sight. You can sit back and study and apparently not greatly influence what you study. In the long run, however, by the summation of all research, historians, philosophers, artists, indeed psychoanalysts, greatly influence the shape of events. How you perceive influences what happens. If you give people a certain self-concept, they will behave accordingly. Furthermore, the most profound research is aware of this fact. It's a matter of having your finger on the pulse.

STROZIER: Like you?

KOHUT: Yes, I guess I would say so. Freud also had his finger on the pulse of his time.

STROZIER: What is the nature of that collective pulse, of that collective sense of time? You mentioned the contrasting sense of time between you and Freud. What is the larger historical sense of time that is presumably reflected in the way you talk about time in psychoanalysis?

KOHUT: You see, what I discovered, I believe, is the pathology of time perception in our time. That patient who felt so blissful when the analyst said, "As you told me a week ago," had his continuity preserved by the selfobject: "By God, I hang together, I am whole." It is this same sense of discontinuity I find painfully present in the work of artists. In mass culture I find the same discontinuity expressed in the frantic need to live only for the moment. There is a deadness in the self. It must be stimulated, enlivened, even if it means going to war. Now nothing in such self-destructive behavior suggests internalized guilt. It is just to feel alive, even if only at that single moment of declaring war. That moment wipes out all the fragmentation, the absent past and meaningless future. That's the pathology I think I have come to understand. It is not the pathology of intense conflict between love and hate or something on that order, but the pathology of feeling wan and feeble and disconnected and disharmonious, without a future or past. Nothing hangs together the way it does in the course of a meaningful life.

STROZIER: Do you think there can be collective cure, and that someone like you can have such an influence?

KOHUT: I hope so, though it is obviously idiotic to think that a single contribution could do more than be a step among many in that direction. There must generally be self-awareness, a kind of subjectivity that enhances objective understanding. Once you realize the meaning of a particular function, you become more objective about non-objectivity, funny as that may sound. When Freud began to show, for example, the importance of drive experience, people were worried the drives would get out of hand and there would be licentiousness. But just the opposite is true. I have been accused in my paper "The Psychoanalyst in the Community of Scholars" (1975), of sentimentalizing science. I think that's an error and that I have been misunderstood by people who say that. Every human activity has to be seen as embedded into a hierarchy of values. In the paper I discuss "tool and method pride (or snobbishness)" in which each particular human enterprise acts as if it were all by itself. This is only acceptable insofar as it deals with the sharpening of instruments. Clearly, the historian has to learn his methodology and how to gather primary data and determine what is reliable and what is not reliable. All this goes without saying. And yet there is a further step: What is history for? It must serve a human purpose; if it weren't there for a human purpose, it wouldn't be there at all. In my mind at least, it serves, like every other human activity, to support life as we cherish it, to make us more human and to maintain our feelings as human beings so that we can be responded to by others and understood by others.

STROZIER: OK, but if you are not being sentimental, would you agree there is a marked optimism in self psychology? This seems to have a theoretical basis—the emphasis on rage, for example, rather than on the death instinct. However, the whole sense of the way you talk also conveys hope. Where do you think that comes from? Is it a part of you personally? Do you think it is an intrinsic part of the theoretical basis of self psychology? As far as I can tell in your writings, the only place you have commented on this was in your discussion of a paper on adolescence by Wolf, Gedo and Terman (Kohut, 1972a). You were not there talking directly about optimism in self psychology, but you did mention some memories of your university life.

KOHUT: You are onto something there, but I'm not sure whether I'll be able to unravel it. Certainly optimism is the wrong word. That much I am certain about. After all, I speak about tragic man when I speak about the very dimension you have in mind. Any observer has a function and operates in a hierarchy of values. I have always tried to be clear about my values. One of the problems with traditional analysis is that it was—and continues to be—a clandestine moral system: Drives need to be tamed. People are born uncivilized and need to become civilized, and, alas, this is not fully doable or achievable. Nobody admits this is so, but it is implicit in the drive primacy theory. So when I say my hierarchy of values—which seems to me axiomatic—is to support human psychological life to its fullest, then the observer's simultaneous function as a selfobject is a supportive one. Now, whether that is optimism, I don't know. We do know that when a child does not get mirroring or approving responses, it despairs. That sense of bringing hope to others is like the role of oxygen in the atmosphere for us physiologically: It is absolutely needed for psychological survival.

Now, is this optimism? It strikes me as the wrong word. I dislike the word love, because it isn't love. Love—at least defined classically—has something to do with the sublimation of the sexual libido. People too easily abandon these old definitions, but it seems to me that is shameful. Freud's system is a marvelous system and you can't just suddenly say, well, he really means something else. Then you haven't even done him the honor of disagreeing with him. It is impossible, to my mind, to conceive of this marvelous system of Freud's without the death instinct. Most analysts say they accept Freud but without the death instinct. How can you? Everything falls down if you remove one of the two pillars on which the system rests.

So, I don't believe that will work for what we're talking about here. I guess I'm talking about empathy: the resonance of the self in the self of others, of being understood, of somebody making an effort to understand you. That is the parental function of selfobjects vis-à-vis the child. But empathy does not mean love or compassion. Empathy can be used decisively for hateful purposes. I figure out where your weak spots are so I can put the dagger in you. Is that dreadful? Well it is dreadful, of course, but it is better than nothing. The worst—and I think I said this most concisely in the final reflections of *Advances* (1980)—is to find oneself in a predominantly nonhuman environment. This is the dreadful fear of our time, to be shot off into space and to be all alone. There is a wonderful symbol of psychosis in dreams. It is that you get out of the gravitational attraction of earth and are by yourself forever. Even a hostile empathic environment is vastly preferable to an indifferent one. That is why Kafka, in a sense, is the literary representative of our time. Over and over again he describes the vacuum that surrounds Mr. K., the everyman of our times. If it were only a guilt that he was punished for, it would be in a human context; but no, he can never find that there is any guilt. They finally kill him like a dog. If there were only some way of getting to the people high up in their castles; you move but you never get closer. There is some ludicrous game being played with Mr. K.; if there were only a battle. Read Homer, for example, about the greatness of these experiences of killing and being killed. But that isn't in Kafka. We strive for a hero who dies for a purpose, like the Scholls who died for their ideals.[1] That baby Marie Scholl put across the crevass shows that she's alive. Her cheeks are flushed with vitality when she was executed. This is not a hysterial fantasy of a masochistic nature. This is someone alive for a cause that will live on; that baby was placed on the other side of the crevass as she was falling. And she said to herself, "It's all right, the baby will live on." So is this optimism? Maybe.

[1] This refers to the discussion in the paper in this collection, "On Courage."

9

Idealization and Cultural Selfobjects

(February 12, 1981)

STROZIER: You once mentioned that the Marxist critique of psychoanalysis does not pay enough attention to the impact of economic considerations on the developing self. Do you think there are class-based self needs?

KOHUT: I have the impression that what I can be most helpful with is not to provide answers to such questions but to give conceptual tools and psychological attitudes with which others can answer such questions. In other words, I interpose between the social milieu and the resulting personality attitudes the psychological question: How does the social milieu provide stimuli or the lack of stimuli? How does it nourish the self or how does it undernourish the self, does it warp the self, etc? In other words, I can't answer the question you ask, but I do believe psychological sophistication, particularly from the point of view of the sustenance and maintenance of the self, enriches what we can understand in human behavior.

Keep in mind that the rich have their own slums. For obvious reasons, I see much more of the rich slums than the poor slums. But not entirely. My patient population is a meaningless sample in terms of making generalizations about the population at large, but it isn't meaningless in terms of seeing connections, in terms of learning something psychological. From what I have seen of those people who come to me with self disturbances, I think those from the rich slums are worse off than those from the poor slums.

In the poor slums I think the real deprivation is not economic but cultural. It would be ridiculous to deny that one needs enough calories and vitamins and proteins to be able to develop physiologically. But as far as I can judge in the United States—though there are pockets of real deprivation to which I don't have access—most of those whom I have treated from slum areas generally had enough calories when they were young. But the food was dreary, and that was the important thing. Everything was dreary. There was no artistry in the apartments in which they grew up. And by that I don't mean artistry in the sense of good taste—but in any taste. It is a world of cultural emptiness. For those who escape it, it leaves a haunting presence and often a lingering need for an idealizable selfobject. It is worth noting that patients I see who have risen out of this world do not necessarily seek an externally victorious father but rather an inner pride and security. Only via such a proud father or parents with a sense of inner dignity, which has nothing to do directly with material deprivation, can one then acquire a sense of one's own worth.

Now it seems to me there are enormous lessons to be learned here for political science, politics, and government. For example, when we think of alleviating poverty we tend to think entirely in terms of food stamps, housing, transportation, and the like. Now I am not a fool. I know one needs food, housing, and transportation. But in the last analysis it is the deprivation of cultural selfobjects that matters most. In this regard one sees among blacks some remedial action in the creation of cultural selfobjects like the baseball players, the boxers, the great athletes. I have no doubt many people have talked about vaguely similar things. But it seems to me that with the armamentarium of self psychology, this could be investigated more scientifically and expressed more explicitly than it has been done before.

STROZIER: Would a corollary of all this be that, in terms of investigating mass psychology, you would expect special importance to be attached to issues of idealization?

KOHUT: We are all inclined to decry some of the horrors of misguided idealization: the Germans flocking to Hitler, the Moonies flocking to Rev. Moon, those following Jim Jones in Guyana. It frightens me a bit. Or take such mass craziness as the sorrow expressed when John Lennon died. Or many other possible examples. Instead of shrugging our shoulders and being down at the mouth at such phenomena, maybe what one should do is to take those things more seriously and examine what legitimate needs have gone astray.

Man tries to support human life, including psychological life. This is behind everything I have to say. The historian supports the continuity with the past so that people can feel better about themselves. When we look at the examples I just cited of distorted and perverse idealization we should look behind them and see what it is that is less crazy and more helpful, how people can feel good without going off the deep end, becoming destructive and perpetuating the misery that runs throughout human history. Obviously, nothing will happen quickly—it's not like injecting penicillin and the fever subsides—but over many generations, over many years, it seeps in, one hopes. Now whether we have enough time to wait with atomic energy on the loose, I don't know. We can only work as our minds allow us to work and hope that people under dire circumstances become more reasonable. Actually, that is often the case. When the stress and anxiety are the greatest, there is perhaps enough survival need in humans that they will suddenly become reasonable. But then maybe I'm too optimistic there.

STROZIER: But to return to my question, in terms of looking at collective needs and aspirations, do you think there is something specially important about idealization?

KOHUT: Absolutely. I think I can say, without false modesty, that in my clinical work I discovered there are two new transferences. Both are reactivations of frustrated developmental needs. They are not drive transferences, which were the only ones that had been recognized until then. One I called the mirror transferences and the other I called the idealizing transferences. I have no doubt—and now 15 years of observation have made no dent in this basic conviction—these are two of the basic needs of the developing self. One needs to be accepted and mirrored—there has to be the gleam in some mother's eye which says it is good you are here and I acknowledge your being here and I am uplifted by your presence. There is also the other need: to have somebody strong and knowledgeable and calm around with whom I can temporarily merge, who will uplift me when I am upset.

Originally, that is an actual uplifting of the baby by the mother; later that becomes an uplifting feeling of looking at a great man or woman and enjoying him or her, of following in his or her footsteps, of a great idea being uplifting, or a wonderful piece of music, etc. That is extremely important. And when I talk about cultural selfobjects, which is the replica of the culture for the group self of what occurs in individual development, I think that these two basic needs are also present, perhaps collectively. I am not sure whether to say "collectively." You used that term. Maybe it is what I mean. Why not? It still means to me a number of individuals, and implies some statistics or the greater majority or the verbal majority or whatever (or whoever) then carries historical action.

STROZIER: The term "collectivity" then seems less evocative to you than "group"?

KOHUT: No, I have nothing against the word. It's just that, being so steeped in individual psychology, it's difficult for me to conceive of the abstraction of a group having as much life meaning as a person. When we talk about a group self, what we mean is a number of individuals who are not necessarily the majority but who determine historical action. That strikes us then as the group. It may be only 30 percent or even only 20 percent of the whole population. But they are the verbal ones; they initiate action and the others follow suit.

STROZIER: That's a crucial point. Are those "spokesmen" representative or do they determine the actions of the group? There's always the problem of the heterogeneity of the group.

KOHUT: I think that's a crucial question. And I don't have the answer, but I have a guess. I think to some extent they must be representative. Somewhere there must be a common denominator, however manifest the diversity of groups. I have no question that the followers of Hitler were originally composed of all kinds of groups: the industrialists who wanted to see the economy revived; the lower middle classes who wanted to get uplifted from their suddenly lowered status; the unemployed who wanted jobs; and those for whom national defeat was the major sore that needed to be healed. And yet, for all of that, Hitler was an unquestioned figure of inner security and power. This man had absolutely no doubt about his mission. In that sense he was an idealizable leader. But in another sense—and that was the uniqueness of the phenomenon—I don't think he was enormously bright. Certainly he was an uncultured person in many ways. His tastes were certainly abominable by any standards: the kind of buildings he wanted to build, the kind of art he liked . . .

STROZIER: The movies he watched.

KOHUT: Yes. But to judge this kind of phenomenon on these levels is foolishness.

STROZIER: In trying to identify historically the sources of self needs and the specific qualities of those self needs, where would you think that the search could begin? Would it be in the family, within the political structure? What are the points of access?

KOHUT: There again, my immediate response is to bow out modestly. Why should I, a rank amateur in the methodology of historical investigation, a rank amateur in the methodology of political and social science, make suggestions as to methodology? What I *can* say—and that is the important thing—is that it would be useful if you were informed by the insights of self psychology. Let us assume, for example, that a good way of investigating poverty would be through the use of interviews. You go into the slum and you have a statistical average so that you have a good cross-section and somebody interviews. That has been done, I am sure, for a long, long time by social scientists. I do not know about questionnaires. But if people who do the interviews, who design the questionnaires, are informed by self psychology and are aware of the importance of people feeling deprived of idealizable objects and of not feeling appropriately mirrored, then I feel the research will yield fresh results.

STROZIER: In some of your discussion of individual leaders you have suggested that the personality and character and public persona of the leader can suggest the nature and shape of the group bound to that particular leader. Is that a misreading?

KOHUT: I would think that is partially at least a misreading. My feeling is that there is a dialectic between the group need and the greatness of the leader. A Hitler at another time would have been recognized as the ludicrous individual that he was. But there's the rub. You see, people now say often—and I must say I am not totally blameless in that respect—that from the hindsight of today, those who ridiculed Hitler when he first came to power were being defensive. They didn't want to see the danger, so they denied it and pushed it away. They grossly underestimated Hitler. To people brought up in the way the leading layers of Western society were and still are it was unimaginable that Hitler could be a serious threat. It seemed so ludicrous, so odd, so poverty-stricken. And yet what it meant was that this upper layer was totally out of touch with the culturally disenfranchised masses in Germany who were yearning for somebody who would turn to them and talk to them and for them. All of a sudden here was a man, strong, unafraid, utterly convinced of his—and our—greatness. All of a sudden people were willing to die for that marvelous image they got of themselves via this particular person. It is an incredible phenomenon that a man can say, "We will all commit suicide," and then we all commit suicide. This is only understandable in terms of this enormous need that people have to merge into some secure greatness. And if that is present, particularly during periods of prolonged cultural deprivation, then people will do anything for it. I think it no more amazing—though obviously less traditionally explainable—that more than 800 people committed suicide in Guyana than that many millions of people went to a war in which 20 million died.

STROZIER: Those are the same in that they are equally hard to explain?

KOHUT: I think they are equally *easy* to explain. They are basically the same phenomenon.

STROZIER: Quite a different question. An important tenet of self psychology as I understand it is that much of drive expression is a result of the breakdown of self organization on the individual level. Is there an analogue in human history about the meaning of war?

KOHUT: Well, let's start from the beginning. I have never claimed that drive expression results only from the breakdown of the self. I believe that isolated drive, a drive in which the self does not participate, is a break-down product. I furthermore say that in individual psychopathology only such an isolated drive leads to psychopathology, while a drive that is part and parcel of the total driven self experience is healthy and constructive. The baby is born in a way as a unit. He lacks a reflective self but he, plus his mother and father, constitute a self-selfobject matrix from the beginning. Now this early self is assertive and loving towards those around him. These feelings are just not yet integrated.

Freud to my mind failed to differentiate these healthy self-amalgamated drive experiences from essentially conflictual infantile sexuality that becomes the nucleus of adult neuroses. A normal drive is not pathological. It is a fabulous experience. It is uniting, creative, and self-enhancing. That is why I differentiate between the oedipal phase and an Oedipus complex. Freud talked about them as though they were the same. If the little shaver at four or five pushes daddy around and is affectionate to mom, then dad's chest should swell with pride. If mom is now affectionately handled by her little boy, she doesn't normally get sexually stimulated. Normal parents respond with pride and pleasure at this developmental phase of their child. This is a joyful, not a pathogenic, experience. It becomes pathogenic only when the parents react in a pathogenic, not self-enhancing, way, in other words when they fail in their oedipal selfobject function. Freud, for example, often used the example of the hysterical patients whose seduction fantasies he originally believed. We have come now to realize that the hysterical patients were right, in a way. They didn't describe real seductions, it is true; Freud had to recognize he had been misled in his credulity. But he went much too far in saying the parents had nothing to do with their children's hysteria, that only fantasy is relevant. Sometimes there are gross seductions with psychotic or crypto-psychotic parents. But usually the issue is the parents' inability to respond to the child in warm, oedipal, accepting attitude. To be uplifted or enhanced by a drive experience first of all requires a cohesive self and, secondly, has a cohesion-producing secondary result. Any intense experience and activity may, and in many instances does, intensify the sense of the self.

Furthermore, I do not believe in the Freudian U-tube theory that if narcissism goes up then object love goes down and if object love goes up the narcissism goes down. A passionate lover feels high in his self-esteem because the intense emotion brings together the sense of who and what he is. At the beginning of a war, for example, people frequently have this sense of united purpose and they feel enhanced. It's often been interpreted that all the flags and the music and flowers at the beginning of a war (at least in past wars; now it's quite different) are because everyone is afraid and they have to overcome their fear by playing up the opposite of their strengths. But that's not altogether true. These are really expressions of the intensifications of the self during such a period of initial activity. That it doesn't last, that then comes the nitty-gritty of death and mutilation and destruction, is a different story. As this disintegration experience comes about, then we have group phenomena that parallel the isolation of the drive: the sadism of troops, plundering, the lack of discipline, the abandoning of their own wounded. Those are phenomena in which the group self breaks apart. An army that abandons its wounded is an army in disintegration. An army that goes plundering and murdering—though it may have to be interpreted historically in terms of what is permissible—is in disintegration.

STROZIER: Like My Lai?

KOHUT: Exactly. There are exceptions, however, that are worth noting. Alexander could say to his troops, "Now you have two days to plunder." This is like a holiday. You know that after two days it will be over. Of course it is just as bad to be raped and killed during a holiday of the invading troops as by an army in disarray. But this is different from an army that moves on. We all need our aggressions. We need to kill our enemies in one form or another, whether through polemics in writing or through punishing icy silence.

10

On the Continuity of the Self and Cultural Selfobjects

(February 26, 1981)

STROZIER: What is the history of your interest in history?

KOHUT: It's not easy for me to give an answer to that, because—how should I phrase it?—it doesn't strike me that my interest in history is so personality-bound, or specifically bound up in some deeply rooted features in my personality, though one can never be sure about that. But I have the impression that it is not the case, that it is just part and parcel of my general fascination, all my life, with how people behave, why they behave, channeled as, of course, much of my intellectual development was, by my secondary school experience. In my school we had relatively less science compared to the humanities. The eight-year program was divided into two periods, the Unter- and Obergymnasium. There was no real standing to this difference, but it had some interesting implications. For example, as I remember it, we had three years of history in the Untergymnasium and three or four years in the Obergymnasium. We had ancient history in one year, medieval history in the second year, and modern history in the third. Then they repeated the sequence in the upper level. You learned the same things once more, except now on a higher level of sophistication. The history teacher that I had—to bring a long story to a simple solution—was one of my great idols. All the teachers, by the way, were male. I never had a single female school teacher in my whole life; they simply didn't exist.

STROZIER: Did your history teacher in the Gymnasium also move with you through all six years?

KOHUT: I don't believe so. But most of those six years I think we had him. Certainly the first three years, and then a certain number of the remaining three years. He taught history and geography. Unlike most of the teachers, we didn't fear him. He did nothing but lecture. He was from the provinces and was very unsophisticated, fat, and he held a huge bundle of keys in his hands. But when he talked he brought a balance and a culturally sophisticated approach to history. He was not interested in quizzing us about dates or names. He gave the flavor of each period. I just loved the man. He was definitely the low man on the totem pole on the faculty of the secondary school, because he was so easygoing. But I remember him talking about the French absolutarian rulers and the type of parks they built, how the trees had to be exactly in line, and how this corresponded with the economic system and the hierarchy of power distribution, and how this contrasted with the English garden and English society and the organization of the aristocracy vis-à-vis the king and the democratization that led them to handle their landscapes differently. Ideas like that were tailor-made for me to listen to. That was probably the source of my earliest interest in history. I did read a great deal of course about literature and art. Culture, art, history were always part of my general interest in the humanities.

STROZIER. Well, I asked largely because it has always impressed me the way you integrate the clinical and nonclinical aspects of any problem. The two seem necessarily blended.

KOHUT: That is my outlook. It estranges me from the great, great majority of my colleagues. Much of the time I am totally unprepared for the opinions of my colleagues. My outlook is so basically different from those who are entirely clinically oriented.

STROZIER: You seem to regard phenomena beyond the clinical setting as important for your understanding of patients.

KOHUT: Absolutely. The two are inseparable. After all, people are people. It's true you don't get free association and certain models can't be applied to works of art or behavior in the political or historical realm. But it is really just what I have called "tool and method pride" that creates that separation between psychoanalysis and the humanities. The phenomena are basically the same. Certainly, there are different tools that people use in their respective fields. But they can't be *that* different. You know, what you learn in one realm will make you sensitive to things in another. And the other way around. The problem is that we all confound the difficulties. Analysts, moreover, don't consider research outside the clinical realm as worthwhile. They see it as frivolous and playful. How, they ask, can a responsible psychotherapist waste time on such things? I happen to be someone who works with individuals and therefore my discoveries come from that realm. I am sure I would never have thought of the idea of "cultural selfobjects" had I not first seen analogous phenomena in individual psychology. But I could well imagine the discoveries could be made the other way around.

STROZIER: Let me pursue further the idea of the cultural selfobject. The concept of the selfobject in psychology is tied closely to the development of the individual person. As you have often stated, the baby is born into a selfobject milieu and matures into an adult with continuing selfobject needs. How does that really work with the group self?

KOHUT: So much depends on how we conceive or what we discover and how we add to our understanding of the essence of that central experience of being a self. There are a number of things that define this experience. The self is the center of initiative. We experience ourselves as the center of initiative. We know we are influenced, we know we listen to other people's opinions, we consider choices. And yet somewhere there is a sense of comparative independence, of assertiveness, of initiative. That's one feature.

Another feature is cohesion in space and continuity in time. There is also a sense of cohesion versus fragmentation; a sense of the harmony of oneself versus the sense of chaos of oneself; a sense of strength about the self versus a sense of weakness, lack of vitality; a sense of feeling alive. We must feel alive. Part of being less than self (as amusing as that sounds) is not to feel alive. People complain all the time about the fact that they don't feel alive or feel alive only under certain circumstances. The selfobject transferences in such people make them function as though they were plugged into an electric outlet; only that charges them. When they leave the selfobject they lose that. So when we talk about the cultural selfobject, I think the answer that I like as an empirical scientist is not a general one but one that addresses itself to all the issues that are to be raised when we define the self, the particular qualities, the particular attributes that in the totality make the self. Now when you may say you have a frag-mented self, you still say "self." But if it were totally fragmented, it wouldn't be a self.

It is in this sense that Proust has to be understood as not inves-tigating a Freudian past. When he remembers his mother visit-ing him in the night and giving him the madeleine that he smells, the major point is not that they are screen memories covering oedipal material of being alone with mamma or wanting daddy to be dead and putting it into a harmless oral sphere rather than in that of sexuality; that would be the classical Freudian inter-pretation and it has its own integrity. But the Proustian search can only be understood when you read—which most people don't anymore—the last volume of his novel, which explains the moment at which he decides to undertake this work, when he suddenly trips on the curbstone and slips and feels out of bal-ance. That comes after he had been away from Paris and returns to find everything subtly changed. Although the people are the same, their opinions and values have shifted. Proust feels totally estranged. He feels more than usually disconnected from him-self. It was at that point he decided he had to write his total life history, not to figure out the past and its meanings in the uncon-scious but to reestablish a continuity within himself. He became his own historian in order to establish the continuity of his indi-vidual self.

This is perhaps a complex way of saying a simple thing: Rather than talking in general about cultural selfobjects, one should talk about which particular functions for the group self a particular selfobject fulfills. The good historian, for example, does this for the group. It is the specificity of the functions of cultural selfob-jects that I, as an empirical scientist, would like to address myself to rather than giving a global answer to your question, "What do cultural selfobjects do for the group self or for the individuals

out of which the group self is composed?" If a group feels his-
tory-less, it lacks an important aspect of a live, vital group self.
It is the same with the individual. We search for the continuity.
"How was I when I was a little boy?" "How were you when you
were a little girl?" "What did you do?" "Tell me about me," we
ask. "Did I really say clever things? Was I bad sometimes?" It
doesn't matter what the questions are exactly. The importance
of these questions is not so much to investigate the past because
of old conflicts that have become unconscious and still bother
you, but to establish the continuity of the self via the reflecting
eyes of the selfobject. The excitement of such questions is not an
object-instinctual one, i.e., "I love you mom and once wanted to
sleep with you." The excitement is the knowledge of *me, me, me.*
You saw me, you held me. Tell me about it. It's the me that's the
important issue, that I was important to you and that you
remember that and that you can tell me about it. Groups likewise
need that sense of connectedness along the time axis. It has
nothing to do with the manifest changes in the group.

STROZIER: I'm not sure I understand. What do you mean by
manifest changes?

KOHUT: I'm an old man. My hair is grey. My muscles are feeble.
Yet I know I am the same person I was when I was 18, and 22,
and six, when I was running and jumping. It's still in me and a
part of me. There is no discontinuity. I have totally changed and
yet my conviction that I have remained the same is absolute. I
never feel myself chopped up in that way, however otherwise
my self might be endangered. There is that sense of continuity
along the time axis from the little boy in the Austrian Alps to
Vienna to the well-known investigator of the self at the age of
68 in a place whose name I hardly knew when I was that young.
I have no question that I am the same. There is a sense of utter
continuity. And it is this sense of utter continuity despite all the
enormous changes that matters. You know, when you think about
it, that little six-year old boy in Vienna and the six-year old boys
in Vienna now have much more in common than that six-year
old boy that was I and the 68-year old man that I am now. We
have very little in common, it seems to me. And yet, I feel we
have everything in common, not only that, but that we are the

same. It isn't somebody else. I'm not estranged from that. I may not remember much about the boy anymore, but he is still within me.

It is this sense of continuity, this indefinable sameness, identity, unalterableness that I believe selfobjects respond to, like the mother who says, "Well, yes, I remember how you were." When I was 60 years old—and this may give you an idea of why I feel so sure (you know, I am free associating)—when I was 60 I was president of the American Psychoanalytic Association. My birthday is the third of May and I was in St. Louis for the meetings. I was on top of our organizational hierarchy. Flowers and other gifts came. And my mother sent me a telegram, unsigned: "To me it seems like yesterday." You get the point? That was all she sent. I will never forget that. It was one of the best things she ever did. It was not a make-up.

The same kind of investigation is possible vis-à-vis the group self. There is no group self if there are no supports; without them it would be nothing. It must have some sense of its continuity. For that historians are needed. I'm not sure how aware black historians are of this role, but I'm sure that in some way they must be aware of it. The same is true for cultural heroes and the creation of myths about cultural heroes; you know, the uplifting experience of:

"Daddy, how did you do it? Did you really come to this country and have only $25? Just enough for a bus fare from Boston to Chicago? Is it really true you only knew one person in the United States? And he was in Chicago, and that was why you spent your $25 on the bus fare? And then you got here and had no money at all? And yet, look what became of you?" "Yes, Tom, that's the way it was."

You know, when the black community hears about Jackie Robinson and how all he could hope for was to be the bat boy and then he became a nationally renowned star, or Ralph Metcalf and Jesse Owens who pitted themselves against the whole Nazi hierarchy, won the 100-yard dash and forced Hitler to leave the stadium—those are things that confirm the sense of group self. That also probably diminishes group violence. Assertiveness and aggression in a group are not at all the same as violence. There is a huge difference between narcissistic rage and assertive action. Narcissistic rage comes from narcissistic injuries, which can never be satisfied because the injury remains. A fragmented self is violent in all directions.

STROZIER: I'm not sure I understand what you mean by a "fragmented self."

KOHUT: You know that one of the crucial concepts in self psychology is that of transmuting internalization. To speak in biological analogies, we need foreign protein in order to build up our own protein. The essence of our biological equipment is the protein molecule. The protein molecule is a highly complex and a very specific molecule; it is specific not only for each race but probably for each individual in its fine arrangement. Now the protein molecule itself is composed of various shifts and combinations of amino acids, which are themselves molecules but not as complex as the total protein molecule. Apparently the body cannot build up protein molecules. It needs foreign protein, which it takes apart into its constituent amino acids; then it reassembles these amino acids again to form its own protein. Our protein is very different from the foreign protein. If we eat beef, we don't become oxen, but we do need meat or cheese or whatever in order to take these proteins apart and reassemble them for our own purposes. This analogy fits well for transmuting internalization. You need other people in order to become yourself.

STROZIER: What about origins?

KOHUT: For one thing, remember that you cannot create the self. It's like creating a language. You know, the attempt to create a universal language like Esperanto is pointless. In the same way, you cannot create a group. It comes into being long before it is strengthened. In the process of psychoanalytic cure, we are always dealing, not with the creation of a self, but putting it in harmony, recreating its vitality, firming it. The awareness of self, by the way—without being extreme in my pronouncements—is often a sign of weakness rather than strength. For example, from the realm of group psychology, sabre-rattling pronouncements of strength, loud protestations of how strong we are and how different we are, more often betray insecurity than strength. The groups that feel most secure don't need so much overt talking about it. They just are.

STROZIER: Would you relate this back to the role of cultural selfobjects?

KOHUT: The cultural selfobject's group self, of course, being simultaneously a responder to the needs and part of the group, will naturally respond to the needs of the group. This is why I have so often stressed the anticipatory function of art. Art, by the way, is clearly ahead of science in recognizing the needs and wants of the group self and responding to it. The artists of the 20th century knew decades ahead of the rest of us that it was the fragmented self that needed to be reassembled, that it was an empty, a nonvital self and not the guilt-laden, firmly structured self that now needed a response. And so the artist began to work on that, although, unfortunately in many ways, in such an eso- teric fashion that it somehow didn't filter through quickly enough to heal the wounds that existed.

STROZIER: In "Forms and Transformations" (see this volume, p. 97 ff) you identify criteria really for assessing growth and change within the personality: humor, empathy, creativity, wisdom. Those criteria have always seemed to me particularly interesting in terms of psychobiography and in dealing with individuals. I wonder how you feel about the relevance of those criteria for the issues of the group self. One of the things that is so striking to me about Nazi Germany, for example, is the utter humorlessness of the period. Is that a valid way of coming to grips with the health or sickness of a group self?

KOHUT: That's a good observation. When I see a patient whom I am really concerned about and wonder if there is much hidden paranoia, I always feel reassured when I see a glimpse of the capacity for humor, enough security in the self to appreciate the relativity of the self and the recognition of other selves. Humor and sarcasm, of course, are not the same. One would also say that in the artistic field in Nazi Germany there was no meaning- ful creativity. Now I know perfectly well that the consuming needs of preparing for and then fighting a war absorbed any potential for creativity in Nazi Germany. Nazi Germany, furthermore, never really became a culture; it was an interlude. So it's very difficult to judge it on that basis. But certainly it had the earmarks of a sterile group that has only one goal—to deny the sense of fragmentation and disconnectedness and become invincible. And this renewal came about by identifying with a leader who personified utter fearlessness and the conviction of his own invincibility. The civilized world was paralyzed in the face of these totally new, unhuman methods that ran counter to anything they were trained to expect or deal with. That was a large part of the success of Nazi Germany—the paralysis of the world before German fascism, which was, of course, quite different from the fascism of Italy. But beyond that, I don't think your question should be examined in terms of a comparatively short phenomenon as that of Nazi Germany, particularly since it was engaged in a total effort to prepare for war that channeled all its energies. For you might well say that the creativeness of Germans all went into their war machine, into the inventiveness and creativeness of waging war. Who's to argue with that? I don't like it, but perhaps if they had been victorious they would have begun something new that might have led into something unforeseen. Human beings, you know, have a way of going on beyond from where they start. But thank God, we didn't have to face that experiment. But I think it would be more interesting to examine these questions in terms of comparatively well established and quiescent groups, to study their creativity and their capacity for empathy and their sense of humor and their wisdom and their ways of dealing with the unanswerable questions of life and death and nonexistence over a long period of time.

STROZIER: But what about Jaeggerstaetter, whom you assess in terms of his sense of humor in the courage paper (see this volume, pp. 17–18)?

KOHUT: I wrote that paper, of course, because it was important for me personally, but how humor can be applied to whole groups is the issue that your earlier question raises. And I do believe that it can be. But what does humor mean? For example, how important is the phenomenon of the *New Yorker* magazine for American culture? How important is the phenomenon of *Punch* for British culture? How important was the phenomenon of *Simplissicimus,* which corresponds to *Punch* and the *New Yorker* in some ways, in Germany? How important in France was the *Canards-Enchanais*? All these four had similar types of humor. Of all of those I would think the *New Yorker,* at least in its heyday, was the most significant, because there was wisdom in it as well as self-humor. There was a sense of the relativity of the greatness of achievement that was continuously held up to people and that connected them to each other. Now, you can say the audience was small compared to the population, but there is again something that we need to investigate, namely, how do values of this type filter into the total population. They do. It would be interesting to investigate even the apparatus by which they filter. How, for example, the sophisticated writing of the *New Yorker* may influence some provincial magazine indirectly, maybe by various intervening links in the chain. But it always does. And the same, by the way, is true for science and for history and for art. Take science fiction. Very important ideas in science are often dealt with in science fiction long before there is real equivalent scientific knowledge. Space travel is one such example. I remember as a kid I loved to read fiction that dealt with space travel. Obviously it was taken from pioneering thinkers in science. It was a beginning preparation for our capacity to accept the idea that really one is not bound to the earth, that really one cannot only think about interstellar space but actually cross it. Ideas now of halting time by stopping biological processes are in the same realm. Such ideas sound crazy at first, but perhaps later they will not sound so crazy.

STROZIER: Is all this part of what you mean by what selfobjects do?

KOHUT: Yes, the question is how do sophisticated cultural selfobjects influence the totality of group belief? It's clear that great historians do not write for the masses. If a great historian can bring alive a period of the past and its meaning for later generations as a developmental stage of the group self, this is not going to be digested by the mail carrier. But yet in some way this awareness filters through, even for him. Media, for example, plays a great role in this filtering-down process.

STROZIER: But it does seem to be that the criteria you enumerate give you the opportunity to assess the quality of that interaction in psychological terms. I think that is an original idea.

KOHUT: You might find group needs that are more easily identified as far as an examination of the group is concerned than secondarily as a part of individual needs.

STROZIER: Do you mean different forms of creativity, like folk art forms?

KOHUT: Yes. There are supports that the growing self, or the forming self, has that we are least prepared to see. All advance in knowledge is as much dependent on unlearning as on learning. I can't tell you how significant that finding is. Many times what one finds are such simple things. It seems incredible that no one has seen them before. But the reason you haven't seen them before is that you were caught up in a learned system that prevented you from seeing them. Take the example of the discovery of perspective in the Renaissance, which is usually dated to the architectual drawings of Brunelleschi, who was the architect of the duomo in Florence. How could it be that they didn't see that people are small when they are far away and bigger when they are closer? Now I'm not talking about you and me back in the early Middle Ages, let us say, but the greatest geniuses of art and vision, ones as great as Michelangelo and Leonardo. The problem was that they were caught up in the knowledge that people are always the same size. That knowledge prevented them from seeing that people are not always the same size. It is not that they seem smaller when they are far away, that it's a prejudice. They are smaller when they are far away. They are bigger when they are closer.

STROZIER: In other words, it's not a value change, but a real change.

KOHUT: Yes. The discovery that this is so was an unlearning rather than a learning, for how could one not see that? We continuously correct what we see in terms of what we have learned. Part of seeing something new is the painful, courageous unlearning of something one has known.

To return to the beginnings of the self, we must shed the learned framework of thinking only in terms of individual interactions. We always think of mother and baby. We have learned that. And I don't think we have learned it from Freud. We have learned it from the Madonna and Child, from the Old Testament, or wherever. To define that relationship precisely is a problem of cultural history. But the point is that it created a theory that orders reality in a particular way. What one does in confirming and creating the self is of the greatest importance. But we pay no attention to it. I have often asked myself: How can one evaluate new art forms? Is it just art that is still beyond my grasp? Is it just noises that this composer makes, for shock effect? Or is it like Alban Berg, of the Vienna School of Music, in his *Lyric Suite?* I remember when I first heard it and how strange it sounded. Now tears come to my eyes when I listen to the violin concerto. I remember that when I first heard it the concerto sounded like someone was tuning an instrument.

How does one separate the wheat from the chaff? Whether you like it or not is surely not the issue. That's for sure. You may intensely dislike something once, but when you learn its language, you may be quite moved by it. One possible criterion is that art which promises to be enduring has an inner cohesiveness. It expresses a unity that comes from the human mind in a form that hangs together. Take, for instance, Tiffany. I used to hate the stuff and thought it was nothing but crazy patterns. Now I love it. Here is some *(points to several examples in his study, where the interview was being conducted).* The beauty is that all these lines hang together. It is an art form that is totally different from all others. It has its own meaningful design and approach to the world. You may say you don't like it and yet Tiffany is something unique that tells you something about a whole time that was an expression of how people felt about themselves. And as such it is genuine. When you look at Picasso's work you can look at the blue period or the antique period with the fleshy women or the hollow period of the skeletons or the cubist period; what makes it great? It is the expression of an eternally restless search to find some tactile-visual orientation. Picasso's work is genuine because it expresses this human search. From the beginning the baby and the small child are exposed to such genuine—or the absence of such genuine—expressions of a human reality. People ask, "How should you bring up children?" You can give them a million answers, but the answer really is: "Be somebody. Then everything will fall in place."

11

"One Needs a Twinkle of Humor as a Protection Against Craziness"

(March 12, 1981)

STROZIER: Last time you said true art has a sense of inner cohesiveness. It expresses a unity that comes from the human mind in a form that hangs together. But how can you determine this unity?

KOHUT: I am trying to explain the experiential criterion that I used for guessing whether something that comes my way is just a hollow new form or whether the new form is in an unbroken contact with the depths of the creator and, as such, offers a new model for self-expression and the way in which one sees the world. There is the cute story—I don't know whether it is apocryphal— of someone showing Picasso a bunch of drawings that included a number of forgeries of his work. He went through the pictures and separated the forgeries from what he had really done. But among the items he identified as forgeries were some that unquestionably had been done by him. And it was pointed out to him, "Look, I know you did these; I watched you while you were drawing them." He said, "It's still a forgery." What he meant, I think, is that when he did those it was a forgery of his own style. It did not come from the depths. If one uses structural language, it was segmental rather than sectorial; in other words, it was not a sector that went to the depths but a slice from the surface. And, likewise, all of us will occasionally imitate our own style or our own mode of thinking, but this is not when we are at our creative best. This is the touchstone of the differentiation betweeen junk or schlock and a serious attempt to express a new vision of the world in art.

STROZIER: Yes, it all fits together. But you are stressing today, as you stressed last time, the unity of the cohesion, and I must say I am a little confused, because the period in the early 20th century, which you have written and talked most about, are described in terms of their expression of the lack of cohesion. It's the exquisiteness of their portrayal of the impending fragmentation.

KOHUT: I honestly don't see any contradiction there at all. If you as an artist are seriously struggling with expressing this fragmented state, then you will, in a genuine way, express the fragmented, empty state. Take Kafka, for example, where in short story after short story, novel after novel, he portrays the empty, rejected, meaningless self. All of Kafka together deals with that. When you look at Picasso's genuine work—not the forgeries, either by himself or by others—there is a restless search. His total oeuvre hangs together, once you understand the restlessness of the search to put together the fragmented visual universe into some kind of a cohesive form after it has fallen apart. There is something unitary about that, unitary about the attempt to repair fragmentation. It is a genuine description of an inner state. So I see no paradox. You might say it is discontinuity or fragmentation itself that characterizes 20th century art—or some of it—and I would say, yes, but that is what gives it unity. Picasso would work for hours over the simplest kinds of things: he would have a square and a circle and would shift them around on paper for hours until at last he would be satisfied. It then expressed just the kind of inner tension that he felt. This kind of genuine art will have a confirming or supporting effect on people who feel understood by it, mirrored by it.

The problem is that the avant-garde may sometimes leave unsupported large numbers of people. That is what happened in the Weimar Republic. Artists reached a constituency in the big cities among the intelligentsia. They also, I think, had some contact with the working classes. But the new art totally bypassed the petit bourgeois that had gotten its support from quite different selfobjects up until then and was suddenly completely deprived of them, in fact held in contempt by those who now produced the modern art. This is something I find extremely interesting and highly complex. The late Romantics, like Wagner, in a sense captured both sides. Wagner, for instance, was highly influential in the transition to modern music. I don't think that one could imagine, for example, Schoenberg without Wagner or the late Romantics (Brahms and Bruckner). There is a cohesion there, but ultimately the great flowering of 20th century art for some reason lost touch with an enormous culturally untutored group in Germany. They derived no benefits from art at all. Whether that is a significant fact in Hitler's success, I don't know, because many of the leaders were cultured people, and they were great Wagnerites.

STROZIER: You mean the leaders in Weimar?

KOHUT: No, I mean in Nazi Germany as well. They were not intellectuals, certainly.

STROZIER: I think I understand.

KOHUT: Well, try another question. The problem is probably that my answer isn't sufficient.

STROZIER: I wonder about this idea of art expressing the creativity of the group, but then saying that its appeal to the masses is irrelevant.

KOHUT: Keep in mind that the borderline between art and political action is not as sharply drawn as we might like to think. Leaving aside—which is very, very difficult to do—our moral abhorrence of the Nazi movement, as a political development, it almost had an artistic quality. The Nazi capacity to tune to large groups of the most diversified people and intuitively offer them an image of cohesion and strength, heal the fragmentation, the weakness, and the underlying depression, suddenly give people a sense that they are worthwhile, indeed better than others, had something truly artistic about it. Leni Riefenstahl, for example, captured this quality in her film of the Olympics or in the one of the party rally (*Triumph of the Will*) which has the plane coming out of the clouds with the Führer in it. The film offered a perfect response to what the population needed.

Now, modern art, to my mind, is a much greater art than that.

But there are layers of art and political action, the same way there are layers of religiosity. There is the kind of religiosity that is a crude mythology on the level of a fairy tale. It is, in other words, primitive science. It gives wrong scientific answers to legitimate scientific questions, like how did the world come about? He made it in so many days, he willed it, etc. This is, in a way, a kind of pseudo-scientific answer. Now, insofar as religion is a crypto-science, Freud was right: It is an illusion. But he was absolutely wrong, I think, in not seeing its values on other levels. Not everything can be judged on the level of accurate, appropriate, and truthful cognition. Life is not to be understood on just the cognitive scale. Science is a very valuable tool, but it is a tool, and its purposes are limited. There are forms of religion that have nothing to do with these pseudo-scientific answers.

When we compare the esoteric art of the 20th century with the easy answers of the Hitler movement or other totalitarian movements, it isn't just that Hitler got defeated. Nazism never really could have endured, because it doesn't lead anywhere. The movement was in part an emergency stopgap measure responding to the intense impoverishment of the self for large numbers of people. There was nothing long-term or curative about it. It's similar to what happens in the cults. A leader can make people feel well immediately if he is clever. People can then have conversion experiences. They are suddenly cured. The same thing, I dare say, characterizes the differences between many kinds of psychotherapy and psychoanalysis. It is sadly easy to establish a gross identification with someone else's strength in a regressive way. But it doesn't lead anywhere. That kind of identification stifles creativity. The confrontation of man with the artistic and scientific elaboration of fragmented and empty states is a very different story. It doesn't cure anybody immediately, but it establishes a context for long-term and really structure-building transactions to take place.

In talking about psychotherapy in the broad sense, including psychoanalysis, I have argued that in most cases gross identification with the psychotherapist as a defense should not be rejected. I certainly do not consider such an identification as a desirable end result to psychotherapy. It is a transitional step. When somebody cannot face his need for supportive selfobjects that reflect him, for those whom he can idealize and next to whom he can work silently—like shaving next to daddy or kneading dough next to mommy—a walling-off takes place. The depleted self becomes arrogant, and falsely self-sufficient. A chronic depression holds the self back from taking on the daring steps of appealing for responsiveness from others. When you get that in your therapeutic relationship, then nothing will happen for a long, long time. But not infrequently, the first step forward will be an act of sudden and gross identification. That I welcome. I welcome it not because that is the cure, but because that is a first move in the right direction.

STROZIER: The gross identification in the therapeutic setting is an interim step toward health. But in the group setting in history, like in Nazi Germany or in Jonestown, it means the opposite, doesn't it? It's an interim step in the wrong direction for the group?

KOHUT: There is of course a tremendous difference between a knowledgeable therapist observing his patient's behavior and a manipulative leader who uses mass reactions for his ends. But who knows what even the grossest unifying influence will lead to? I think one might have to look, let us say, at the history of religions for some insight here. What happens to a religion over the course of the century *after* the messianic leader? What happens to the great leaders of a historical past of a nation? How are they used in people's sense of cohesion, of their feeling connected with the past, of giving them a sense of how they want to move forward? I just don't know. Certainly, in the short run of history, you are right. In the short run, this is not desirable.

STROZIER: What about some examples from the 20th century?

KOHUT: Churchill rallied the anti-Hitler forces around him by making fun of Hitler's statement that he was going to twist the English chicken's neck. Churchill responded: "Some chicken, some neck." Everybody drew courage from that, as they did from his tough speeches and his whole demeanor with the cigar and the civilized anger that would courageously stand up. People identified with this leader's courage; thank God they did.

STROZIER: Group self awareness, however, probably leads to a diminution of messianism and a dramatic assertion of leadership. Is that a fair conclusion from what you have been saying?

KOHUT *(hesitates):* No good psychotherapy makes total, dramatic changes. It just makes what is there more controlled, sensible, human, balanced. But the person remains the same. You can't create somebody new. The direction of personality development is one way, so far as I can judge. A childhood can only be had once. What you do in psychotherapy is to remedy things that were left undone in that childhood or things that were not completely done, but you cannot create a new childhood. The same holds true for what I think you said about group awareness counteracting the influence of charismatic and messianic leadership. I would not be comfortable simply saying yes. I think it is part and parcel of good human equipment to be able to be enthusiastic for the great. In some people this capacity needs to be liberated rather than curbed. The capacity to admire a great leader figure, even a messianic and charismatic one, is not pathology. However, what you rightly implied is that there must be awareness of that process, there must be insight. It is like the difference between paranoia and normality. To my mind, one of the outstanding symptoms of a paranoid person is his deadly seriousness. One needs a twinkle of humor as a protection against craziness. Neither the people who followed Rev. Jones into death nor Jones himself had a twinkle in their eye. The same was true of Hitler. Hitler could be very sarcastic and make people laugh about his enemies and the abberations of Weimar democracy, etc. He had that kind of humor. But not the true humor of wisdom that knows the limits of the self. He couldn't laugh about his own strut. That doesn't mean one should never strut. It doesn't mean one should never feel triumphant.

STROZIER: Is that feeling of triumph a creative expression of narcissism, so to speak?

KOHUT: Look at Freud. I have always greatly admired an essay by Freud (1917a) in which he proudly compares himself to Copernicus and Darwin in terms of the insights in the history of man that have shaken up people's narcissism. Copernicus said that man is not in the center of the universe; Darwin said that man is not created separately by God; and Freud said that man is not even master of his own psychological household but is subject to unknown forces in the unconscious through which he is lived rather than which he controls. Well, that was a nice set of ideas, but Freud's interpretation of the hostility that he, Copernicus, and Darwin faced was wrong. Were people really mad because Copernicus' new system took away their centrality in the universe? Or was it not just the other way around? It seemed an immoral hubris to claim that space went into all directions and that man, from a position at the bottom of the heap in a stable universe, roamed free in the world. The powers that be, especially the Church, felt threatened by that revolution, and that's why he was attacked. It was not because he took away something great. He made man great. And who knows about Freud? I can't believe that the great resistance against Freud was because of his fancy idea that there is an unconscious. It was much more that people were accustomed to thinking in certain ways about themselves and all kinds of power positions would be undermined if this new system of psychology were to supervene.

STROZIER: What about the researcher's empathy with the past? When I read about Nazi Germany, after a certain point, I find it difficult to continue. Beyond a certain point I can no longer empathize with and communicate with students the meanings of what's going on. I wonder whether that kind of distance, the inability of an historian to empathize with a period, is not like in psychology or psychoanalysis the inability of the therapist to relate to severe forms of pathology.

KOHUT: The borderline, with the psychoses, is a relative one. It depends not only on the observed field, that is, on the patient and his pathology, but also on the ability of the therapist to extend his empathy to the patient. Insofar as you can truly build a bridge of empathy to a person, to that extent he is not psychotic. You have not cured him from his psychosis; he isn't psychotic. Once you are with him and have built this bridge, he has ceased to be psychotic. I think many people are thus erroneously diagnosed as psychotic. I am calmly treating people now who are delusional. And it doesn't particularly frighten me, for I understand what's going on. The delusions are in response to things felt

about me and the world. They become a psychologically meaningful way of expressing states.

In the case you like so much, Mr. E, there were two episodes
that might be called psychotic. Once a fish looked at him after
his mother's death and at one time or another he had his mother's face. It was a bodily delusion. But the therapist and I (as
supervisor) understood what was expressed by that. Delusions
are no more difficult to grasp than dreams people have that they
don't understand. You wake up with this gibberish thought from
the night. You go to your analytic hour and you and your analyst
see how it fits into all the things you are doing. It's just that the
dream is expressed in an archaic way. Once it becomes part and
parcel of your interchange with another human being it becomes
a part of your communications. It's not psychosis, even though
it doesn't fit into the normal mode in which people converse. In
a good analysis, a dream does not become something one ana-
lyzes as if it were set aside, a product that is being translated like
hieroglyphics.

Analogously, when you are first studying a new culture, you
first learn how to make the translation of the hieroglyphics, but
once you learn that it becomes merely a means to an end, a path
toward understanding the whole culture. So long as another culture is totally foreign to us, it is like psychosis. It's so easy to say
the Nazis were beasts and that Germany then regressed to
untamed callousness and animal-like passions. The trouble is that
Nazi Germany is understandable. There is an empathic bridge,
however difficult to maintain.

STROZIER: If psychosis is defined by the inability to establish and
maintain empathy, is there a group analogue to that?

KOHUT: That's what I'm talking about. Can we build an empathic
bridge to those who committed these horrors? As soon as we can
they are no longer a psychotic culture. I don't know whether we
can. I think up to now we can't; it's too close. But I would not
say that in principle we should agree it is not possible. In principle, it should be possible. After all, millions of people at that
time understood and were able to live in accordance with Nazism. It came at enormous cost to their humanness and their ability to understand other people's sufferings and feelings. They
switched from feeling human themselves to feeling like the only

humans or almost the only humans. That was obviously a pathological solution, it you want to apply this term, but still the
pathology is bridgeable, and I think that unless we try there is
no hope. And it is necessary to make some progress toward control of such events. For instance, I have often gotten into arguments with friends of mine, for I am always on the side of
transacting things rather than legislating things. I'm sure this
can be overdone, but in the borderline areas I am always in the
area of transaction. I am against total freedom of print, for
example. An attempt should be made to define what is poison
and what is not poison. People will say any such decision is arbi-
trary and it is better to have total freedom; I say no. It is only
the eternal struggle that will maintain us. I would much rather
have *Ulysses* prohibited and then vindicated in a great trial than
say everything is publishable. Not everything should be published. I don't see any real value at all to gross pornography.
Now, you can struggle with this and say, well, how about the late
works of Picasso, is that gross pornography or is it art? I would
say it's art, though I wouldn't say it is his greatest art. But I think
it should be argued. Do you understand?

STROZIER: I understand, though I am trying to link it up to your
earlier point.

KOHUT: Well, it's the same idea. One struggles to understand
even a Hitler, even those beasts in concentration camps who were
apparently not beasts.

STROZIER: Are you saying that the same spirit that would lead to
allowing any form of expression would lead to dismissing any
attempt at understanding the Nazis?

KOHUT: You don't have to worry about it anymore. You just
describe facts.

STROZIER: Would you also say it is more than just interesting; it
is important in the process of group self-awareness?

KOHUT: Absolutely. I think I have helped some by showing the
intensity of the narcissistic injury that often needs to be undone.
Over and over again, from Captain Ahab to Michael Kohlhas to

the Palestinians today, people will go to extraordinary lengths to undo narcissistic injury. These people would much rather die than live with shame. One has to study this dispassionately. What else can you do? You have no other choice.

12

Civilization Versus Culture

(May 7, 1981)

STROZIER: Freud said (1927a, p. 6): "I scorn to distinguish between culture and civilization." Could you talk about this distinction?

KOHUT: Well, it certainly is implied in all my dissertations to you and in my writings on what I call the cultural selfobject. It is not a civilizing selfobject. "Civilizing" is embedded in the concept of civilization. I don't know whether you realize this. Freud's paper (1930), "Civilization and Its Discontents" was, in German, "Das Unbehagen in der Kultur." To become civilized may create some tensions. It can be painful to be domesticated, for it limits free drive expression. In the framework of a drive psychology, of a drive processing psychology, the concept of being ill at ease in culture makes some sense. But that is mental apparatus psychology. As soon as you begin to think of man as essentially motivated by the maintenance and growth of his self, and by the living out of the destiny of the self, the program of the self, in a life curve, you think of culture only as supportive or as nonsupportive of the maintenance of the self. It can never be a *Unbehagen*. The *Unbehagen* can only be when support is not provided. You hear the familiar sounds of one's language. You hear the familiar sounds of national music. You hear the voices of those you know. You recognize the habits of those you see. You are nourished by the art, the philosophy, by the political leadership of those you idealize. Where is the *Unbehagen*? The absence of all that supportive framework of language, art, music and tradition of all kinds leads to those disintegration problems that Freud considered the essence of man. Then the animal must be domesticated. In that conceptual framework civilization becomes something conceptualized as discontentful. Man wants to kill, man wants to fuck, man wants to eat ravenously. However, everybody says don't eat quite so much or quite so fast, these women are to be subdivided, and you can't kill or they will put you in jail. The result of all these restrictions is drive pressure. The model is one of a machine. There is a certain tension, and when the tension rises you put the lid on. That was the concept of *homo natura* à la Freud. It is a marvelously consistent early model. I have often expressed my admiration for it and how it clarifies so many aspects of symptom formation. It's lovely to behold. It's an esthetic pleasure. But I think it misses the essence of man. Undoubtedly, self-psychology in turn will be superseded someday by a better concept of man, but I think for the moment self psychology is closer to grasping the essence of human nature than Freud's machinery concept. The self psychology framework fits better and explains far more of human life in culture. Freud, for reasons of his own, was contemptuous of the differentiation between culture and civilization. Culture was supposed to be the high falutin' stuff. He wanted to show that it is just drive-taming and drive process.

STROZIER: Would you scorn to use the term "civilization"?

KOHUT: No, I don't think so. There is some value in looking at man from that point of view. Certainly, (and this is something that people now have begun to realize), when you colonize some so-called savage tribes and impose the standards of western culture upon them, you try to civilize them. But colonization does far more than stabilize drive expression. Colonization is a kind of civilizing and only now have people begun to realize to what horrors that leads. Look at the Native Americans and their depression. Are they depressed because they cannot kill anymore and so have turned their aggression against themselves? That would be Freud's *Unbehagen* in their new civilization. But don't they drink because their all-sustaining culture, their own traditional self, has become valueless? The children grow up with fathers who have no means and no strength worthy of idealization. There must be a continuity of culture if you really want to maintain psychological life. You kill people when you take their culture. This is not because they are suddenly asked to tame their drives. They have their own drive-taming mechanisms built into their whole culture system. It was their own way. They had pride in themselves as warriors and a fully integrated culture.

STROZIER: Is there any legitimate drive-taming purpose to civilization?

KOHUT: Yes, but let me answer that in terms of psychotherapy. As you know, I work with two theories side by side: the theory of the self in the broad sense and the theory of the self in the narrow sense. The theory of the self in the narrow sense is something that Heinz Hartmann, for example, accepted. Hartmann once made a very interesting point—a little one, but an interesting one (1964, pp. 114 and 127). He differentiated between ego and self. That was an important refinement in nomenclature. When Freud spoke about ich, he sometimes meant the self and sometimes meant the ego as a part of a mental apparatus. Hartmann said we should differentiate the two clearly. That was helpful. But to him the self was only a content of the mental apparatus. He thought of man as an abstraction. I accept that up to a point. There are certainly clinical situations in which one can look at drive expression and defenses against it. The question is only: why do these situations come about? They do because the self has not been supported.

The Oedipus complex is a pathological formation—not, as Freud thought, the normal state of the child between the ages of four and six. The normal oedipal child is assertive and affectionate. It is only when the selfobjects do not respond with pride and pleasure to this growth of the next generation, or respond by becoming sexually stimulated, that regressive development occurs. Then lust appears instead of affection and hating and killing wishes instead of assertiveness. But lust and hate are not the primary psychological products. They are derivative and secondary. The primary thing is the assertiveness. It is nonsense to consider a baby as a bundle of chaotic drives. He becomes that only when there is no selfobject milieu to greet him. To say, well, after all when you give the baby culture and selfobjects you have added something to the baby is absurd. You haven't added anything. It's just like saying you are born into this world and you start to breathe, and then you add oxygen. You are constructed to be born into a world of oxygen. You are constructed psychologically to be born into a matrix of responsive selfobjects. It is an artifact to disregard that.

STROZIER: So murderous and incestuous impulses have to be civilized but they are not the norm?

KOHUT: Exactly. Then you are in struggles about them and parents will secondarily relate to them, since there are always imperfections in selfobject milieus.

STROZIER: In that sense, civilization becomes a breakdown product of culture.

KOHUT: That's a nice way of putting it.

STROZIER: Let me change the subject and ask you something from earlier. When you talked about Tiffany, you claimed that the way to determine whether art will endure is whether it expresses a unity that comes from the human mind. Is there an analogue there for politics and leadership?

KOHUT: I would think so. I am not an historian, unfortunately, and in that sense I cannot speak with absolute conviction. But I have often seen—at least I believe I have seen—something that I'm sure may seem a little trite: the fit between the leader and the group at certain historical moments. At other times the same leader has no influence on the group. Now, by that I do not mean only political leaders. Take Jean-Jacques Rousseau. As a social or political scientist, he is a hazy thinker. The *Contrat sociale* is awfully functional, and certainly his novels border on the junky. And yet look at the enormity of the response that this man evoked. Somehow he grasped people's deepest commitments in reassembling a self that was on the edge of destruction. I don't know enough about it, but it would be interesting to see what had happened to the absolute monarchy in France at that time. It wasn't real anymore, it seems. There was discord and debauchery at the court. They had nothing but cooks and enormous meals and ever more fanciful dresses. Royalty had outlived itself culturally, and that is why the court went to pieces. It became hollow, leaving only etiquette in its wake.

STROZIER: You mentioned Rousseau once before.

KOHUT: He's such an interesting character. He grew up in Geneva, and I believe his mother died very shortly after he was born. He had a brother who was a ne'er-do-well, I believe, who left the house and was never found again; there was also an apprentice or a watchmaker or something. I forget now. But he obviously had a very unsustained life early on and he was always searching. He attached himself to a much older woman, a Madame de Warens. His own deep sense of not belonging was therefore personal. It matched perfectly the population at large. Rousseau thus expressed something important at an historical moment when a major reshuffling of the group was occurring.

STROZIER: So what defines the genuineness is that intuneness?

KOHUT: Yes, but this is only one criterion of real leadership. It must also come from the depths. I am sure there were hundreds of thousands of people with shaky selves in Rousseau's time.

STROZIER: When you say from the depths, you mean from the depths of the relationship between the leader and the group self?

KOHUT: I mean from the depths of his personality. He himself was able to reorganize himself by certain creative acts. But these creative acts spoke generally to Frenchmen of the time who needed the group qua group reassembled. The political leaders who came later were action-oriented people. At the time of Rousseau the idea of action was impossible. The police were too strong, for one thing. Rousseau himself was something of a paranoid character. He got involved with Hume, for example, and suspected him of persecuting him. Rousseau operated on the borderline between severe pathology and the creative reassemblage of the self in a way that is characteristic of many significant figures. The influence of many modern fascists leaders are of that kind. They offer a quasi-paranoid solution to their own ills and to those of the disturbed selves of their followers. Now I would think that in a thousand years—if a human world still exists on earth, which is doubtful, though I have some confidence in human resourcefulness—that man will feel genuinely connected with the future. Historians then will see these fascist regimes as little bubbles in a transitional phase of the renewed self that man once acquired. Nothing creative comes without trauma, and while what the fascists did—and do—is enormously ugly and inhuman, yet in a vast overview they may very well come to be seen as conditional phases towards something positive. That is why I say that so much of modern art is genuine when it is from the depths and describes a creative search for a reassembled self. The eternal search of Picasso is what makes him so great in my mind.

STROZIER: In the political example therefore the issue is resonance between the leader and the depths of the group self?

KOHUT: I'll agree with that way of putting it. But keep in mind that we are talking about great leader figures. During crucial moments of self survival—not just biological survival but *self* survival—something fundamental is threatened. At such moments, the gifted and successful leader experiences danger on a personal level but can realize and express that danger on the group level. He experiences it at a personal level because he himself lacked the sustenance of selfobjects as a child. He is threatened by disintegration and goes through phases of near fragmentation frequently in late adolescence or early adulthood, then reassembles himself with a set of creative ideas that happen to fit the overall needs of the group. He and the group then become each other's selfobjects. They come to form a unit that is exhilarating and full of vitality. The self that was fragmented clicks firmly back into place. It is for these experiences that people gladly will die. Biological survival is nothing by comparison to this experience. Is it now clear?

STROZIER: Yes.

KOHUT: You know, we see the same thing in psychoanalysis. At first there is usually an uplifting experience when a positive selfobject transference establishes itself. But then comes the nitty-gritty of years of work and many disappointments, which is the essence of cure.

STROZIER: Could you say that the unity would describe the empathic bonding of the particular relationship with the leader, whereas the dialectic captures the inevitable frustration?

KOHUT: That's very well put. What you call empathic bonding is not an intellectual thing. It is not based on insight as it is on psychoanalysis. If it were ever verbalized, it would be counter-productive.

13

Religion, Ethics, Values

(June 6, 1981)

STROZIER: You have written and talked a great deal about politics, culture, art and the like. What about religion?

KOHUT: Let me begin with Freud, who attacked religion as being poor science. Now, of course, that's true. Religion is poor science. To say that the world was created by some prescient superhuman being called God who divided up his work into seven days is poor science. It is an understandable attempt to find explanations for things, but as science it is poor. However, as a supportive selfobject, religion is not poor by a long shot. Freud's concern was with religion as irrational dogma. But he ignored the supportive aspect of religion. Religion constitutes a set of cultural values which he totally underestimated; there was no opening in his system for such things. He operated on a different level of generalization, as he did when he talked about culture and civilization. Western religion at least has a civilizing influence to it, because it is, of course, anti-drive in many ways. But it is also more than that, for religion is a very complex phenomenon.

STROZIER: What about the question of ethics?

KOHUT: Ethics and values interest me in both religion and science. There is no science of man that is thinkable without some value system behind it. One can only demand that a value system fit the dominant needs of the generation. There are two things that can happen to values. They can change their position on the hierarchical scale. And the other thing that can happen to a value is that values can become an ego function. A value that once was considered as somewhat separate from the self, that one looked up to but with a degree of foreignness, can become totally integrated into the personality and thus lose its ethical definition as a value. To take an extreme example, the value of not killing could cease to exist. That would obviously be a peak value. But, if there were no more impulse to kill, it wouldn't be a value anymore.

STROZIER: I find your use of the term "peak" here confusing.

KOHUT: Peak values change all the time. Each generation has its own peak values. Self psychology, being a child of our century, has different peak values from those values of a scientist still fighting obscurantism (like Freud). In a hundred years there may be other peak values that will gain ascendancy. But, as I said, two things are needed: One must be able to be aware of what the peak value is by which one is guided, and hidden moralism everywhere must be acknowledged.

STROZIER: In psychoanalysis is it a hidden moral that drives are bad?

KOHUT: Exactly. Drives are bad, and everybody is a recalcitrant child who resists even knowing that, let alone changing it. Another example would be the seemingly scientific concept that we must move from the pleasure to the reality principle. Such an idea is a moral value, which is not necessarily wrong—but you must understand it for what it is. You must determine your own peak values, which in turn fit specific peak needs. The values, let us say, of the need for a selfobject matrix throughout life by which we are, as it were, guided fit into our specific self-needs. Values of independence are phony, really. There is no such thing. There can be no pride in living without oxygen. We're not made that way. It is nonsense to try and give up symbiosis and become an independent self. An independent self is one that is clever enough to find a good selfobject support system and to stay in tune with its needs and the changing of the generations. To that system one must be willing to give a great deal.

14

"Stranger, Take Word to Sparta: Here We Lie Obeying Her Orders"

(July 16, 1981)

STROZIER: An issue that you hinted at last time is whether, for the psychologically healthy individual, death is not feared. I'm curious about the ethical implications of that idea.

KOHUT: I don't understand what you mean. I certainly did not intend to imply that. And I wouldn't say that one could reverse it and say that a person who is afraid of death is therefore psychologically ill. It depends a good deal on the setting. It depends a good deal on the makeup of the individual. First of all, health is such a doubtful concept anyway. What is healthy? I would be perfectly satisfied to say that death doesn't necessarily have to be feared. It goes without saying that everybody is deeply afraid of dying, but for the healthy individual it isn't really fear. It depends both on the inner makeup of the person and on the selfobject milieu. This is what I think I was telling you about. Under certain circumstances death is not feared at all. I described this in the paper "On Courage" (see this volume, pp. 20–21) particularly in the last dream of Sophie Scholl. If a person has given over his total self to an ideal—the baby that she places on the other side of the crevasse that opens up in front of her on the day on which she is going to be guillotined—if a person is capable of doing that, then he will die without a trace of fear, die as a matter of fact proudly. He knows that he has supported his real self, which lives on. When the Spartans died at the Thermopylae, the famous inscription was: "Stranger, take word to Sparta: here we lie obeying her orders." They lost their lives but only their lives. That was their feeling. If you're thinking in terms of biology, of course, then they lost their lives, but if you think in terms of psychology they didn't lose their selves. They lived on in the habits, the standards, the ethics of the Spartan city-state. That's one example where the inner commitment to the ideal outweighs the fear of death. Another one would be when somebody tells a dying person what an example he is to him when he will have to cross that barrier, that line, and how he admires him for the way in which he handles and faces this trying moment, the last moment of his life. A dying person hearing that may die proudly. The opposite occurs when the selfobjects retreat from the dying person and abandon him, either by not visiting him anymore or by emotionally walling themselves off. This is so beautifully described in the *Death of Ivan Ilich* by Tolstoy. In that story everybody goes about his way blissfully, not wanting to be reminded of death. The wife does this and the friends do that. The man would have died miserably had there not been one selfobject, a servant or serf, who stayed with him and massaged him and at least stayed in some degree of emotionally meaningful contact with him. That is what made the dying bearable.

STROZIER: In religion, the question of death is so central to the whole question of an afterlife. It's prospective and a matter of having . . .

KOHUT: You see, the way religion has always been seen, and this is what I've stressed so many times, is that it is a poor science. That is Freud's mistake and Freud's correctness. It is poor science. But if it's good, it may be outstanding psychology. In its best and central part, religion puts into words an awareness of what is in people. When you talk about paradise, the idea is that there is something greater than the individual life. Although some ideas become debased and vulgarized and popularized in terms of very specific concrete images, like hymn-singing angels, I think in the eyes of a deep searcher for religious truths these things fall by the wayside.

STROZIER: That's very important. But what grounds ethics? For religion that's such a clear question; God imposed it.

KOHUT: That's how a child remembers it, as something imposed on him, something that he inherited. But a mature man will go beyond that. Ethics is something to be struggled for. I think that's what makes Luther an impressive figure. He was not satisfied with the idea of God handing things down. His struggle with God, it seems to me, was on a much higher level than simply believing that God imposes and one has to obey. One searches inside oneself. It was his own conscience that he struggled with. I cannot say more about it at the moment. As I've told you many times and as I've written a number of times, ethics change. The only unchangeable thing about them is that if ethics are to be meaningful they address the psychological needs of a particular generation. The ethics of the unsupported and support-needing self is different from the ethics of the strong self that is faced with other types of problems. Too much prohibition doesn't allow it to expand and assert itself and fulfill its program.

STROZIER: It's all therefore culturally variable? You said one time that what are apparently the most solidly grounded taboos could themselves change. Such as murder.

KOHUT: If the aggressive impulse were negligible and became negligible in our race, the prohibition against murder would melt away. It would lose its relevance.

STROZIER: So taboos can change. What about cultural variability of issues of the self, like idealization?

KOHUT: Of course they can change.

STROZIER: They can change and therefore there is a history of them?

KOHUT: Yes, I think so. It's like what I have described with artists in the way they prefigure what the scientist later discovers.

STROZIER: So what grounds ethics is the human experience?

KOHUT: It responds to a particular need to fortify the individual in problematic areas, in weak areas. Now of course if you assume, as Freud did, that the essence of man is determined by an unchanging central conflict, then you have no such variability in ethical existence. Because you will always in the last analysis address yourself to that central conflict. My feeling is that this is an error.

STROZIER: There's only lower and higher forms?

KOHUT: Yes. You know I would imagine that the course of history would show that we have not totally done away with certain values. I can't be sure that that's true.

STROZIER: That what's true?

KOHUT: That certain values have not totally disappeared. It would be very difficult for a contemporary historian to pick up values, let us say, that motivated a people long ago, like the Greeks or the Romans or the Egyptians, because they wouldn't know the configuration and detect it. For example, I am almost certain that we misunderstand the essentials of the ancient Greeks. I can't tell you why, but something in me tells me that we have missed something that's completely out of our understanding.

STROZIER: It's not because of the time gap, but something in the cultural difference?

KOHUT: Take the discovery that Greek sculptures were painted. We had always believed the Greeks were surrounded by these simple stones. To find out they were painted was a shaking experience for me. It throws a totally different light on what, for instance, their aesthetic values were. Can you imagine yourself being surrounded by painted sculptures with red lips and blue eyes and dark hair, or whatever?

STROZIER: Is there something special about the Greeks in terms of the difference you are talking about that, say, would not apply to Medieval Europe?

KOHUT: I'll tell you why I said this. I said it for a personal reason. With my humanistic education I have always been more at home in ancient Greece than in the present time, given my secondary school training. Rome also seems understandable to me. But I have never felt I could understand Egyptian culture under the pharaohs. I suppose if I devoted a lifetime to it something finally would click. I don't mean to say that it is forever ununderstandable. It's the same way with patients. Nothing interferes more dramatically with acquiring a deep understanding of a patient than premature closure. If you think you know, then you cut yourself off from taking in more and more details with that pleasurable expectant puzzlement, until you finally see a totally unexpected configuration. It just comes to you. Then, of course, you can confirm it or not confirm it by other kinds of mental processes.

I think the same would have to be true in the study of foreign cultures. In a sense everything from yesterday backwards is a foreign culture. It is very difficult to think oneself into another person. Some years ago I analyzed a patient who had been born and raised in Kansas. The family came from a farming background and had made a tremendous move upward in wealth and education over a few generations. But they retained something of the American Gothic, as in Grant Wood's painting with two farmers, a man and a woman, standing side by side, with a pitchfork between them. There was a kind of practical pragmatic puritanism in this man's background. He suffered tremendously from it in a variety of ways that I can't describe. But at one time he said something that I've never forgotten. He said, "You know, you too are very provincial." And I said, "How?" He said, "You are provincial in your cosmopolitanism." And he was right. That Kansas background has its own reality and validity and so does mine. But one can't be stuck with the one or the other. It is only provincial as long as it does not retain openness to the perception of the cohesion, the synthesis, the meaningful unity in another's outlook on life. That is very difficult to do, and it may be even more difficult over the ages.

STROZIER: Indirectly that raises another question I have, and that is whether you feel there are any ethical concerns for the practice of psychohistory?

KOHUT: Ethical concerns?

STROZIER: Yes, a lot of people feel strongly that it is not ethical to study the dead psychologically.

KOHUT: You know, one needs courage. Always. Anything that is good needs courage. There is always an interim period with something new. People are outraged before they'll finally accept it. People once shouted down modern music; now they fill the concert halls to hear it. When Béla Bartók's beautiful piece for percussion and celesta was first performed in no less a musical city than Vienna, they couldn't finish the performance. There is hardly anybody now who wouldn't listen to it with pleasure. The same is true for Stravinsky. The outrage against Stravinsky never was quite as great. These things simply become accepted once you get used to them. But of course they have to be handled with skill and meaning. Just to go bedroom spying into the lives of great political figures and to have no other interest but showing perversions and homosexuality—that puriant kind of interest should be condemned. I think there are some psychohistorical studies that have this kind of appeal. There's some kind of a psychohistorical publication I once saw with obscene advertisements . . .

STROZIER: *The Journal of Psychohistory?*

KOHUT: Yes. The advertisements had an appeal that bordered on the obscene. Now, you know, I have no way of judging whether I am diagnosing this correctly. But certainly a solidly based psychohistorical investigation does not remain focused only on those details of psychology that are discovered. It must, as with a work of art, show how these things became interwoven with a variety of other motives and led, let us say, to significant redeeming action as far as the group is concerned. You might say, "Who cares what Lincoln's childhood hangups were?" Well, if you don't care, then don't care, that's fine. But the human mind is interested in establishing connections and getting fuller and fuller pictures of the world. If a significant aspect of adult (and historical) actions was influenced by childhood events, then I think it's very important to establish the connections. Take Kafka, who was clearly sensitized to death by something in his early life. There were millions of people who were exposed to these same experiences. But there was only one Kafka who, with the aid of crystalline, brief sentences and realistic prose, could spin out these understandable stories that hit everybody right where it hurt the most. Now what's wrong with wanting to investigate how personal experience is woven into his art? Why is that debunking? And the same is true for historical figures. When I said about Churchill that there must have been something in his early life that made him particularly prone to repeat one situation and to thrive on it and to do the best in it—namely, the one of being seemingly hopelessly enclosed and then finding a gigantic way out of it—it does not in the least debunk his performance (see this volume, p.   ). It explains partly why this man could perform so well when called upon by history. As a child, of course, he nearly killed himself when he jumped over the ravine with outstretched arms. But then, when all of England and the rest of the civilized world seemed uncertain, then he could rise to his greatest firmness and serious, courage-inspiring strength.

STROZIER: So people should not be choked off from speaking?

KOHUT: I think some people should be choked off. But now why don't we stop.

Heinz Kohut died
October 8, 1981

References

Adler, A. (1907), *Study of Organ Inferiority and Its Physical Compensation.* New York: Nervous & Mental Disease Publishing Co., 1917.

Alexander, F. (1938), Remarks about the relation of inferiority feelings to guilt feelings. *Internat. J. Psycho-Anal.,* 19:41–49.

———, and French, T.M., et al. (1946), *Psychoanalytic Therapy: Principles and Application.* New York: Ronald Press.

Baumayer, F. (1956), The Schreber case. *Internat. J. Psycho-Anal.,* 37:61–74.

Benedict, R. (1946), *The Chrysanthemum and the Sword.* Boston: Houghton Mifflin.

Bing, J.F., McLaughlin, F., & Marburg, R. (1959), The metapsychology of narcissism. *The Psychoanalytic Study of the Child,* 14:9–28. New York: International Universities Press.

——— (1957), *Sigmund Freud: Reminiscences of a Friendship.* New York/London: Grune & Stratton.

Bonnard, A. (1963), Impediments of speech: A special psychosomatic instance. *Internat. J. Psycho-Anal.,* 44:151–162.

Bracher, K.D. (1969), *Die deutsche Diktatur: Entstehung, Struktur, Folgen des Nationalsozialismus.* Berlin: Kiepenheuer & Witsch. Tr. Jean Steinberg, New York: Praeger, 1970.

Buber, M. (1967), Das echte Gespräch und die Möglichkeiten des Friedens Friedenpreis des Deutschen Buchhandels. *Reden und Würdigungen* 1951–1960. Frankfort: Börsenverein des Deutschen Buchhandels, 1961. 2 Auflage, 1967.

Bullock, A. (1964), *Hitler: A Study In Tyranny.* New York: Harper & Row.

Churchill, W. (1942), *My Early Life.* New York: Macmillan.

——— (1959), *Memoirs of the Second World War.* Boston: Houghton Mifflin Co.

Eckermann, P. (1836–1848), *Conversations with Goethe*. London: Dent, 1930.

Eidelberg, L. (1954), *An Outline of a Comparative Pathology of the Neuroses*. New York: International Universities Press.

────── (1959), A second contribution to the study of the narcissistic mortification. *Psychiat. Quart.*, 33:634–646.

Eissler, K.R. (1962), *Goethe: A Psychoanalytic Study*. Detroit: Wayne State University Press.

────── (1963), Freud and the psychoanalysis of history. *J. Amer. Psychoanal. Assn.*, 11:675–703.

────── (1971), *Discourse on Hamlet: A Psychoanalytic Inquiry*. New York: International Universities Press.

Ellenberger, H. (1970), *The Discovery of the Unconscious*. New York: Basic Books.

Ellman, R. (1959), *James Joyce*. New York: Oxford University Press.

Epstein, L., ed. (1962), *Hebrew and English Edition of the Babylonian Talmud*. London: Soncino Press.

Erikson, E.H. (1956), The Problem of ego identity. *J. Amer. Psychoanal. Assn.*, 4:56–121.

Federn, P. (1936), On the distinction between healthy and pathological narcissism. In: *Ego Psychology and the Psychoses*, ed. E. Weiss. New York: Basic Books, 1952, pp. 323–364.

Ferenczi, S. (1913), Stages in the development of the sense of reality. In: *Contributions to Psychoanalysis*. New York: Basic Books / R. Brunner, 1950, pp. 312–339.

Fergusson, F. (1949), *The Idea of a Theater*. Princeton: Princeton University Press, pp. 111–112.

Fermi, L. (1954), *Atoms in the Family*. Chicago: University of Chicago Press.

Feuchtwanger, L. (1925), *Jüd Süss*. English translation: Power, tr. Willa and Edwin Muir. New York: The Modern Library, 1926.

Freud, A. (1936), *The Ego and the Mechanisms of Defense. Writings*, 2. New York: International Universities Press, 1966.

────── and Dunn, S. (1951), An experiment in group upbringing. *Writings*, 4:163–229. New York: International Universities Press, 1968.

Freud, S. (1887–1902), *The Origins of Psychoanalysis*. New York: Basic Books, 1954.

────── (1896), Further remarks on the neuro-psychoses of defence. The Standard Edition, 3:159–185. Edited and Translated by James Strachey. 24 Volumes. New York: Norton, 1976. Hereafter cited as the *Standard Edition*.

────── (1900a), The interpretation of dreams. *Standard Edition*, 4 & 5.

────── (1900b), Die Traumdeutung. *Gesammelte Werke*, 2 & 3. London: Imago Publishing Co., 1942.

────── (1901), The psychopathology of everyday life. *Standard Edition*, 6.

────── (1905), Three essays on the theory of sexuality. *Standard Edition*, 7:125–245.

—— (1908a), Character and anal-eroticism. *Standard Edition,* 9:168–175.

—— (1908b), Creative writers and day-dreaming. *Standard Edition,* 9:141–153.

—— (1909a), Analysis of a phobia in a five-year-old boy. *Standard Edition,* 10:3–149.

—— (1909b), Notes upon a case of obsessional neurosis. *Standard Edition,* 10:153–249.

—— (1910a), Leonardo da Vinci and a memory of his childhood. *Standard Edition,* 11:59–137.

—— (1910b), The psychoanalytic view of psychogenic disturbance of vision. *Standard Edition,* 11:209–218.

—— (1911), Psychoanalytic notes on an autobiographical account of a case of paranoia (dementia paranoides). *Standard Edition,* 12:3–82.

—— (1913), Totem and taboo. *Standard Edition,* 13:1–164.

—— (1914a), On the history of the psychoanalytic movement. *Standard Edition,* 14:7–66.

—— (1914b), On narcissism: An introduction. *Standard Edition,* 14:69–102.

—— (1914c), Remembering, repeating and working-through. *Standard Edition,* 12:145–157.

—— (1915), Instincts and their vicissitudes. *Standard Edition,* 14:117–140.

—— (1916a), Some character types met with in psychoanalytic work. *Standard Edition,* 14:310–355.

—— (1916b), On transcience. *Standard Edition,* 14:305–307.

—— (1917a), A difficulty in the path of psychoanalysis. *Standard Edition,* 17:137–144.

—— (1917b), Mourning and melancholia. *Standard Edition,* 14:239–258.

—— (1920), Beyond the Pleasure principle. *Standard Edition,* 18:7–64.

—— (1921), Group psychology and the analysis of the ego. *Standard Edition,* 18:7–143.

—— (1926), Inhibitions, symptoms and anxiety. *Standard Edition,* 20:87–174.

—— (1927a), The future of an illusion. *Standard Edition,* 21:3–56.

—— (1927b), Humour. *Standard Edition,* 21:161–166.

—— (1929), Some dreams of Descartes'. A letter to Maxine Leroy. *Standard Edition,* 21:203–4.

—— (1930), Civilization and its discontents. *Standard Edition,* 21:59–145.

—— (1932), The acquisition and control of fire. *Standard Edition,* 22:185–193.

—— (1933), New introductory lectures on psychoanalysis. *Standard Edition,* 22:3–182.

—— (1937a), Moses and monotheism. *Standard Edition,* 23:3–137.

———— (1937b), Analysis terminable and interminable. *Standard Edition*, 23:211–253.

Gay, P. (1968), *Weimar Culture: The Outsider As Insider*. New York: Harper and Row.

Gedo, J. (1972), On the psychology of genius. *Internat. J. Psycho-Anal.*, 53:199–203.

———— and Goldberg, A. (1973), *Models of the Mind*. Chicago: University of Chicago Press.

Gedo, M. (1980), *Picasso: Art as Autobiography*. Chicago: University of Chicago Press.

Glover, E. (1940), *The Psychology of Fear and Courage*. New York: Penguin Books.

Goethe, J.W. (1828), Selige Sehnsucht. In: *Goethe's Werke: Vollstandige Ausgabe letzter Hand*, Vol. 5. Stuttgart: Cotta.

Goldstein, K. (1948), *Language and Language Disturbances*. New York: Grune & Stratton.

Greenacre, P. (1957), The childhood of the artist. In: *Emotional Growth*. New York: International Universities Press, 1971, pp. 479–504.

———— (1964), A study of the nature of inspiration. In: *Emotional Growth*. New York: International Universities Press, 1971), pp. 225–248.

Grinker, R. (1962), "Mentally Healthy" young males (homoclites). *Archives of General Psychiatry*, 6:405.

Hammarskjöld, D. (1965), *Markings*. New York: Knopf.

Hartmann, H. (1939), *Ego Psychology and the Problem of Adaptation*. New York: International Universities Press, 1958.

———— (1950), Comments on the psychoanalytic theory of the ego. In: Hartmann, 1964, pp. 113–141.

———— (1953), Contributions to the metapsychology of schizophrenia. In: Hartmann, 1964, pp. 182–206.

———— (1956), The development of the ego concept in Freud's work. In: Hartmann, 1964, pp. 268–296.

———— (1964), *Essays on Ego Psychology*. New York: International Universities Press.

———— Kris, E., and Loewenstein, R.M. (1964), *Papers on Psychoanalytic Psychology. Psychological Issues*, Monogr. 14. New York: International Universities Press.

———— and Loewenstein, R.M. (1962), Notes on the superego. In: Hartmann, Kris, & Loewenstein, 1964, pp. 144–181.

Heiden, K. (1966 [1936]), *Hitler, A Biography*. New York: A.A. Knopf.

Hitler, A. (1941–1944), *Hitler's Secret Conversations*. Tr. Norman Cameron and R.H. Stevens, 1953. Intr. by H.R. Trevor-Roper. New York: Octagon Books, rep. 1972.

Jacobson, E. (1954), The self and the object world. *The Psychoanalytic Study of the Child*, 9:75–127. New York: International Universities Press.

———— (1964), *The Self and the Object World*. New York: International Universities Press.

Jones, E. (1913), The God complex. In: *Essays in Applied Psycho-Analysis,* 2:244–265. London: Hogarth Press, 1951.

———— (1953, 1955, 1957), *The Life and Work of Sigmund Freud,* 3 Vols., New York: Basic Books.

———— (1954), *Hamlet and Oedipus.* New York: Doubleday.

Jung, C.J. (1961), *Memories, Dreams, Reflections.* New York: Pantheon.

Kleist, H. von (1808), *Michael Kohlhaas.* Clarendon German Series, ed. J. Gearey. New York: Oxford University Press, 1967.

Kohut, H. (1957), *Death in Venice* by Thomas Mann: A story about the disintegration of artistic sublimation. *The Search for the Self: Selected Writings of Heinz Kohut: 1950–1978,* Chapter 1. Ed. Paul H. Ornstein. 2 Volumes. New York: International Universities Press. Hereafter cited as *The Search for the Self.*

———— (1957), Observations on the psychological functions of music. *The Search for the Self,* Chapter 13.

———— (1959), Introspection, empathy, and psychoanalysis: An examination of the relationship between mode of observation and theory. *The Search for the Self,* Chapter 12.

———— (1960), Beyond the bounds of the basic rule: Some recent contributions to applied psychoanalysis. *The Search for the Self,* Chapter 19.

———— (1964), Values and objectives. *The Search for the Self,* Chapter 27.

———— (1966), Forms and transformations of narcissism. *The Search for the Self,* Chapter 32.

———— (1968), The psychoanalytic treatment of narcissistic personality disorders: Outline of a systematic approach. *The Search for the Self,* Chapter 34.

———— (1970), Discussion of D.C. Levin's paper: "The Self: A contribution to its place in theory and technique." *The Search for the Self,* Chapter 38.

———— (1971), *The Analysis of the Self.* New York: International Universities Press.

———— (1972a), Discussion of Ernest S. Wolf, John E. Gedo, and David M. Terman's paper: "On the adolescent process as a transformation of the self." *The Search for the Self,* Chapter 41.

———— (1972b), Thoughts on narcissism and narcissistic rage. *The Search for the Self,* Chapter 40.

———— (1975), The psychoanalyst in the community of scholars. *The Search for the Self,* Chapter 43.

———— (1977), *The Restoration of the Self.* New York: International Universities Press.

———— (1980), Summarizing reflections. In: Goldberg, A. *Advances in Self Psychology.* New York: International Universities Press.

———— and Seitz, P.F.D. (1963), Concepts and theories of psychoanalysis. *The Search for the Self,* Chapter 3.

Kramer, P. (1955), On discovering one's identity. *The Psychoanalytic Study of the Child,* 10:47–74. New York: International Universities Press.

Kris, E. (1936), The psychology of caricature. In: Kris, 1952, pp. 173–188.

───── (1952), *Psychoanalytic Explorations in Art*. New York: International Universities Press.

Levin, D.C. (1969), The self: A contribution to its place in theory and technique. *Internat. J. Psycho-Anal.*, 50:41–51.

Lewisohn, L. (1934), *The Permanent Horizon*. New York & London: Harper.

Loewenberg, P. (1971), The unsuccessful adolescence of Heinrich Himmler. *Amer. Hist. Rev.*, 76:612–641.

Ludwig, E. (1926), *Kaiser Wilhelm II*, tr. M. Colburn, London & New York: Putnam.

───── (1947), *Dr. Freud: An Analysis and a Warning*. New York: Helman, Williams, 1948.

McGuire, W. ed. (1974), *The Freud / Jung Letters*. Princeton: Princeton University Press.

Manvell, R. and Fraenkel, H. (1960), *Dr. Goebbels, His Life and Death*. London: Heinemann.

Mercier, L.S. (1781–88), *Tableau de Paris: études sur la vie et les ouvrages de Mercier*. Ed. Gustave Desnoiresterres. Paris: Pagnerre, 1853 [1781–88].

Miller, S.C. (1962), Ego autonomy in sensory deprivation, isolation, and stress. *Internat. J. Psycho-Anal.*, 43:1–20.

Mitscherlich, A. (1957), Meditationen zu einer Lebenslehre der modernen Massen. *Merkur*, 11:201–213, 335–350.

───── (1963), *Society Without the Father*. (Translated by Eric Mosbacher.) New York: Harcourt Brace & World, 1969.

───── (1965), *Die Unwirtlichkeit unserer Städte*. Frankfurt a. M.: Suhrkamp.

───── and Mitscherlich, M. (1967), *Die Unfähigkeit zu trauern*. Munich: Piper.

Niederland, W.G. (1951), Three notes on the Schreber case. In: Niederland, 1974, pp. 39–48.

───── (1959a), The "miracled-up" world of Schreber's childhood. In: Niederland, 1974, pp. 69–84.

───── (1959b), Schreber: Father and son. In: Niederland, 1974, pp. 49–62.

───── (1960), Schreber's father. In: Niederland, 1974, pp. 63–67.

───── (1963), On the "historical truth" in Schreber's delusions. In: Niederland, 1974, pp. 93–100.

───── (1974), *The Schreber Case: Psychoanalytic Profile of a Paranoid Personality*. New York: Quadrangle / New York Times Book Company.

Ornstein, Paul H. (Ed.) (1978), *The Search for the Self: Selected Writings of Heinz Kohut 1950–1978*, Vols. I and II. New York: International Universities Press.

Petry, C. (1968), *Studenten aufs Schafott: Die Weisse Rose und ihr Scheitern*. Munich: R. Pieper & Co.

Piaget, J. (1937), *The Construction of Reality in the Child.* New York: Basic Books, 1954.

Piers, G. and Singer, M. (1953), *Shame and Guilt.* Springfield, Illinois: Charles C. Thomas.

Rangell, L. (1954), The psychology of poise. *Internat. J. Psycho-Anal.,* 35:313–332.

Rank, O. (1911), Ein Beitrag zum Narzissmus. *Jb. Psychoanal. Psychopath. Forschungen,* 3:401–426.

Rauschning, H. (1938), *Die Revolution des Nihilismus.* New edition with introduction by G. Mann. Zurich: Europa Verlag. 1964.

Reich, A. (1960), Pathologic forms of self-esteem regulation. In: *Psychoanalytic Contributions.* New York: International Universities Press, 1973, pp. 288–311.

Sachs, H. (1942), *The Creative Unconscious.* Cambridge, Mass. Sci-Art.

Sadger, J. (1909), Heinrich von Kleist: Eine pathographisch-psychologische Studie. *Grenzfragen des Nerven- und Seelenlebens,* 70. Wiesbaden: Bergmann, 1910.

Sandler, J. Holder, A., and Meers, D. (1963), The ego ideal and the ideal self. *The Psychoanalytic Study of the Child,* 18:139–158. New York: International Universities Press.

Saul, L. (1947), *Emotional Maturity.* Philadelphia: Lippincott.

Schafer, R. (1973), Action: Its place in psychoanalytic interpretation and theory. *The Annual of Psychoanalysis,* 1:159–196. New York: Quadrangle Books.

Scholl, I. (1953), *Die Weisse Rose.* Frankfurt: Fischer.

Schur, M. (1972), *Freud: Living and Dying.* New York: International Universities Press.

Silberer, H. (1909), Report on a method of eliciting and observing certain symbolic hallucination-phenomena. In: *Organization and Pathology of Thought,* ed. D. Rapaport. New York: Columbia University Press, 1951, pp. 195–207.

Speer, A. (1969), *Inside the Third Reich: Memoirs of Albert Speer.* New York: Macmillan, 1970.

Spitz, R.A. (1946), The smiling response: A contribution to the ontogenesis of social relations. *Genet. Psychol.* Monogr., 34:57–125.

Sterba, R. and Sterba, E. (1954), *Beethoven and His Nephew.* New York: Pantheon.

Szekely, L. (1967), The creative pause. *Internat. J. Psycho-Anal.,* 48:353–367.

———— (1970), Uber den Beginn des Maschinenzeitalters: Psychoanalytische Bemerkungen über das Erfinden. *Schweiz. Z. Psychol.,* 29:273–282.

Tausk, V. (1913), Compensation as a means of discounting the motive of repression. *Internat. J. Psycho-Anal.,* 5:130–140, 1924.

Terman, D. (1972), Summary of the Candidates' Pre-Congress Conference, Vienna, 1971. *Internat. J. Psycho-Anal.,* 53:47–48.

Tolstoy, L.N. (1866), *War and Peace.* New York: Simon & Schuster, 1942.

Trilling, L. (1947), *Review of Emil Ludwig's Dr. Freud.* New York Times, December 14.

Trollope, A. (1857), Baby worship. In: *Barchester Towers.* New York: Doubleday, Chapter 16, pp. 133–144, 1945.

Wangh, M. (1964), National Socialism and the genocide of the Jews. *International Journal For Psychoanalysis*, 45:386–395.

Zahn, G.C. (1982, rep. 1964). *In Solitary Witness.* New York: Holt, Rinehart & Winston.

Index